THE CULINARY PLAGIARIST

The Culinary Plagiarist

(Mis)Adventures of a Lusty, Thieving, God-Fearing Gourmand

---

by
JASON PETERS

Front Porch Republic *Books*

THE CULINARY PLAGIARIST
(Mis)Adventures of a Lusty, Thieving, God-Fearing Gourmand

Copyright © 2020 Jason Peters. All rights reserved. Except for brief quotations in critical publications or reviews, no part of this book may be reproduced in any manner without prior written permission from the publisher. Write: Permissions, Wipf and Stock Publishers, 199 W. 8th Ave., Suite 3, Eugene, OR 97401.

Front Porch Republic Books
An Imprint of Wipf and Stock Publishers
199 W. 8th Ave., Suite 3
Eugene, OR 97401

www.wipfandstock.com

PAPERBACK ISBN: 978-1-5326-8980-2
HARDCOVER ISBN: 978-1-5326-8981-9
EBOOK ISBN: 978-1-5326-8982-6

Manufactured in the U.S.A.   October 5, 2020

Permission to quote from the following has been kindly granted by the authors:

Staying Put, by Scott Russell Sanders, copyright © 1993 (Boston: Beacon Press)

Secrets of the Universe, by Scott Russell Sander, copyright © 1991 (Boston: Beacon Press)

Consulting the Genius of the Place, by Wes Jackson, copyright © 2010 (Bekeley: Counterpoint)

New Collected Poems, by Wendell Berry, copyright © 2012 (Berkeley: Counterpoint)

Our Only World, by Wendell Berry, copyright © 2015 (Berkeley: Counterpoint)

"The Futility of Global Thinking," by Wendell Berry, copyright © 1989, *Harper's Magazine*

Till We Have Built Jerusalem: Architecture, Urbanism, and the Sacred, by Philip Bess, copyright © 2006 (Wilmington, DE: ISI)

"Imagine a collection of essays with all the wit and polish found in *The New Yorker*. Subtract the nasally, condescending tone and the moral vacuum also found there. Add in an authentic Midwestern accent and a Christian sensibility (e.g., always slice asparagus stalks so as to honor the Holy Trinity). Let it marinate in a fanciful wine over several days of reading, and you have Jason Peters' *The Culinary Plagiarist: (Mis)Adventures of a Lusty, Thieving, God-Fearing Gourmand*."

—ALLAN C. CARLSON
Author of *The Natural Family Where It Belongs: New Agrarian Essays*

"The funniest writer in America is a broken-down hoops star of irrepressible high spirits, an astringent Christian wit, a cussedly independent rhapsodist of olive burgers and local beers, and a whipper of creams and puller of pork and minter of apothegms. Jason Peters is the (gaunt) Chesterton of Dumb Ass Acres, Michigan. Read him while it's still legal to do so."

—BILL KAUFFMAN
Author of *Dispatches from the Muckdog Gazette*

"Imagine Falstaff finds God, gets lucky in marriage, and retreats to a farm, where his epic appetites, redeemed at last by person and place, inspire him to share his wit and wisdom (much of it stolen from his well-stocked bookshelf) on the joys of food and drink. In *The Culinary Plagiarist*, Peters puts the gusto back into gustatory, serving spicy verbs and gutting sacred cows. Consumer warning: don't swallow while laughing."

—DAVID BOSWORTH
Author of *The Demise of Virtue in Virtual America*

"In the kind of whimsical and lyrical prose that is all too rare these days, Jason Peters artfully combines the best of what has been thought and written with the best of what has been cooked and fermented to produce a thoroughly entertaining and rewarding book. I could not wait to turn the page and see what was next from Peters' delightful and slightly devious brain."

—MICHAEL P. FOLEY
Author of *Drinking with the Saints*
and *The Politically Incorrect Guide to Christianity*

"This book is delicious—every chapter a little *amuse-gueule*. If Roger Scruton was a beer connoisseur, he would have written this book. If Robert Farrar Capon weren't high church, he would have written this book. Put this on your shelf between *Supper of the Lamb* and *I Drink Therefore I Am*. Wonderful!"

—RICHARD AVRAMENKO
Author of *Courage: The Politics of Life and Limb*

"Jason Peters' writing on food, drink, and other earthy pleasures is like the most candid essayist—Montaigne, say—on truth serum. He may be the raunchiest gourmand ever to publish kitchen (and bedroom) musings, and also the funniest. Beneath the libidinous arias on martinis and mushrooms, however, there is a reverent man at work, as devoted to topsoil as to pasta, as versed in the Bible as in bourbon. The book is a wise romp. Read it with your favorite dish or darling."

—SCOTT RUSSELL SANDERS
Author of *The Way of Imagination*

"I've never met anyone who takes more pleasure than Jason Peters in working out the implications of the Incarnation, and his delicious prose spreads the pleasure around. If you enjoy outlandish similes, learning subversively deployed, and great throwaway opinions voiced as if any sensible person will agree, this book is for you."

—JOHN SHELTON REED
Co-author of *Holy Smoke: The Big Book of North Carolina Barbecue*

to Mike,

who could never even get the bread dough to rise

lux perpetua

See! That which we have chosen is given us, and that which we have refused is, also and at the same time, granted us. Ay, that which we have rejected is poured upon us abundantly. For mercy and truth have met together, and righteousness and bliss have kissed one another!

—Isak Dinesen, *Babette's Feast*

Ooh that gastronomic epicure culinary crepe suzette!

—Yosemite Sam, *Shishkabugs*

Contents

Preface | ix
Introduction: The Argument of His Book | 1

I: Spring | 13

1. Apple Blossoms and Horseshit and Divine Intention: What Happens Before We Eat | 15
2. After All, It Almost Rhymes With Bikini | 18
3. The First Morel, the Skipped Meeting, and a New Verb Infinitive | 27
4. Primary? What Primary? There's a Tournament on and a Woman to Impress | 33
5. Well, It's Not like After the Risotto | 37
6. Casting Asparagus on Another Person's Character | 41

II: School's Out | 45

7. An Expostulation Upon the Morning B.M. | 47
8. In the Season of Sweet Basil | 51
9. Turn the Turnip to Good Account | 55
10. The Lamb Shank Redemption | 59
11. Cioppino in the Heartland and the Cost of Misbehaving | 64

III: High Summer I | 73

12 Hungry for Meatless | 75
13 She's Headed for the Pollo Side of Town | 81
14 How to Cheat on Your Wife in the Kitchen | 84
15 Chicken Erotica and the Venus Transit | 89

IV: That's Some Pig! | 93

16 Carbonara-Based Life | 95
17 Carbonara *Redux En Toto* in the '80s Kitchen | 98
18 *Carpe* Bacon | 102
19 Baconation on a Theme | 107
20 The Blouse, the Pig, and the Fox | 109
21 She Don't Lie, She Don't Lie, She Don't Lie . . . Propane! | 113
22 Indirect Heat: 1; Miami Heat: 0; Or, Ode to the Porcine Dead | 119
23 Barbecued Ribs and "The Best That Ever Was!" | 124

V: Vegetarian, Hell! | 129

24 Tuesdays with Jesus | 131
25 Careful Exegesis and the *Au Bleu* Ribeye | 136
26 The Thoughtful Carnivore Eats Raw Beef | 141
27 Cutting the Mustard | 147

VI: Interlude: A Miscellany | 153

28 The After-Dinner Cigar | 155
29 Men, Women, and the Dishwasher: A Non-Sexist Dissertation on Female Guile and Incompetence | 159
30 Agricultural Potential, Real Wealth, and the *Gold* Gold Standard | 165
31 Haber-Bosch and the Problem of Whom to Tickle | 171

VII: Fasting (Sort of) | 177

32 Against Breakfast | 179
33 For Breakfast | 184
34 And Now For a Little Abstinence;
    or, Approach to Clean Monday #1 | 189
35 Lenten Humility, Bar Jester Style;
    or, Approach to Clean Monday #2 | 192

VIII: High Summer II | 199

36 Cool as a Cucumber—In *This* Heat | 201
37 The Pick-Up and the Pasta | 205
38 Chicken Aioli with a Seventeenth-Century Wag and the Greatest Living Guitarist (Not Counting Phil Keaggy, Tommy Emmanuel, Neal Schon, or Chet Atkins) | 209
39 O Summer! O Saturday! O Barbecued Chicken! | 213

IX: Adult Beverages | 219

40 Beer. It's What's For Dinner | 221
41 The Neighborhood Bar and the Chief End of Man | 226
42 Bourbon | 230
43 James Bond, The Poet Laureate, and a Plagiarized Drink | 235
44 The Teleology of Vodka | 241
45 Variation on the Theme of Vodkaean Teleology | 245
46 Concerning Spite; or, Metaphysics as a Guide to Porters | 247
47 How to Write History and Practice Bourbon Politics | 251

X: Back to School | 257

48 Something's Fishy—But Not Very—At Suppertime | 259
49 On the Conversion of Grass and Sunlight; or, Round Steak in a World Gone Mad | 263
50 Skillet Penne Sausage and The New Year's Dissolution | 267

Afterword: Curiosity Killed the Keg: A Tribute | 271

Preface

I am a valiant flea indeed, thus to dare perch upon the lip of such a lion as the literature of feasting!

—M.F.K. Fisher, *Here Let Us Feast*

These short essays were written over the course of about eight years, almost all of them for the Front Porch Republic (FPR) website. I drafted the first of them, "In the Season of Sweet Basil," on the evening of July 28, 2009, in response to a call that FPR president Mark Mitchell sent out saying, in effect, that there was no new material in the queue for the next day. And what an incipient electronic magazine needs above all else is new material each day. Site meters must spin. Did anyone have anything that could go up?

I didn't, but as a founding contributor to FPR with a vested interest in its success I figured I could try to whip something together. Sometimes you have to do that, whether at the writing table or the stovetop. So I sat down and tried to describe what I'd done late that afternoon with the basil from my herb garden. At the time I had no intention of writing anything more on the topic of food (or drink).

But then I found myself in the grip of something. The *genius loci*? The ugly stepsister of one of the muses? Whatever it was, it got me thinking in a new way about an old concern: how to be entirely present in the world—how to be a man who fully inhabits his place, not some half-assed version of a humanoid staring stupidly at a screen. ("It is important," said a fellow Michigander, "not to miss the world that is actually there.") Before I knew it the line between cooking and composing had blurred. I was writing, almost without meaning to, about garden, grill, and kitchen. And now, a decade later, at the gentle insistence of a few friends whose judgment may prove to be untrustworthy, I have decided to collect the essays into a book that combines two of my interests, writing and cooking, neither of which I claim to be any good at but both of which I happen to enjoy. The surprising discovery I made along the way is that these two interests are very much alike. I also discovered—or maybe confirmed an old suspicion—that, whether at my writing table or my cutting board, I am a wholly derivative person, a dwarf standing on the shoulders of giants, as Bernard of Chartres once put it. Hence "plagiarist" in the title.

To speak of an organizational plan here would be to make promiscuous use of two words: "organizational" and "plan." These essays, when first written, were never intended to cohere. But of course a book must cohere, so I have imposed on them something like a movement from spring to winter, but I have had to allow for a few disruptions in the pattern. This is a defect we're all going to have to live with. Besides, there has never been a perfect book, and I didn't think it fair to all the other writers in the world to produce one.

Other oddities may be accounted for by a few facts of biography. One is that I did the writing not in one place but two, Rock Island (Illinois), where I used to live but still earn my miserable keep, and Williamston (Michigan), where I currently live but fail miserably to keep what I earn. So both places impinge on the work. But I think I have provided enough in the way of cues and context to render clearly what otherwise might be confusing on that score.

Another biographical fact is that during the writing nearly a decade passed. In one piece an eight-year-old boy rides his bike with me to the farmers' market early on a Saturday morning; in another the same boy has hairy legs and sleeps till Saturday afternoon. But whether on the banks of the Mississippi or the Red Cedar I have tried very hard to *be* where I am, to be fully present in my place, to shape myself, "body and mind, to fully inhabit this earth," as Jim Harrison—the aforementioned Michigander—once put it. I also hope I never have to sell a house and move again. The prodigal has come home, though in my version he throws his own feast and doesn't have a pissed-off older brother.

I wish to acknowledge the advice and friendship of Jeff Polet, Mark Mitchell, Dave Crowe, Jeff Bilbro, and Bill Kauffman. I raise a glass to them. If this book has any faults, if any of its jokes or recipes are in bad taste, these five scoundrels are to blame. Blame them for not insisting more vehemently that I listen to their suggestions or else remove their names from the preface. (Also bear in mind Rumpole, the great defense barrister and swiller of Chateau Thames Embankment: "the food here is like my jokes—not always in the best of taste.")

But I raise the after-dinner glass, the snifter, to the woman whose favorite pastime is to count the number of times I refill it. She can wind my clock beyond all mortal hope of repair—just to pilfer a felicitous phrase from a more talented food writer. A woman of such immense variety, as Chesterton observed, can make a perfectly monogamous man feel as if he's living in a spiritual harem. And so it is with me. I have no doubt that when God realized His first computational error—that is, when He said (and here I paraphrase) "Uh, hold the phone. It is not good, *not good at all*, that man should be alone"—He had the likes of me in mind. This accounts for the presence in the world of such longsuffering and shimmering creatures as Kristin, wife of my youth and companion through time, ageless and *nonpareil*.

Introduction

The Argument of His Book

The world may or may not need another cookbook, but it needs all the lovers—amateurs—it can get.
— Robert Capon, *The Supper of the Lamb*

Curiously, in both writing and cooking you're a dead duck if you don't love the process.
— Jim Harrison, *The Raw and the Cooked*

The book you're holding and have already resolved to buy ten more copies of for Christmas gifts isn't really a cookbook. Or, if it is, it's a cookbook only in an accidental sort of way. It is certainly a book about food and drink, but it is also about music and poetry, work and play, repulsion and desire, heaven and hell, sunshine and snow, friendship and enemyship. It's about all things that pertain to both flesh and spirit. For the most part, however, it is a book about love, and maybe a little about lust too, but not the bad kind. Not goat-like lust. I mean the lawful variety—the lust that's like your good cholesterol engaged in dubious battle with the bad. I'll pilfer a line from that seventeenth-century wag, Robert Herrick, and call it "cleanly wantonness." And, having pilfered, I'll confess that there's plenty of stealing going on here as well. What is a plagiarist if not a thief?

But what I want to say first is that I have written this book as an amateur: out of love—love of place, of home, of earth and air and fire and water—and firewater too—of the goodly frame and excellent canopy and the brave o'erhanging firmament, of the simple, sensuous, and passionate, of love itself, and especially of the bread we do not live alone by, of food glorious food, of beer and cream and butter and cheese, of meaty sentences and seasoned meats alike: what oft was et but ne'er so well convexed.

Of course there are some recipes here too, or what might pass for recipes, so if recipes are what you're after, then by all means keep reading. And if you've already paid your money, I won't even mind if you use the book for kindling when you're done, especially if you resisted those pernicious discounts at amazon dot hell and paid full price for it at your local bookstore. Burn your books if you want to, and your bras and boxer briefs too. You won't offend me. I write because I like to and because the royalties keep my chain saws in bar oil for about an hour each year. Plus I subscribe to the Edward Abbey doctrine: I write to amuse my friends and annoy our enemies.

I'll admit, plagiarist that I am, that most of the dishes you'll find here don't exactly benefit from originality, that adolescent nineteenth-century obsession that afflicted so many of the Romantic writers. Nor do they satisfy the Modernist's demand to "make it new." But as someone who finds pound cake more palatable than Pound's *Cantos*, I'm not exactly vexed by this. "Originality," said James Russell Lowell in his delectable (if disapproving) essay on Thoreau, "consists in power of digesting and assimilating thoughts"—note the gastronomic metaphor—"so that they become part of our life and substance." So Montaigne: "The bees steal from this flower and that, but afterwards turn their pilferings into honey, which is their own; it is thyme and marjoram no longer." And as for making it new, I have always been baffled by this demand, so I don't see why I should heed it in the kitchen. Newness seldom impresses and often horrifies me.

But I would also be hard-pressed to say for certain that there are *no* original dishes in this book, or that I have never taken anything old and made it new. It is possible, I suppose, that I invented something here, if not a recipe then at least the paragraph in chapter 29 consisting of a single italicized exclamation point. That's something I've never seen done before. But readers hoping to discover new frontiers of delectation and sensory delight, and *real* gourmands demanding a *bocconcino* of savory piquancy plus lexicons of other inscrutable foreign words on every page, will find themselves in the position of the young bride looking out at Niagara Falls and admitting a little sadly that there are now *two* major disappointments in life.

So I make no claim to originality. As for Romantic obsessions or Modernist demands: falling upon the thorns of life has absolutely no appeal, and running with the bulls is just damned foolish.

But stealing is easy, so I steal.

Now that isn't as unlawful as it sounds. Borrowing and citing sources and knowing for sure where you got something are all tricky business. Not for undergraduates, mind you, and maybe not for your odd historian, who are the clumsiest thieves around. I mean for people who have been reading for a long time and for whom the parallel lines of the past, having been drawn in strict perspective, are all merging now. I mean people for whom to speak is to quote.

And besides, what you mean by "plagiarism," once you're beyond the blundering undergraduate or Ambrosial stage, ultimately depends on a lot of things. "Verbal plagiarism," wrote that neglected genius Owen Barfield, "is a matter of determinable fact." But "psychological plagiarism, or 'borrowing,' . . . depends on a number of imponderables such as the way a man reads, the way he thinks and, in the last resort, on your view of the nature of mind"—where "mind" might mean the fundamental principle of the universe and a whole host of other things that litigious copyright lawyers and other brain-dead materialists couldn't begin to get interested in, much less comprehend.

So there you have it. Notwithstanding the doctrine of one food writer—that "attribution is important in cooking"—I'm not going to cite all my sources, whether literary or culinary. There are too many of them. And here's a warning to each and every one who thinks I should have spent another eight years tracking down permissions: if all of you file suit, you'll go bat-shit crazy trying to divide a $30 royalty check thirty thousand different ways. Theft is the running gag here. I'm going to proceed with what I admit, and you should assume, are sticky fingers.

(Your fingers are sticky? So lick them. I'll use the $30 to throw a party for all of us.)

But I also want to point out that theft is part and parcel of one of the most interesting styles available to us, the allusive style, and that this is true in writing and cooking and music and everything else. Few of us ever utter a word or a phrase we haven't borrowed from somewhere else. There are no originals. Even Concord's dull sage figured that out—once he'd had a couple of decades to rethink the callowness of "Self-Reliance." "Originals are not original," he wrote in 1859, and "genius borrows nobly." And even if Eliot and Stravinsky and Faulkner were wrong, it's flattering to remember what they said: that lesser artists borrow while great artists steal. Whenever I need reminding of this I put Brahms' first symphony on the hi-fi. For, as Brahms himself said, even a donkey can hear the allusions to Beethoven's ninth.

Food is on a lot of people's pens these days, at least to judge from the newspapers and magazines and the remainder bins that await this little masterpiece. There is no paucity of reading material. (There's also no paucity of *viewing* material, and whenever I'm reminded that my retirement account is thinner than carpaccio I'm almost sorry I wasn't called to be a toothy Italian celebrity chef with her own cooking and cleavage show.) But about the time I started writing these little exuberances—having already learned from Anthony Bourdain's *Kitchen Confidential* how to use the phrase "hot nut" properly, and having on more than one occasion been shamed by Jacques Pépin into thinking I haven't even earned the right to pour milk over Fruit Loops—I picked up a book on food that was published in 1969: Fr. Robert Farrar Capon's *Supper of the Lamb*. I liked it so much that I was prepared to drop my pencil for good and admit that we'd come to the end of writing about food. Capon, God rest his soul, had done it so well, and with such care and patience and insight—and hinting all the while at the "heights and depths of the sexuality which is our glory"—that it seemed the only thing left for me to do was recommend his book. But then I remembered the words of Holy Writ: of the making of many books there is no end.

Who was I to disregard a clear injunction from Above to keep producing them?

And then, misery of miseries, Jim Harrison died. *The Raw and the Cooked* would need to undergo a renascence, and I was just the acolyte to lead the sacred procession: after all, Harrison was born near my fishing shack along the Au Sable river, and he graduated from a high school a mile and a half from where I grew up. Talk about another clear injunction from Above.

And here's the clincher: whatever Capon's and Harrison's merits, the really important thing about them, I realized, was that they agreed with *me*. Handling and preparing food, drinking wine (and calling it "wine," which is its name, not "alcohol," which isn't), eating, conversing with friends, looking at things and loving them for what they are, not for what they mean to us, ignoring the loathsome pronouncements of food ninnies and nutritionists and "foodies" (a term to be used as a sneer or not at all)—these remind us that, as I will repeat in this book, the fullness of man is the incarnate condition. (That's stolen from Bishop Anthony of Sourozh and slightly modified.) We aren't disembodied spirits floating above the earth. We are creatures of flesh and blood, sometimes stumbling clumsily and sometimes gliding gracefully across the flat and rolling and infinitely various surfaces of this splendid spinning planet, awaiting expectantly, as we should, the resurrection—*not* the fabled departing flight of the ungrateful Platonic soul but the *resurrection*. We should want to get down into the grasses, as David Brower once put it, not drive over them like a Gnostic spastic on his way to McDeathknell's or Burger Thing or KF(ing)C.

The problem, however, is that Capon was a man of the cloth and Harrison a kind of anti-clerical honorary Ojibway, whereas I am neither of these. Also, they both belong to the Three-Strikes-And-You're-Out Club: they're dead white males, whereas I'm a living one. So we don't even share a common ontological status.

This, I recognized almost immediately, was clearly a problem that required some serious plagiarism. I was going to have to think of myself as a "renovated spirit singled out." I might even have to go so far as to say that a

> bond unknown to me
> Was given, that I should be, else sinning greatly,
> A *dedicated* Spirit,

which, let me tell you, clarified things perfectly, as I'm sure you can imagine. (Who says *The Prelude* has no utilitarian value?) The task before me was plain: I was to carry on their work. All I had to do was keep from being as tedious as a nineteenth-century lacustrine stamp distributor and erstwhile poet who in his younger days had knocked up a French girl. Capon had the dishes and the drinks; he especially had the indispensable theological flights of fancy so lacking in Harrison, and also the notes of dissent ("I do not, so far as I know," he writes, "own a pan with Teflon"). He had all this and much else. Harrison had the appetitive nature and the whimsy and the irreverence lacking in Capon, and also the right amount of well-aimed contempt ("I had become a writer," he says, "to avoid shitting through my mouth like a politician"). So I set out to attempt a proper synthesis. I would make it all my own and add the stolen moments, when love is caught off-guard, just to pinch a phrase from Dan Fogelberg, may he and his scattered ashes also rest in peace: I mean the moments when you're in the kitchen and the music is on and the scent of onions sautéing in butter reaches the cartilage bisecting your face and you just can't *not* pat the fanny of the one you love or pick up your daughter and squeeze the stuffing out of her or sneak a quick shot of bourbon to hasten the sacred ministry of the slow-working beer at hand.

And I would insist, as my forebears had implied, that the kitchen is where all good folk belong—at least until lights-out—and that these good folk belong there *with* one another, handling a pomegranate like a relief pitcher rubbing down a baseball, chopping fresh garlic on a *wooden* cutting board, not on one of those plastic abominations, tasting sauces from a *wooden* spoon, swirling deep inky red wine in a balloon glass or peaty Islay scotch in a thick rocks glass, and singing along to the music.

Always make sure there's music. And I don't mean the garbage that the kids these days listen to.

It is said *le style c'est l'homme même*, at least it's said in France, whenever the native snobs take a break from viewing foreign cuisine down the slopes of their cowardly Gallic noses. And right they are to say it. But man is not made by style alone. Style, like presentation, is only an aspect of the fare, a mere part of the board. And so because my readers, whether they be amused friends or annoyed enemies, may encounter both stylistic *and* prejudicial idiosyncrasies in this book—opinions, let us call them, not widely held though certainly proper to a creature of flesh and blood—I think it prudent to provide a little context to help clarify some of the diversions and flights of fancy here, to offer a short profile of the eccentric impecunious author and to list a few articles of his stalwart unwavering faith: to give, as that wag Herrick did in *Hesperides*, an argument of his book. (Even Capon paused to explain his prejudices, which included an aversion to all diets.) So what follows is meant to help you make sense of both the book and the author, the *Plagiarist* and the plagiarist.

1. Don't be confused by the several aliases, *noms de plume*, and *noms de guerre* that I go by in this book. They include: the Bar Jester, Dumb Ass, Chief Dumb Ass, Lucky Bastard, and Cheap Bastard, just to name a few. I'm not really a bastard. I'm as legitimate as Edgar. But I *am* lucky. I'm also cheap.

My wife likewise goes by many terms of endearment, some of them uncharacteristically original with me and some not: Sweet Precious, Chief Eye-rolling Officer (C.E.O.), Counter of Cocktails—not a name or role that becomes her, in my opinion—Sleepy Pie, Goddess Excellently Bright (that's stolen from Ben Jonson), Espouséd Saint (and that from Milton), and so on. For some reason using given names has always embarrassed me a little—the way a Polish Catholic would legitimately be embarrassed at being asked by the pastor of *Shout!* Ministries to "open with prayer" before their sons' church-league baseball game. There's a certain unsettling sincerity to given names, and in my view being sincere is something people aren't nearly suspicious enough of. Too much sincerity, and the next thing you know you're in grave danger of becoming a millennial guest on NPR and starting every answer with the word "so." So you can bet the children go by a whole other set of labels here as well, especially the older boy, whom we're all prepared to see tricked out fairly soon in a fetching orange jumpsuit.

2. Even after three decades of marriage my wife sometimes forgets that I'm not an especially serious person. Once when I cracked a joke and she took me seriously I said, "How long have you known me?" She looked me straight in the eyes and said, "Too. Damn. Long." What a girl! She's the bright center of my irregular orbit. She's the main dish, as I like to tell my feminist friends, who really go for that kind of talk. Plus at present writing we have two teenaged boys, so we find ourselves after thirty plus years at a new and unexpected stage in our marriage: automatically allied in all household battles. Allied by default. You have heard it said that a common enemy will unite people? Nothing unites you and your Counter of Cocktails like having a common conundrum in size ten adidas living under your roof.

3. I'm an unreconstructed sports nut who favors the standard American pastimes. But I abominate soccer and must ask you to forgive me for believing that the mascot of all soccer teams should be the penguin. If you're going to behave as if God didn't provide you with hands and arms—*and* bore the hell out of everyone on your way to a 1–1 tie—then what you are is a penguin.

I'm loyal to the Big 10 in general, even though (as of pub date) it has suffered a foreign invasion from Penn State, Rutgers, Maryland, and Nebraska. 10≠14. I'm loyal to Michigan State in particular, because green and white are God's favorite colors (*q.v.* Song of Solomon 1:16 & 5:10) and because I had season tickets during the Magic Johnson era. I also filched a couple of my credentials from this noble university, our nation's first land-grant college. But I *hate* the NBA. Pox take it! I didn't hate it in the age of Bird and Magic, and before them in the glory days of Clyde Frazier, Earl the Pearl Monroe, the Big O, Jerry West, Lucius Allen, Dollar Bill Bradley, Bill Russell, John Havlicek, Jo Jo White, and the sky-hook assassin formerly known as Lew Alcindor.

(Once upon time the names of athletes were glorious, were they not? Think of Alberto Juantorena and Steve Prefontaine and Fred Biletnikoff and Garo Yepremian and Aurelio Rodriguez and Auld Tom Morris—and even, way on down the line, God Shammgod. What names! Not a "Mackenzie" or "Jaden" or "Dakota" among them.)

4. It is true that I am an English professor, though I usually try to keep this embarrassing fact a secret. Indeed, I try to keep concealed facts and revealed opinions somewhere near the vermouth-to-bourbon ratio of a good Manhattan. My friend Jim, the farmer, says I'm a farmer who got lost in the English department. On most days I can believe this is true: "lost" is certainly an appropriate epithet for most professors. We're a convocation of politic worms. What we do to the great artifacts of human culture is inexcusable. It was aptly articulated by G.K. Chesterton when he attempted to explain what we have done to the "bubble blown from the pipe of poetry": we have robbed it of "much of the lightness of the bubble, and retained only the horrible healthiness of the soap." So it should surprise no one that, wherever I can, I take swipes at "hire" education, as Gene Logsdon called it. (See especially chapters 7 and 31.)

5. I don't like the split infinitive any more than I like split-pea soup but I have nothing against the stranded preposition. That's one thing I'm sure of.

6. I worked my way through college and graduate school doing manual labor and found that I preferred it to intellectual "labor." I like carpentry, plumbing, engine repair, gardening, and felling dead trees on cold fall afternoons, Michigan State football on the radio of my beautiful ugly brown '83 Dodge Ram pick-up, a.k.a. The Babe Magnet. I admire capable men who can do necessary things; I abominate people who look down on them.

7. In politics I'm a fair-minded man, which means I'm an equal-opportunity hater. That's the salutary effect that our two-party system has had on me. I've never once pulled the lever for a Republican and I don't intend to start. Democrats hoping for better treatment from me will die unhappy, which is fine with me so long as they die. My view is that while these two utterly clueless groups of social planners pursue their pet social projects, one to arm

kindergarteners with assault rifles and the other to supply them with ribbed condoms, the rest of us should get on our knees and thank God for giving us two middle fingers—and then use them. (Let us not forget Harrison: the government is "the world's most powerful autistic child.") You might say I'm against everything—everything that isn't local, which means just about everything. I especially hate bigness and centralization. Give me the small and decentralized. "Subsidiarity" is one of those words schoolchildren should learn before they're taught the Pledge of Allegiance, and they should learn "subsidiarity" in unconsolidated schools that enjoy autonomy and local control. I realize that local school boards and teachers and parents can be wrong sometimes. But being wrong and being free to be wrong is *way* better than living under the kind of "expert" compulsion that issues from wronger people in distant places. Distant places and the people in them should mind their own damn distant business. Each place should be free to make its own trouble—*without*, I hasten to add, some smug-mugged Rand-retching Libertarian trying to take the credit for saying so. We'll all be fine if we just read enough Chesterton and Belloc and follow old Wendell, the poet of Port Royal, down to where the wood drake rests in his beauty on the water and the great heron feeds.

8. I love my country, even though it went to hell in the late 1780s. Not even Elijah Craig's salutary discovery, first distilled that same ill-fated decade, could prevent the downward spiral. I'm an anti-federalist, which makes me a true federalist. I would have voted for the New Jersey Plan. Constitution-worship baffles me.

9. I like new things once they're old but not until then. And so, as with my pick-up trucks and flannel shirts and jeans and basketball shoes and books and sports heroes, so with my religion: the older the better. "Contemporary worship" is a contradiction in terms, like "mobile home," "microwave cooking," and "new tradition." (In my racket there's always a dean who's trying to implement a "new tradition." This is also known as auditioning for a presidency somewhere *else*. I'll have none of it.) If you want to make certain that you're in church instead of therapy, check to see if you've confessed an ancient creed. On this point I'm quite sure that Robert Capon would have agreed and Jim Harrison not, though I bet he does now.

(Here I must extend an olive branch to the blue-jeaned guitar-strumming members of *Shout!* and to Pastor Todd, with his shirt untucked and the electronic gadget he's reading the Bible from—"a new dynamic translation updated for today's multi-tasking believer!"). I write as much for these good folk as for the Papist at his beads and the Anglican at his sherry. I would have no one go away hungry or use this book for kindling *yet*. I have read it. I know how it ends: rich like a reduction and assertive like a salice. And if you're reading it on a Kindle, you can't burn it anyway. A Kindle, being a new thing, isn't flammable, though it can be thrown with great enthusiasm at a brick wall—and *should* be, preferably Al Hrabosky style, especially if you bought it on amazon dot hell.

10. I try not to buy things that can't be burned and I never shop on amazon dot hell.

11. And while I'm at it, I might as well quote the upright Nicolás Gómez-Dávila on the topic of preaching: "sermons undermine faith."

12. It may be that I'm a thief, but I'm not a liar—or not much of one—and I don't always prize transparency. Transparency in and of itself satisfies no categorical imperative. So, for example, if you can see through a thing, it's not beer. It's an advertisement or a promise from an administrator—or, if you're a lucky bastard, an article of clothing. (Someone *else's* clothing—a woman's.)

13. All change is bad. (I pilfered that from Bill Kauffman, the Sage of Batavia.) As Lord Falkland said during the English Civil Wars, "When it is not necessary to change, it is necessary not to change."

14. There is no such thing as too much garlic, too much irony, or too much thigh—provided the thigh is a good one. For, again, Gómez-Dávila: "A nude body solves every problem of the universe." *Et alibi*, "The modern world shall not be punished. It is the punishment."

15. There's no excuse for not liking to cook, even if you're no good at it. (Have you stopped woggling just because you're clumsy in the clutch?) And you *do* have time to cook, if only you would cancel your cable package, throw away your "mobile device," and quit going to the gym to use that machine you climb and climb and climb on while ascending to no heights. (Harrison: "If you don't have time to cook your dinner quit your job.") It is in keeping with our true nature and end to enjoy good food, prepared carefully, and eaten gratefully and slowly in the presence of other people who

can laugh at jokes, recite good poems, and who have figured out that food is more than "little invisible spooks called calories," as Capon put it. ("The calorie approach," he said, "is the work of the devil.") Anyone who says food is just calories might as well go all the way and say sex is just friction. Life is too short for people blessed with wheat and water and yeast, with tarragon and basil and tomatoes, with bacon and bourbon and butter, to be that unbelievably wrong about something as important as food.

16. And, unlike pretty much everyone else—certainly unlike almost everyone in my racket save the incomparable Scott Russell Sanders ("I wish to consider the virtue and discipline of staying put," he wrote)—I believe in being at home and staying there. Where I am is where I belong. I love my place. In accordance with the decentralist principles that Moses brought down from one mountain and that Jesus ratified on another, and in order of decreasing size but increasing importance, my place is: my state, my county, my town, my pastures, my barns, my house, my front porch, my study, my kitchen, my family, my marriage, and my side of its bed. To quote Nikon Don (and this won't be the last time), I like where I am now.

On these noble principles the culinary plagiarist stands; from these noble principles *The Culinary Plagiarist* rises—like a mushroom from the compost pile.

And now a word about the dedication: my good friend and colleague Mike died at 54. His professional legacy includes a book titled *American Humor*, but his real legacy isn't measurable and never will be, no matter how many Evil Quantifiers robbed his students of their time by forcing them to fill out course evaluations. (By Evil Quantifiers I mean those assessment-mad midlevel-management maniacs who reduce the world to little bubbles scribbled in with #2 pencils. They are ruining my day job, turning a once-august profession into a sub-species of half-assed social-science and accounting, and forcing me—*against my will*—to seek refuge in breweries.) Mike was a friend in an age when "friend" had become a meaningless word, thanks mainly to a pusillanimous television show and then, later, to what is known as "social media," which is obviously anti-social in pretty much every respect.

Mike was no cook. He could make only a couple of dishes well, and as a result he reciprocated the hospitality of his friends by hosting too few dinner parties. None to be exact. But he wasn't above recognizing a good dish when he ate one—or *saw* one, for he was a red-head, after all. He loved all the right books (the ones I love, especially *The Moviegoer*, which I steal from frequently here) and all the right beers. He also would have agreed with Gómez-Dávila about the explanatory power of the nude. Mike and I disagreed on the big issues, and I address this in the Afterword, but he was a tremendous friend to me, and I did what little I could to repay his kind offices.

Mike took his qualities and his faults and all the many mysteries that his life was made of and carried them into an early grave. Betimes he carried them, verily. I miss his good company, and because I do, and because the poor bastard could never even get the bread dough to rise, I dedicate this book to his memory.

And now (just to steal a strategy from the novelist Graham Swift) let me tell you about . . .

I
Spring

And the unfailing sense of being young
Spread out like a spring-woken tree, wherein
That hidden freshness sung,
That certainty of time laid up in store . . .
   —Philip Larkin, "Love Songs in Age"

Frhüling ist wiedergekommen. Die Erde
ist wie ein Kind, das Gedichte weiß;
viele, o viele . . . Für die Beshwerde
langen Lernens bekommt sie den Preis.

(Spring has come back again. The Earth is like a child who knows poems by heart; so many poems, so many verses, patient toil winning her prizes at last—or something like that.)
   —Rilke, *Sonnets to Orpheus*

1

Apple Blossoms and Horseshit and Divine Intention

What Happens Before We Eat

The earth's annual stunt of renewal—to plagiarize from John Updike—is fully underway here. It's pretty far along, actually. The first "green" of nature, which as Robert Frost said is actually gold, is no longer gold. It's fully green now.

My apple tree blossomed so quickly this year, and with such speed and brevity, that I barely had a chance to regard its radiant flashing white against the regal purple of the redbud tree in front of it, now also green.

And this puts me to thinking once again that Frost's great strength as a poet was that he always got the details right: Nature's

> early leaf's a flower,
> But only so an hour.

And yet some of that early gold of which he wrote still abides. You can see it in the air—if you can see at all. I can see it through a kind of liquid irritation that will persist until the seed-head is off the grass. But until that time I'll be the willing sufferer of itching eyes and sneezing fits—the *willing* sufferer, for the earth, thank God, is performing its annual stunt of renewal.

Each year at about this time I'm a little nervous the stunt will fail. I always wonder whether this will be the year the big green thing doesn't happen. This wondering is more like an intellectual exercise or an occasion to indulge in what I would call a healthy little dose of fear. But things aren't so bad yet. "There lives the dearest freshness deep down things," as Hopkins said.

> The Holy Ghost over the bent
> World broods with warm breast and with ah! bright wings.

Or, to paraphrase, there is shelter under the shadow of a wing but also a divine intention at work. You might say, if you were inclined to, that the three-personed God whom Donne did battle with *acts for* us but also *thinks toward* us.

True, it didn't appear back in April of 2010 that we were going to get a mulligan in the Gulf of Mexico after the BP oil spill, and oddly enough no oil-dependent TV preacher at the time declared *that* technological disaster to be a vengeful act of God such as Katrina obviously was. But the big green thing does seem to be happening. We commuters and buyers of plastics have dodged another bullet.

Here at Casa Cashdrain our herbs are in. Most of our flowers are in, save for the sweep of Impatiens that by mid-summer will form a curving swath in a riot of colors along the front of the house. We're waiting to put them in until I've fetched a load of horseshit. The soil needs it. We all need it. If there are going to be annual stunts of renewal, the earth must manure itself, and we must help. We must help by putting shit in the spreader.

We'll need everything that lived but that now goes among the wastes of time if we're to manure the earth properly, because spring isn't really a stunt. It isn't an escape trick or a sleight-of-hand or anything like that. And it certainly isn't a series of mechanisms responding to other mechanisms in the absence of a dove-like brooding. It isn't anything but what it is—life emerging from death, then living, then dying so that new life might again be possible, a shadowy picture all the while of a death and resurrection to come, seen from the here and now through fear and hope alike. And we must be very careful when, in trying to understand it, we presume to say what it is, or what it is *like*.

It is true that nature takes its color from the eye—a sober coloring from the eye, as Wordsworth said. Nature as plagiarist! And Pope reminded us that all appears yellow to the jaundiced eye. But it is also true that there is little we can do about this relation of the eye to the world except be careful. "The charming landscape which I saw this morning," said Emerson, "is indubitably made up of some twenty or thirty farms. Miller owns this field,

Locke that, and Manning the woodlot beyond. But none of them owns the landscape. There is a property in the horizon which no man has but he whose eye can integrate all the parts, that is, the poet." If not to see the landscape is a failure of imagination, and it is, then it follows that cultivating the imagination is indispensable, for there is little we can do about the fact that the world we have is, in part, the world that we have called into being by perceiving and naming it. We must be careful lest we see farms and woodlots only and not a landscape—or, worse yet, not a woodlot but a quantity of board-length poised to fetch the going rate.

No: spring is not the rinse cycle. It is resurrection. The poet who said that the world "will flame out, like shining from shook foil" was being careful, as was the poet who said that

> leaf subsides to leaf,
> So Eden sank to grief.
> So dawn goes down to day.
> Nothing gold can stay.

And I reckon they both knew the relation between apples and road apples, as so few poets do today—except, of course, for Old Wendell, the Mad Farmer, Kentucky's finest gift to the world not counting bourbon:

> The fertility cycle is a cycle entirely of living creatures passing again and again through birth, growth, maturity, death, and decay. Industrial technologies may shortcut the cycle *for a while*, but such shortcuts also interrupt it, bringing it, and us, presently into danger and eventually into disaster.

Apples become road apples, which become apples. The former become the latter, which become the former, which become the latter, and so on and so on and so on, so long as we pay our debt to the soil, as Steven Stoll so usefully put it. And *then* we can eat.

But how about a cocktail first?

2

After All, It Almost Rhymes With *Bikini*

I like to drink martinis.
Two at the most.
Three I'm under the table,
Four I'm under the host.

—Dorothy Parker (attributed)

When their drinks were delivered, he looked at his a moment as though it were the Holy Grail. "Even normally, there's nothing like that first ice-cold, razor-edge sip of a martini. But now. Cheers, my love. And may there be many more together." His glass being brimful, he raised it very carefully so as not to spill a drop. "Ah!" he whispered, as though giving thanks to the gods.

—Peter DeVries, *Peckham's Marbles*

An Englishman's gin bottle is his castle.

—Rumpole

R oger Angell, in a lovely little essay titled "Dry Martini," published in *The New Yorker* in August of 2002, quotes Ogden Nash's "A Drink with Something in It":

> There's something about a Martini,
> A tingle remarkably pleasant;
> A yellow, a mellow Martini;
> I wish I had one at present.
> There is something about a Martini,
> Ere the dining and dancing begin,
> And to tell you the truth,
> It is not the vermouth—
> I think that perhaps it's the gin.

And later he quotes *Harper's* columnist Bernard De Voto: "You can no more keep a Martini in the refrigerator than you can keep a kiss there. The proper union of gin and vermouth is a great and sudden glory; it is one of the happiest marriages on earth and one of the shortest."

I know this not because I keep back issues of *The New Yorker* around but because I have in my possession *Secret Ingredients: The New Yorker Book of Food and Drink*, edited by David Remnick, who could leave off writing about politics and do more of this sort of thing.

At any rate it's a book I recall having read from one Wednesday afternoon after I'd come home to the Thanksgiving break. The children were much younger, and I had exiled them to the basement with threats of dismemberment should they disturb me as, in the tradition of Robert Traver, whom I'm about to plagiarize from, I built myself a sky-high drink, put on a mile-long piano concerto—must have been Delius—and sat down to read something I wasn't going to have to explain to sophomores flummoxed by the Puritans and outraged at having to sit through an explanation of the Total Depravity they all suffer from.

And I read again Angell's piece, and a few others, before the growling of young stomachs called me to the kitchen and such intrusive parental duties as feeding children. ("But *father*," you could almost hear them say as if they had just stepped out of some sentimental novel, "we're *cold* and *hungry*. *Please*, father. *Please* don't go to the tavern tonight.")

But ere those creatures summoned me to the stove, I was at leisure, if only briefly, to think about this most civilized of drinks, the martini, which almost rhymes with a noble sartorial combo made of a little bit of string and four variations on a three-sided geometrical shape, a shape that coincidentally resembles a martini glass.

If you put at one end of things the thirsty man who fills his glass with a roaring torrent of tap water and then chugs it down, and at the other end of things the host who, before his guests arrive, has placed his martini glasses in the icebox to chill them and who has stabbed his olives (or pearl onions or capers or who has shaved his lemon), and who, once his guests have arrived, shakes or stirs his gin and vermouth and at last lovingly pours drinks all the way around—if you do this you have in bold relief the thing that distinguishes the martini from chugged water and every drink in between them, for in between the thirsty man and the martini drinker stand all other drinks and all other drinkers, all of whom dwell on a kind of continuum that excludes no one, not even Carrie Nation. The weekend beer drinker who pulls a tab or twists off a cap is nearer the thirsty man than the host chilling his glasses. Mind you, he is no less noble than anyone on the continuum, but the distance between his lips and his elixir is not so great as that between the host's and his gin. In the one case preparation reduces to opening a can or a bottle. And that is preparation only in the sense that rapidly undressing your lover is foreplay.

But the host who thinks ahead and chills his glasses and who at the end of a lengthy process enjoys (with his guests) a martini has submitted himself to a kind of discipline. He has given himself time to anticipate. Or, to extend the apt and noble analogy, he has demonstrated a degree of respect, as it were, for the function of buttons and clasps and the way a soft garment can fall noiselessly to the floor. Drinking a martini is a desideratum, like the apogee of amore. It is itself an end. But it is an end that the anticipation and preparation participate in. It is an end *precisely* because of all that precedes it. The thirsty man at the tap knows nothing of this. He doesn't have making love on his mind. Not yet, anyway. He wants his thirst quenched.

And that's fine, because he's *thirsty*. But the host and his guests are not thirsty. They don't want water. They want martinis. They want to satisfy their great longing for common ground, a place where sweet uncensored talk, so necessary to friendship, can enjoy its beginning, move toward its middle, anticipate and then finally reach its end.

And so they must decide upon their drink. And, to state only the most obvious fact, the martini is a much more efficient catalyst for conversation than, say, buttermilk. No one ever parted with a nasty delicious secret, or told a joke he might normally suppress, under the influence of buttermilk.

Now I would no more be mistaken on the matter of preparation than on foreplay: time is not the transcendent value here. There are drinks that take longer to make than a good crisp clean clear martini, and some of them are worth the investment in time. You drinkers of Manhattans and Old Fashioneds and White Ladys (and especially you millennial connoisseurs of those weird concoctions invented by bartenders in establishments where the men have "hairstyles" and the women peer through designer eyeglasses at obsessively thumbed DumbPhones) know whereof I speak.

But some drinks are not worth the investment in time. I, for one, will spend considerable care on a pomegranate "martini" (explanation of sneer quotes forthcoming) for my own Goddess Excellently Bright, or for a friend's wife, but not a minute on one for myself. There is no such drink in my future. And if you're a man and you ask for one in my house, I will make you one but I will also impugn your manhood. Expect to be treated like a league golfer whose putt makes it only half-way to the hole. Expect to be asked, "does your husband like cocktails too?"

So the value at stake here is *preparation* itself, preparation *as such*.

One thing that makes a martini a martini is the chilling of the glass, whatever your preferred method. (I myself do not care for the iced glass; I prefer to put the glass in the icebox, as, tonight, I have done.) There is a certain something, a certain *je ne sais quoi*, about a piece of delicate stemware silently submitting itself in the dark to the secret ministry of frost. It's like knowing that there is a beautiful woman at home of a Friday evening waiting for you to walk through the door and reassure her—with one of your wonted wanton well-placed pats—that all shall be well and that all manner of thing shall be well.

And, again, to extend the analogy, a really fine martini glass chilling in the icebox is like the expectant woman, ready with her smile and her incomparable kiss, who loves you enough not to ask about your day—as if, even bidden, you could feign sufficient interest in it to rehearse the desultory affair. The turn toward a martini at the end of all *that*, at the end of go-nowhere committee meetings (as if there were any other kind) or such questions as "what do I have to do to get an A in this class?" (Answer: "Be born someone else")—the turn at the end of all *that* is nothing less than a turning toward the light, which even house plants have the good sense to do.

But there is more that makes the martini: measuring the vermouth, for example. And it is worth saying that some men are precise about this and some are not, just as some golfers read a putt deliberately and others play it by feel. And then there's the shaking or stirring, either one recommended by certain aesthetic considerations or dispositions about "bruising" the gin, and then there's the garnish, and the temperature of the drink, to say nothing of the martini glass itself.

Let us consider the glass first. The stemless martini glasses that you sometimes see used in postmodern establishments—you know: places of precise geometric designs packed with people consciously living out their "lifestyles"—have a very limited appeal. As a novelty they satisfy something, like the baffling Modernist demand to "make it new," but they will never manage to compare to that eternal shape of the martini glass, which Angell calls "the slim narcissus stalk rising to a 1939 World's Fair triangle above." The stainless steel variation on that classic design is, I warrant, very nice. (I won't drink pomegranate "martinis," but I grant that they look lovely in stainless martini glasses.) The crooked (pronounced as one syllable) or zig-zag stem is interesting enough, I suppose, and there are others as well, of course, but the best departure from the straight stem I've ever seen is the stem in the shape of a treble clef sign. If you can find one of those and have the good sense to buy it, you have a premium martini in your future.

But what is meant by "premium"?

That begins first with the condition of your inner man (even if you're a woman), which subsequently and perforce points toward your gin. First you must have something really fine on your mind, like Elgar, or the Petrarchan sonnet, or a book of dirty limericks, and then you must honor that intellectual or spiritual disposition with something commensurate to it. No one is saying there is no place for the run-of-the-gin-mill martini made with ten-dollar swill. Sometimes Sibelius and Seagram's are in your future: not the brightest future imaginable, granted, but a future nonetheless. It just so happens that at present we are concerned with something other than a dim future.

We are concerned, that is, with gin, for the martini has evolved to the point at which it seems the vermouth is not much of a concern at all, at least to judge by the way it has been backing out of the drink, from the insane ratios of those that verge on the so called "upside down martini" to Tom Lehrer's 6:1 to the Queen's 11:1 to Colonel Cantwell's 15:1. You may, if you like, purchase an expensive vermouth so that you can say you use an expensive vermouth in your martini. You may, if you like, use Kina Lillet and think of yourself as a kind of Double-O-Seven, going so far as to name your drink after a double agent, herself named for a liturgical hour (see chapter 43). But vermouth is not the point. It is barely even *beside* the point. Was it Churchill who famously said that you make a martini by shaking the gin while facing France and whispering the word "vermouth"? I've heard that this is so and I'm prepared to believe it, just as I'm prepared to believe that some people simply turn the vermouth bottle so that its label faces the gin and then proceed to shake straight gin. But the point is that a martini is a drink composed mainly of gin and only slightly altered by vermouth, ice, and perhaps a garnish. Some folk swirl vermouth merely to coat the martini glass and then pour the vermouth back into the bottle. That's a way never to run out of vermouth, unless you've got a real problem. I myself allow as many as, but no more than, three drops of dry vermouth in a martini, one drop for each person of the Holy Trinity, though I usually stop at two, one for each of the two natures of Christ. The drops go directly into the shaker (or pitcher), but I freely admit that their pedigree is no concern of mine. Because I'm just a poor country English teacher, and also a cheap bastard, I'll spend less on the vermouth so that I can spend more on the gin, and this brings us back to what is meant by "premium."

It means the gin.

For many years I preferred Beefeater because I could get it cheap and because it seemed to me a clean uncomplicated gin, which it is. And, to tell the truth, I still prefer it.

But it seems to have something against me personally, for what reasons I cannot divine—except maybe that "gin" also means "trap," as in Psalm 141: *Keep me from the snares which they have laid for me, and the gins of the workers of iniquity.* So, although I haven't left off drinking it altogether, I drink it less frequently, and rarely at my age risk a second Beefeater martini—notwithstanding the trustworthy axiom attributable, I think, to John Doxat: that there is no such thing as one martini. (I think it was James Thurber who said, "One martini is all right. Two are too many, and three are not enough.") Something about Beefeater doesn't always reciprocate my admiration. I have sometimes called it Memoryeater.

I like Tanqueray, mainly out of respect for David Brower, the great Archdruid, for whom Tanqueray was the gin of choice and who believed fervently in the "preventive martini," and I'll buy Tanqueray now and then. I like Hendrick's but rarely spring for it. I like Citadelle and have bought it at least twice, and Boodle's too, and Broker's. But my gin of choice, in some measure influenced by a friend who knows his way around a shaker, is Bombay Sapphire. I'll say this about it and then leave off: Sapphire is fruity but clean, complex but uncomplicated, at least for my Teutonic palate. It satisfies my nose and tongue and doesn't inconvenience me on mornings after. I can't say I actually prefer it to Memoryeater, but I usually choose Sapphire in its stead.

Now I wouldn't be mistaken here for one of those wankish cosmopolitan critics, one of those sophisticates who pronounce upon the "subtle notes of vanilla" in the bourbon or the "implications of anise in the robust finish" of this or that liqueur. I want to say nothing more than that Sapphire really satisfies, that it satisfies in all the ways that the lesser objects of our longings satisfy. A premium martini requires a premium gin. I have no need of anything premiumer than Sapphire. There are other gins under the Bombay label, but I don't happen to care for them.

Garnishes are another matter, however. Brower, who said that only a madman would put an olive in a martini and displace three cubic centimeters of gin, didn't like how the olive changed the taste of his martini, and I'm inclined to agree with him. (What he would think of the so-called "dirty" martini—an abomination unto the Lord worse, maybe, than fornication and evangelical fundamentalism—is not difficult to imagine.) In a lovely little book titled *Martini, Straight Up*, Lowell Edmunds, a classicist clearly schooled on epigrammatic efficiency, wastes no time weighing in on the matter. Recalling that Sherwood Anderson came to grief because he swallowed the toothpick that his very last terrestrial olive was impaled on, Edmunds says, "I know that the fear of death is not going to stop people from rash behavior, so let me give a stronger reason for not using olives: They ruin the taste of the drink."

Now I like an olive or two fine. I especially like a blue-cheese-stuffed olive, or an almond- or a jalapeño- or a garlic-stuffed olive. But I will usually stab and then rinse the olive before dropping it into the glass. I want as little of the olive interfering with the gin as possible. I also like a pearl onion garnish or a caper garnish. But these, too, I will stab and then rinse. Gin should taste like gin, not gin plus olive or caper. Even the vermouth, finally, is a gesture in the direction of tradition only. No martini drinker at your dinner party would refuse gin in a martini glass simply because you're out of vermouth—or olives, for that matter. Any martini drinker who says otherwise is a scoundrel and a damned liar and ought to be forced to read Adrienne Rich for a whole afternoon—in an uncomfortable straight-back chair.

(And, briefly to revisit the matter of the gin itself, if you fancy a martini, then ninety-nine times out of a hundred you will drink a martini made from shitty gin rather than not drink one at all. Deny it and we'll force Robert Southey on you. Just see if you survive *that* punishment.)

My garnish of choice, if given the choice, is a lemon twist. I like the look of it. I also like the suggestion of citrus, less assertive than the olive, which, as Brower said, displaces too much gin. I don't lace the rim of the glass with lemon or do any of that extra nonsense. I like a crisp clean clear martini: two drops of vermouth adrift in a sea of Bombay Sapphire or Beefeater gin, shaken vigorously over ice and drained into a cold and frosty martini glass, where bathes, naked, like Bathsheba in the moonlight, a thin lemon twist.

(And let's be clear: a martini can also break your throne and cut your hair and, from your lips, draw the "hallelujah.")

Coldness matters. Keeping the gin in the freezer and taking it without the cut of ice is, I warrant, a mighty fine way to go, though I tend not to go that way. Not anymore. And there's a simple solution, as Edmunds points out, to the annoying tendency toward room temperature that the bottom half of a very cold martini inevitably shows: make two small martinis instead of one large one. Even if you're married to a Counter of Cocktails, as I am, two small martinis only count as one martini. If this allowance is not in the Bible somewhere, and that includes the deutero-canonical books, or if it's not a part of Holy Tradition, it should be.

Some would solve the temperature problem by taking their martini on the rocks, the mere thought of which can cause me to fall into a debilitating apoplexy. Edmunds again: "The martini on the rocks is an abomination, and must be classed with fast foods, rock and roll, snowmobiles, acid rain, polyester fabrics, supermarket tomatoes, and books printed on toilet paper as a symptom of anomie."

And I should probably weigh in on the "shaken, not stirred" debate. I have a cousin who can write as fine an English sentence as anyone I know and who also tends a mean bar. He tells me that no one behind any bar he's tending is allowed to shake a martini. And I have heard it said that shaking a martini is barbarous—a memorable expression I disagree with but admire for its elegance, efficiency, and honesty. I own a martini pitcher and will sometimes stir martinis in it. The sound is lovely and the result pleasing. But I myself have no personal feud with the shaken martini. What I do have something against, James Bond notwithstanding, is the so-called vodka martini. ("Ian Fleming," writes Fr. William Dailey, "may have known cars and guns, but on drinks he was out of his depth.") Martinis are made with gin, not vodka. You may shake vodka to your heart's content and pour it into a martini glass if you want to. But don't call it a martini. Call it what it is: a pour excuse. To be sure it's a profanation of the martini glass (*q.v.* Hezekiah 4:13).

It follows that a pomegranate "martini" is not a martini, but on this point I will sustain no domestic dispute with my C.E.O. She looks lovely holding to her sensuous lips a stainless steel martini glass brimming with citrus vodka, triple sec, and pomegranate juice.

My guests have arrived. They sit on the stools at the counter. My Espouséd Saint has prepared an attractive, not to mention delicious, hors d'oeuvres. Do my eyes deceive me, or is that baked brie? It is. The smell of something simple and delectable—onions sautéed in butter—hangs in the air and promises a meal fit for puns and irony and campus gossip. But no one has tasted anything yet. First comes the martini, which, like the Eucharist, requires that you come at it clean. Above everything a little Mozart floats in the dim Chablis glow of under-cabinet lighting. The noble bottles, blue and green, stand ceremoniously to the side, near which awaits a stately shaker, a bowl of ice, and the garnishes.

An overture of ice crashes into the shaker. Over the ice rolls a torrent of Sapphire and a trickle of nameless vermouth. I shake—and shake some more. From the icebox I retrieve the chilled glasses, into which go the garnishes—to each his own. And then, at last, as if from an ancient laver of regeneration, the gin and an implication of vermouth baptize the evening properly.

And to think that some poor sods persist in saying there is no God! They haven't been informed of the principal disadvantages of atheism: no one to call out to *in flagrante delicto* or after the first sip of a very cold premium martini.

3

The First Morel, the Skipped Meeting, and a New Verb Infinitive

---

Yikes! One of my enemies—no time to narrow *that* down—is heading up the hall toward me.

I do an about-face, which is good practice for the imminent pivot into summer. I can get where I'm going by means of another and equally grim stairwell, toward which I now head. Will my enemy be at all curious that I am carrying a gas can through an academic building?

Maybe. Probably not. Let me give you a definition of a professor: someone too caught up in the realm of desultory thought to wonder why a colleague is walking down the hall of an academic building carrying a gas can.

Or someone who doesn't even know what a gas can is.

An idea moves slowly across the dimmed screen of my brain. (This building puts everyone into screen-saver mode.) I could turn and walk toward her, hold up the gas can, point to it, and in a calm but alarming tone say, "Leave. *Now*. I'm going to set the building on fire."

It's possible that would elicit perplexity instead of the usual carefully guarded grievance. To be a professor these days you have to have special training in how to take offense—especially if you're someone whom a Foghorn Leghorn cartoon might have lampooned for having square britches. (Whoops! Did I write that? I just meant to Jimmy Carter it: to think it in my heart.)

Down the stairs and across the alley to the building occupied by "Grounds," that happy lot of men in work jeans and work boots who get to manicure the campus without the trouble of attending committee meetings or dealing with the problem of under-enrolled classes staffed by childless academics on mood stabilizers. (Whoops again!)

I'll steal a little gas—I'll get by with a little help—from my friends. The garden tiller down at the student-run organic garden that I serve as advisor to, a tiller that needs man-handling, also needs combustible material in its combustion chamber. The boys in Grounds will hook me up. This is called "Institutional Support." It's the only kind I get.

I fill the tiller, crank it up, and show a couple of unskilled strapping lads how it works. Once they get the hang of it, I tell them I need to see a man about a horse. A sublunary indicator tells me that in a few minutes there will be a meeting of the full faculty in a grim windowless room, but a cosmic indicator tells me that *at this very moment* there are morels in the woods. Sidereal influence, like common sense, is pretty strong, so I decide to go with "cosmic." And besides, all the Abrahamic faiths clearly teach that moral duty is just a derivative of morel duty. Off to the woods I go in search of dead elms, red oaks, and apple trees, whereunder the darling spores of May await my ravenous fingers.

The wooded acres of this campus are steep, inhospitable to foraging, and short on dead elms (though not on dead wood, which has always proliferated in the garden of tenure). After about thirty minutes I have four pretty good morels. Not a good haul but not a bad one for a man on the average walk home, a soporific meeting of the full faculty at his back. Most people have naught but their little screens to stare down at as they walk or drive wherever they're walking or driving to. Me: I've got the ground, God's good earth, moss, dead wood, and the hope of another morel mushroom. I'm a man on a mission and I don't give two hoots about what a screen says Mackenzie, Colt, and Kayleigh are up to—aside from going through life strapped with names that should be outlawed. (Three whoopses already!)

I feel a very slight twinge of guilt about the meeting being held down campus. It could be that those gathered need me for a quorum. But too bad for those gathered. I'm over it. Hamlet has taught me that there's nothing either good or bad but thinking makes it so, and what I think at the moment is that morels are good and meetings are bad. Plus I've got something more honest to do than vote on whether to approve the wasted minutes from the last meeting I skipped.

Home I go with four good-sized morels and a plan for dinner.

The First Morel, the Skipped Meeting, and a New Verb Infinitive 29

I once heard it said that during the war Evelyn Waugh came into rare possession of a couple of bananas and that he proceeded to eat them both in front of his children. I don't know if this is true, but I can tell you that the story gives me an idea: prepare these mushroom as first-fruits for The Goddess and me and eat them in front of our children. And I'll tell you another thing: Waugh's got nothing on me. He might have been a talented satirist, but I'll bet his potato-fed English ass never skipped a meeting for as good a reason as mine just skipped one for.

Absolved! It turns out that the children—who in the age of Mackenzie, Colt, and Kayleigh I might have gone ahead and named Astralacity, Mendacity, and Pugnacity—have no memory of the morel omelets I made them a year ago and have now decided that mushrooms are "gross." Awesome! God bless the ingrates and amnesiacs!

But into the kitchen walks the Counter of Cocktails and C.E.O. "How do you know they're safe?" she asks after I proudly display my haul on the cutting board.

I point to Pugnacity and ask: "Who's the best that ever was?"

"You are!" says my future lawyer triumphantly.

"You always *were* my favorite," I say. "Now run along and play," and for once he doesn't argue.

I turn, tumbler in hand, to the Counter of Cocktails. (If I'm not mistaken her eyes, normally wont to roll, light upon my glass as if to say "that's *one*. And it had better be the last.")

"Not good enough," she says. "What if I wake up dead because you poisoned me?"

"Look," I say, pointing to a morel. "It's hollow all the way through. And the head's attached. It's a morel."

She folds her arms and shifts her weight from one splendid hip to the other.

I accept my invitation from Her Honor to continue with the evidence. "Remember: I eat raw beef. This won't kill anyone," in proof whereof I put the smallest morel in my mouth and send it down.

As she walks away my eyes smart at the sight of her divine back pockets.

I think to myself: a man could roll the remaining three morels in beaten eggs and flour, or he could sauté them plain in butter or olive oil, which I'm willing to do, when lo! the Counter of Cocktails appears again and sees to her disappointment that I'm not dead. Her eyes, so skilled at rolling and counting, tell me she'll have the morels sautéed in butter.

Handling a morel is a profoundly aesthetic and maybe even an erotic experience. The morel is, *nonpareil*, the crowning feature of the spring harvest. It is as rare and therefore as admirable as pitching a no-hitter, rarer than a teetotaler with a degree from Notre Dame or a sane academic or a competent administrator, though you'll hardly find the latter two in such good places as the woods and forests of this Midwestern region, which is exactly why you *will* find me there.

But *finding* morels is the whole point.

I'm not an expert forager. I know that morels can be found under apple trees and dead elms, and dead elms are, by their shape, known to me. And I can point out to you your wild cherry, your sycamore, your shag-bark hickory, your birch, your locust, your mulberry, your oak, your catalpa, and your tree of heaven (which heaven can take back for all I care, along with the mulberry). But most other defoliated trees are as mysterious to me as the wives of other men.

But I'll be hanged if any of that or if a full faculty meeting—in which it is altogether possible that the singular "they" will be approved for use in the handbook—is going to interfere with hunting morels. Come early May I'm in the woods, just as, come summer, I'm on the river with a hot nut for hoppers, because foraging for mushrooms has at least this much in common with fly fishing: both are characterized by The Search. Both mean you're on to something. Ain't that right, Binx? A man who calls it quits on the river will keep looking for a rising fish and keep casting until he's taken his last step in the water; likewise, a man hunting morels will look to the ground until at last he's in the clearing.

Okay. Music. What music goes with morels? Diana Krall's *All For You* is the correct answer to that metaphysical question.

And was I smart enough to set out two pounds of frozen ground beef? I was. I'm the best that ever was. The Counter and I are having burgers with morels, the Waughlings mere burgers.

I light the charcoal. You wouldn't want Diana Krall catching you doing burgers on a gas grill.

But, Diana, you leggy siren, you: it all wants a bourbon. So why not take all of it? Why not? Because of She Who Must Be Obeyed. So a couple more fingers will do. For now.

I slice the morels long-ways, then chop them. Into a buttered pan they go. I make the hamburger patties. We'll have early beans and some potatoes with lemon and oregano.

The First Morel, the Skipped Meeting, and a New Verb Infinitive

Out to the grill with the burgers. On they go, each accompanied by a short prayer for all vegetarians who haven't figured out, at least in these parts, that their diets—especially their winter diets—are at the mercy of cheap oil. (That is, they're doomed.) Four patties go on and get flipped at the appropriate times. The fifth, mine, goes on with about two minutes to go: ninety seconds per side will satisfy this carnivore.

I've glossed over the steaming of the beans and the baking of the quartered potatoes to bring you, my reading friends and enemies alike, to the table: We have something like an early summer meal before us: no basil or tomatoes, no sweet corn, no robust salad (because, having sat through too many faculty meetings, I have declared a moratorium on the word "robust"), but burgers off the grill nonetheless.

I place a burger before each child (two with cheese and one without, according to custom, with ketchup, mustard, and BBQ sauce available to all, though I strongly object to the use of any of these on burgers), and a fourth on a Kaiser roll before the Roller. And then I make a show of spreading atop the dead cow and its mantle of cheddar a layer of sautéed yellow morels. A bowl of olive-mayonnaise and a plate of lettuce stand at the ready.

Tomato? There's not a real tomato available for five hundred miles, and I won't eat one until it presents itself to me from within twenty. A tomato is a tomato if and only if it smells like one when you cut into it. And, Lord, haste the day when my faith shall be sight.

We settle in. Gratitude is in order. One waggish child begins "Praise the Savior." The rest of us join in. "All we are and have" ends with the sign by which Constantine is said to have conquered—I have my doubts about that whole affair—and we dig in.

The first morels have been put to good use, as has the verb "to Jimmy Carter," and a mind-numbing meeting (but I repeat myself) has been studiously avoided. I'll find more mushrooms tomorrow if I can think of something else to skip out on.

(I can see it now: "Why weren't you at the meeting?"

"What meeting?"

"I sent you an email. Didn't you get my email?"

"No."

"Are you sure? I'm sure I sent it."

"I'm sure I didn't get it."

"Hmm. Why not, I wonder."

"It might be because I filter all your emails.")

Saturday morning the morels will go into omelets with white cheddar, onions, and capers—to fortify us against the evil days when the encroaching singular "they" and other signs that the end is near get majority approval in a meeting of the full faculty. And I *didn't* meant to Jimmy Carter that.

4

Primary? What Primary?

*There's a Tournament on and
a Woman to Impress*

When both the Santorum and Romney campaigns condescended upon my region in March of 2012, I found myself needing to borrow a line from Hawkeye Pierce: the instrument has yet to be invented that can measure my indifference to that.

Forget "seriously," I remember thinking; it's getting harder and harder to take any of this *comically*. And to think some people go so far as to wear buttons and hold signs and get excited.

But things were looking up in Illinois that spring: as I recall, Duke got eliminated in round one of the tourney, which was worthy of convention-style hype. Like everyone else I lost money off that improbable Lehigh win, and everyone I knew considered it money well spent.

No disrespect to the other bracket wrecker of 2012, Norfolk State, but, as everyone knows, Duke-loathing in March is a national sport in itself. Whether Blue Devil self-knowledge extends this far I don't know, but someone should probably let university officials in on a little secret: No one outside of Durham is pulling for Duke. Ever.

Ah, the season of Arch Gladness. What a time. Grown men shout at their televisions, roll off their recliners in agony, go silent as tombs or giddy as schoolgirls for days on end. Wives, high percentages of them, become unaccountably interested in their husbands' obsessions. They allow that watching sports counts as "quality family time." (It counts because what the wives really like is seeing herds of buff young men with actual muscle definition. They're a nice reprieve from belly-fat, navel lint, and shoulder hair.)

And men actually talk to their wives. After I got both 12–5 upsets right, I parted with an unprecedented string of three meaningful remarks expressing agreement about the children's schoolwork. Michigan alone failed me in my Big Ten picks that year (though in the greater East Lansing area folks have come to expect failure from Little Brother), and I found myself actually being kind to someone at work. I was thinking that if no one cheats against the mighty Green & White and they waltz to a championship, I might be able to remember the next two household birthdays plus a wedding anniversary.

And wouldn't two birthdays just happen to fall in March, one of them The Big One? They would. And it's a tough one, toughest of them all. A man needs a quick first step when going up against this one. What would NCAA Basketball Junkie Husband of the Year do?

Here's his plan every time a certain day in March rolls around.

What she deserves is a break from the Lenten fast, which, in honor of the season, we'll call a fast break. I even depart from my wonted taciturnity and consent to a conversation.

But to the menu: there's a time and a place for zucchini-crust pizza, and I'll get around to that, but not now. I'm thinking something along the lines of a stuffed skin-on chicken breast and then maybe a quasi-fussy starch, like sliced purple potatoes under the broiler sprinkled at the very end with rosemary, or maybe a complicated pasta dish—you know, something to make me look extra special on someone else's special day. Either dish will answer.

But first, the dead bird. I think I'll sauté some onions in butter and set them aside. Then I'll brown the chicken on the stovetop, remove it, cut a little pocket in each piece, and then into each piece I'll place the onions, some chopped mushrooms, some fresh basil, a few bits of chopped sun-dried tomatoes, and a dollop of gournay cheese.

I don't know. Maybe spinach instead of basil, maybe sage instead of spinach. That will be a game-time decision.

Into the oven the chicken will go. Three-fifty, three-seventy-five. We'll see. And not too long. Thirty minutes tops.

Lo! On the cutting board I'll see garlic, green pepper (very little, mostly for color), and more sun-dried tomatoes. The tomatoes and peppers I'll chop, the peppers very finely, and I'll press the garlic—in spite of the heretical opinions of those anti-garlic-press Pelagians and Arians whom the devil begot upon Mary Hunt and Carrie Nation, respectively. All of it, along with crushed red peppers, will go into about twelve ounces of *al dente* linguini, oiled like a body-builder's pecs and sprinkled with dried oregano. (It appears I've decided against the purple potatoes.) That'll get covered and, for warming purposes, put in the oven about ten minutes before tip-off. I'll serve it with shredded asagio cheese—which, by God, I'll shred as if it were a zone defense like in the glory days. (The older I get, the better I was.)

Beside the cutting board will be a salad of spring greens. Someone nearby has figured out how to raise them all winter. Even arugula! There will be enough cheese going on everywhere, so no caesar with parmesan or feta in the line-up. It won't be rebounding we need so much as quickness.

So, quickly: crushed caramelized walnuts, croutons, and balsamic vinaigrette with strawberry freezer jam stirred in for good measure.

French bread? Why not. This is the team captain we're cooking for. Don't want any blown assignments.

How will it play out? I'll call her to dinner, and we'll line up on either side of the table. She'll look around the circle and say, "Where are the children?"

"The who?"

"Our *children*."

"Oh, them. Right. I fed them dry toast and water. They're downstairs scarfing down popcorn and watching Looney Tunes. The racist ones from the 1950s."

"Did they get a vegetable?"

"I think I saw each of them sneaking a spoonful of sugar. That grows from the ground."

She'll reach for her glass. "Wine. Mmm. Nice touch."

"Speaking of touch. How about a little one-on-one, full court press?"

After the obligatory rolling of the eyes she'll say, "There are no games tonight. They start up again tomorrow."

"I wasn't talking about . . ."

"There are *no* games tonight."

"Well, then, open this." I'm not worried about the stuffed chicken. I can make the food happen. It's the presents that make or break me.

She'll open up a gift. Ear rings. "Wow, honey. These are really pretty."

"Pretty" is good, but surprise is not. I know what she's thinking: who helped me picked them out? Why, after three decades of marriage and several years of courtship, am I still no good at this?

"Yes, well, I have very good taste. Also I'm quite at home in jewelry stores. They're almost like dusty old gymnasiums to me."

"What's for dinner?" she'll ask. "Why don't you lift the lid off of that dish and show me?"

"That's what I was getting at earlier."

"*That* dish. *That* one there." More rolling of the eyes. 'It never ends,' they say.

I'll lift the lid. "Recognize that?"

She does. An old favorite from a preferred restaurant that time and miles and children and a thousand other obstacles prevent our going to.

"It looks like. . ."

Her voice will have that slight modulation that suggests one of those transitionless subject-changes women are famous for. I assume—wrongly, as it turns out—that, because she was flipping through the newspaper earlier, this remark will be about the primaries, which I can't bear to have spoiling my dinner. "Let's stick to basketball," I say, interrupting. "Shall we?"

"I was *going* to say 'it looks like another swish from downtown to send it into overtime,'" she'll say, admonishingly. But I just clanked one off the front of the rim. "Pass that, please."

"Passing is how . . . "

". . . is how *I* get the ball. Yes, I know," she'll say, finishing an old joke that only one of us thinks is still funny.

But then she'll tip her head in that way of hers, shake back her hair, and put the ear rings in. They *are* pretty. Even *I* can see that. Put them on a woman like her, and you're winded like a pizza-fed power forward in transition.

5

Well, It's Not like After the Risotto

What the sam hill is this? I'm asked merely to *flavor* the olive oil by heating a single clove of garlic in it? And then *discard the garlic*?

No, no, no. This won't do at all. In the first place, no one uses only one clove of garlic—not for anything. That's like coming home from a bad day at work and having half a beer. First rule: triple the . . .

Wait a cotton-pickin' minute! The kitchen is as silent as that spot which no vicissitude can find! Onto the hi-fi go the Ozark Mountain Daredevils—the *Car Over the Lake* album, which I usually listen to only while 'zarkin' (that is, while standing by an outdoor fire and puffing on a corncob pipe), but it's been too long.

Ah, there we go. That's right. Keep on churnin' till the cows come home.

(The Ozark Mountain Daredevils won't sue me for quoting them. I'm their truest fan and best apostle.)

First rule (as I was saying): triple the garlic. It's like irony: there's no such thing as too much. I peel three cloves and chop them.

I've committed myself to something called "Pasta Risotto with Peas & Pancetta" (if I quit now, croon the 'Zarks, it'd surely be a sin), except I ain't got no pancetta, so I pull out a half-pound of that miracle meat commonly known as "bacon."

Now I'm not sophisticated enough to know whether what I'm making actually qualifies as risotto. It's made not with Arborio rice but with orzo pasta, which, I know, is an etymological departure from "risotto" and is therefore, strictly speaking, not risotto. But I see no reason that my orzo pasta shouldn't be allowed to take full advantage of identity politics or thumb a ride from the very *Zeitgeist* itself and *identify* as risotto. So there you have it. I'll be adding grated cheese to this, as to risotto, but that doesn't mean a damned thing. (The Daredevils: it just don't mean a thang.) Adding grated cheese to metal shavings doesn't make the shavings risotto. So I'm going to have to go ahead and leave that fine point of distinction to you members of the culinary disputocracy.

A *New York Times* article of blessed forgetfulness says, "It is not hard to make a good risotto. But you have to stand over it for at least 20 minutes and this makes it difficult for dinner parties."

Utter nonsense. Standing over the stovetop is what you *do* in the kitchen. You stand over medium heat, you sing along with the music—down in Leatherwood country love's gonna steal your mind—and you sip something very hoppy. And, as with most pleasurable activities, including country matters, you do it for *way* more than twenty minutes.

Outside my kitchen window there's a fickle March sky, now slate-grey and furious with flurries, now pale blue and shot through with late shafts of sunlight. If my eyes do not deceive me, house sparrows have already taken up residence in the bird houses I didn't even clean out last fall. Cardinals are aloft, and several robins have returned. Last year at this time a confused spring coaxed the darling buds of May out two months early. The ScamLawns and ScrewGreens of the world were applying pre-emergent herbicides to the neighbors' lawns on this very day last year. But not today. I see snow—and how I love it still.

March! When a young man's fancy turns to basketball. March! As in the old that's-what-she-said-joke: in like a lion, out like a lamb.

Whoops! Did I write that? I only meant to think it in my heart.

Dice the bacon and toss it in a big sauce pan, where wait two tablespoons of olive oil—unnecessary, of course, since I'm using bacon rather than pancetta. But a man likes the look and smell of the oil.

Sip a little Modus Hoperandi. Here's to you, Steve Cash (RIP) and the 'Zarks, and to the magic and the mortar in a cobblestone land. And to you, Bacon! Could there be a meat more miraculous, a more fit vehicle of grace? It's a little-known fact that in Antioch, where the faithful were first called Christians, the Eucharistic elements were bacon and IPA.

Stand over the heat to spite that snotty *NYT* writer. If this were a dinner party, my guests would willingly stand here while I amused them with cracks about the Eucharist in Antioch. Watch and listen to the heat do its job. And smell it! Soon we will taste and touch it as well. Ah, the fullness of man: the incarnate condition! Show me an *NYT* food writer who knows anything about *that*.

Drain some of the grease but not all of it. The bed-time statin will want something to work on, after all, and you can retain what you drain for lathering your burger buns—if you're the bun-toasting kind (and I am). And now into the finished bacon goes the chopped garlic. The aroma improves apace. I stir. Round and around and around and around, round and around and around. It does seem to me that the Daredevils wrote "Gypsy Forest" for just this occasion.

But where is the Goddess Excellently Bright? The Chief Eye-Rolling Officer? Nurse Goodbody? The Conscience? The Counter of Cocktails? As yet there have been no sightings. No high-heeled sound of her feet.

Add about a cup and a half of peas—seasonal peas from the freezer. Stand over the heat and stir. And now for the orzo pasta—about eight ounces—and a little over two cups of white wine and chicken broth, boiling and ready in another pan. I've got ten minutes of groping time to spend and no one to spend it on.

But lo! It appears I'm a conjurer. I merely imagine those splendid back pockets, and in they walk!

"What's this?" they ask.

"You'll want a cigarette afterward."

"I don't smoke."

"That's one woman's opinion."

She inspects the workmanship. "Is that enough liquid?"

"You just walk to the other side of the kitchen and then walk back over here and leave the inspecting to me"—a line that hasn't yielded a rise in at least a decade.

"You're going to need more stock," she says.

"You know what I need?"

"More stock."

She takes a hit of the IPA.

I say, "Drink to me only with thine eyes," which, upon my recitation, roll.

Whereupon I hear the high-heeled sound of her feet leaving the kitchen.

"How do I love thee? Let me count the lays."

No response whatsoever except from the hi-fi:

> And she would shine like a diamond
> Trapped in a clear crystal ring.

Ten minutes are up. The bonehead who wrote this recipe, who suggested I merely flavor the oil with one clove of garlic and then toss the garlic, now wants me to add a single tablespoon of butter. But how am I going to get sympathy from the Eye-Roller for suffering a massive myocardial infarction if I add only 1 T of butter? As with garlic and irony, so with butter: triple it.

And now the grated Parmesan. I stand there and stir and think about the *NYT* writer worried about his mePhone-toting guests, most of whom are no doubt bores of the first water in designer eye-glasses: those who disrupt solitude without bringing the benefit of good conversation. Not a one of them could spot an eye-rolling goddess in splendid back pockets.

Okay. We're assembled. The two older children are well-mannered enough to eat what's in front of them. The youngest, half-Eeyore and half-Oscar-the-Grouch, is the variable. He might pitch a fit and make things difficult, though the bacon's in my favor.

He devours the "risotto." The Goddess Excellently Bright and I are relieved. At the last bite he holds up a pea. "But I don't care much for these but it's alright."

I knew the peas might pose a problem, and I agree that peas are best et raw. And if he were ready for a lesson in style and grammar I'd tell him that "but" used twice in close proximity is a real rhetorical no-no, and I'd call him out on the singular-plural problem, but he isn't ready, so I dismiss him with a wave of the hand. Another day's food has been savored and swallowed, and we are grateful.

"Well?" I say. How do you feel after the risotto?

And she, co-plagiarist showing her happy Ozark glow, says, "I feel full."

6

Casting Asparagus on Another Person's Character

Damn me if the asparagus isn't coming in, green and purple and stiff and tender! A mere sixty square feet of garden space devoted to this graceful stalk will yield God's own bounty, and up here in God's country a fresh local pound of it will fetch a good price.

I've got my own well-established patch, and let me tell you the asparagus is ready for the heat.

And as for that heat, let's be clear about one thing. It is an offense punishable by the fires of hell to blanch your asparagus. Unless you live on a damp island, have bad teeth, and occasionally croon "God Save the Queen" disingenuously, do not boil your vegetables. Boiling the asparagus will get you drawn and quartered, tarred and feathered, and hanged at dawn—not to mention put on bread and water for a month. Asparagus is a noble manifestation of the earth's increase. Boiling it is blasphemy of the greatest magnitude.

I'm afraid that the bibulous reader might be disappointed to know that the foreplay to this Asparagasm involves no lovingly prepared potable. The reason is that my asparagus salad is best prepared in the sobriety of late morning or early afternoon, when the anticipation of an evening cocktail hasn't yet presented itself to the longing heart—and also because you want the salad to cool before you feast upon it. You want it to spend the day in the deep-delved earth or, if you don't have a root cellar, in the fridge.

But get yourself a pound of fresh local asparagus. *Local*. Not that stuff shipped in from California, unless you live in California. Cut as much as an inch off the fat end of the stalk, depending on the fatness, and put the stubs in the compost pail. The stubs were made to be turned into soil anyway, so don't lament this profligacy. It isn't profligacy. And you don't have to break the stalks instead of cut them, as some kitchen snobs say. They say this because (1) they're snobs and (2) they think breaking asparagus by hand magically trims each individual stalk, as if the stalk itself knows what its waste parts are. (The truth of the matter is that the stalk *does* know this, but it's important to avoid snobbery and even more important to distrust the judgment of anything that's long, hard, and purple.) Trust thy knife: every asparagus stalk vibrates to that iron string.

If you're going to grill the asparagus, cut each stalk in half so that you have one piece for each of the two natures of Christ. If you're going to sauté the asparagus, cut the stalks in thirds, one for each person of the Trinity.

GRILLERS: brush the asparagus with olive oil (*local* olive oil if you live in Greece or Italy); put the fat ends on the grill first, then, after a minute, the thin ends (& tips). Four minutes on a hot grill will be too much heat. The stalks will need salt and pepper during the grilling.

NB: as with beef, always undercook.

Remove.

STOVETOPPERS: heat olive oil (*local* olive oil if you live in Greece or Italy) in a large saucepan over medium heat. Put the fat thirds of the asparagus in first, then (after about a minute) the middle thirds, then (after about another minute) the tips. Using a wooden spatula, move them around in the pan for a total of about five or six minutes. They'll need salt and pepper during all this.

NB: as with beef, always undercook.

BOILERS: Go to Hell. But first . . .

Boil a pan of water. Throw a palm's worth of sea salt in and then drizzle in some olive oil. When the water has reached a boil, put in about a half-pound of linguine or fettuccini, depending on your preference. Be sure that you break the pasta into thirds, one piece for each time St. Peter denied the Savior, so that the strands are not too long. Strain after nine minutes and reserve.

Put the asparagus aside and think about a nice light white wine—but do not open one.

Now you must toast some sliced almonds. You probably can't get local almonds, but try. If you can't, remember that it is better to ask forgiveness than permission. Toast three or four handfuls of sliced almonds either on the grill or in the oven. Don't burn them. Put them aside.

Get yourself a minimum of eight ounces of mushrooms and slice them about a quarter-inch thick. Put them aside. *Don't* put them anywhere near the heat.

Now just as Jesus needed a forerunner, so your bourbon (or martini or scotch) will need an iced tea. Make one. Sweeten it depending on proximity to the Mason-Dixon line.

All the ingredients heretofore prepared and reserved (the asparagus, pasta, almonds, and mushrooms) should be placed in a single bowl and cooled. You are now ready to make your vinaigrette.

Briefly fondle two big lemons and then, as you squeeze their juices into a bowl, recite Commelyn, that seventeenth-century Dutch pomologist, who said that the lemon "is Oval, or longish Round, sharp at the End, with a long Point sticking out, almost like the Nipple of a Woman's Brest." Add about five or six finely chopped garlic cloves and at least a quarter teaspoon of red pepper flakes. Add a palmful of salt and a drizzle of olive oil—three tablespoons or so.

Wait. Wait longer. Wait longer still. Go make love or something.

Now, having put the reserve ingredients into the same bowl, stir and then pour the vinaigrette over it, sprinkle over everything some grated asagio or parmesan cheese (not that sawdust Kraft sells), crack a light white wine—a Frascati if you can find one—and serve both. After dinner, read aloud some summer poetry.

Or maybe, just for the fun of it, sit down and rehearse the bizarre demise of Mr. Organic himself, J.I. Rodale, who in 1971 told Dick Cavett he never felt better and then promptly died right there on the set during taping. Rodale, sitting next to Pete Hamill, leaned his head back—or maybe his head leaned itself back—and then began making snoring sounds, which according to some reports induced Cavett to ask, "Are we boring you, Mr. Rodale?" In fact they were not boring him. They were killing him. (Television talk shows will do that to people.) Hamill at least had the good sense to say, on camera, "this looks bad." But the bad part was apparently over, for, as Cavett would later say, Rodale had already joined the silent majority. Cavett said this while managing to stay alive on someone else's hazardous television talk show (Seth Meyers'), during which he also got off a couple of good cracks on tricky Dick Nixon.

But the point is this: it is scurrilous to assume Rodale's death had nothing to do with the fact that he had just parted with his recipe for asparagus boiled in urine, though he had. I shit you not. If you're patient enough you can read about this in *The Wizard and the Prophet*, and also in other sources.

The culinary plagiarist has known asparagus to alter the scent of his wee-wee; he has never asked wee-wee to alter the taste of his asparagus. Nor does he recommend that anyone try, because the consequences could be dire. You could end up on the Dick Cavett Show.

II
School's Out

In the first place God made idiots. This was for practice. Then he made School Boards.

—Mark Twain, *Pudd'nhead Wilson's New Calendar*

7

An Expostulation Upon the Morning B.M.

You can imagine the scene. If not, I'll describe it. The hour is bit late for the morning rite. A quarter of noon. Baccalaureate is over and done with—an ecumenical affair suggesting that we believe in pretty much nothing. (It was Muggeridge, I think, who said ecumenism is for those who agree on much because they believe in little.)

This means that august figures in gay regalia, learned men and women, doctors of the academy and their spouses, will soon be arriving on my back deck for Post-Baccalaureate Bacchanalia, a compressed affair of intense high festival. That solemn soporific somnambulant ceremony known as Commencement commences at three o'clock; it will put a quick and terrible end to my purposeful misbehavior, so there is no time to waste.

I arrive first to find my Tabulator of Tanquerays in her summer whites. She looks as if she has just stepped off the cover of a magazine. I take a quick gander at my watch, then at her, then at my watch. Damnation! Not enough time. But off go the flowing robes anyway. On go the cargo shorts. In no time at all I'm lighting the peanut oil. The traditional turkey will soon fry and, while frying, be given a ceremonial name. Whom do I and my friends like least at the end of *this* academic year? Whose hot air has scorched us the most in faculty meetings? Who filibustered the most egregiously? (No doubt someone in Speech Communications, that minor league to Associate Deanery.) Which of our high-output colleagues believe they're too good for this place? With so many deserving candidates, renaming this tom will not be easy.

The guests arrive, smiling. We all love this one. Dishes appear on the tables, bottles on the counter, cans and bottles in the coolers. The sound of popped corks, of ice clinking against the sides of glasses, the smell of lime wedges, gins and tonic, baked brie, artichokes, and maybe even the under-whiff of sebum and sweat. (We have, after all, some of us, been secreting under our long flowing monkey suits while being assured that there are no significant differences among the Abrahamic faiths.) No matter. We'll dry off ere we start secreting again.

We're all in excellent spirits, and by their means we'll be in better spirits still. There's time for improvement.

But, as God is my witness, I'm as sober as synagogue beadle. So, to rectify the offense, I mix myself a little concoction and stand there in my own kitchen, the very lord of the manor, the ecstatic patron of recurrent light.

Lo! A colleague's wife, half-way into a G&T, is already pronouncing the party a success. So I go serious. "Tell me," I say, taking a long pull on a very spicy bloody mary, "don't you find it very satisfying to have a great big B.M. in the morning?"

I drink again.

She's a ready wit, by my troth. She herself is Sympathy in White Major. Swirling her G&T she takes up the gag with aplomb. "Well, maybe not so satisfying as *you* find it," she says, "my own preferences running toward a modest G&T, but, yes: a big B.M. in the morning can be very satisfying, or so I'm told."

I turn to my wife and pose the same question: "How about you? Do you like to have a big B.M. in the morning?" She rolls her eyes, turns, and resumes a conversation with someone else. What splendid blithe shoulder blades she has! It does one good, as Hawthorne almost said, to see such fine indifference so fitly cast.

Let us take a closer look at, let us undertake a more intimate investigation of, the morning B.M.

It should be an event of considerable magnitude. It should be a burning viscous affair. I myself begin with a spicy bloody mary mix, which, of course, is usually not spicy at all except when compared to plain tomato juice. (Some mixes, because of their names, are to be preferred above others. Major Peters comes to mind, as does Irish Dog, Hoosier Momma, Kick Ass Classic, Willie's Hog Dust, and Dr. Swami & Bone Daddy's Spicy Cajun.) I then proceed to improve upon it: two large spoons-full of hot mustard, a torrent of some kind of hot sauce (Tabasco sauce will answer nicely, of course), an ellipsis of Worcestershire sauce, salt, freshly-ground black pepper, the squeezed juice from a large lime wedge (plus the lime wedge), and, of course—and here I break one of my rules—cheap rot-gut vodka, a liquor otherwise used for cooking only, not for drinking.

I stir vigorously, add ice, and feel the relief.

Okay. You can add a celery stick or a long column of skewered olives if you must. (A local bartender skewers an olive, then a pickle, then another olive, displays it suggestively, and calls this garnish "cock and balls." When you order a B.M. at his bar and he asks you, aloud, for everyone to hear, whether you want cock and balls, you have to resist the urge to

> take the shortcut
> between flesh and spirit

and punch him in the face, as Tony Hoagland once put it.) Cajun spice around the rim of the glass is a nice touch. It's all good. No argument here.

I stand at the counter peppering tom and injecting him with melted butter, a long involved process that lasts for a whole B.M.

I make another at 11:59 a.m. There are two days a year a man may reasonably take a drink in the morning: this day, and Saturday of the British Open. Luckily the two days have so far never coincided and thereby cheated us out of one of them.

I step out on the deck. Here's a delicate creature, wife of yet another colleague. She's carefully placing on a table the salad she made. It's lovely. She's lovely. We're all lovely. She looks at me as I sip my bloody mary. I smack my lips and say, "let me tell you about the B.M. I just had." She knows me of old. Her husband is even more juvenile than I. She shakes her head, rolls her eyes, and returns them to the task at hand. I move off the deck, my words trailing behind me in an affected Anthony-Blanche-style stutter: "It was *m-m-most* satisfying. I *assure* you."

Out to the oil. Temperature is almost 360. I want it at 400 when the bird goes in, because tom or whomever we name him for will cool it a little, and 360's the magic number. About three minutes per pound at that temperature, and you've got yourself a fried turkey. You can't do one faster in a volcano.

The house buzzes with year-end complaining, rejoicing, bitching, bad-mouthing, and doxologizing. We're here to launch the summer properly: with the exquisite mixture of disillusionment and euphoria. We'll eat well, drink well, and gossip well. We'll sit in the shade, pronounce judgment on the baccalaureate speaker, complain about colleagues, students, wages, benefits, administrators. We'll tell jokes—I certainly will—and we'll take surreptitious glances at our watches, for the sad and bitter truth, the dark cloud above this day of obligation, is that this party is life in miniature, life accelerated: it will make us ache with joy, and then, too soon, something unpleasant will bring it to an end, which in English is called "Commencement."

We've settled on a name for the fried bird: a certain someone who—ah, best not to say. He or she has spent about forty-five minutes in the oil and is crispied-o'er with the pale cast of grease. And now I'm stabbing him or her with my steely knife.

We throw ourselves on the various foods. Look at us celebrating diversity! We float in the afternoon warmth, held aloft like airy spirits on the spirits' airy wings.

And then, almost of a sudden, we downshift. There's an unending ceremony to endure and stay awake through and not pee during, and probably, when it's all over, a few parents to greet with obliquely set visages and, if we've remembered them, breath mints. At once we're cleaning up. Without knowing it I'm changing back into the flowing monkey suit, another school year's promise come and gone.

Time was my pal Mike, who, as a mid-level administrator didn't have to march, would stay behind and help with the heavy cleaning (and no doubt flirt with the hostess), but he was untimely ripped from this and all parties by the swift hand of death. And my pal C—, who made all parties better, would get lubed and talkative with anyone in earshot, but weary retirement took him hence. And my good friend D— graces us no more. He descended into administration at another institution.

The changes are unbearable, but, having no choice, we bear them—we bear them until life itself bears down and pinches us out, reminding us, to its own great satisfaction, that we too among the wastes of time must go.

8

In the Season of Sweet Basil

The awning above the west-facing kitchen window was doing what it was made to do as the all-seeing Illinois July sun beat our cedar-shake siding like a red-headed step-child. I stood at the sink, looking out the window and down the ravine to the gentle slope near the bottom where the previous summer a small flat vegetable garden struggled for the last time in the encroaching shadows.

Young trees that I didn't want to take out, including a wild cherry, were casting down too many penumbral patterns, and the garden, too much i'th'shade, did poorly to say the least. The woodchucks fattened themselves on what little the ground did produce, though for some reason they left the jalapeños and habaneros untouched, and the retaining wall that held the east edge of the garden was straining mightily to hold what in its younger days it retained with ease and grace and conviction.

So in the spring I removed the long rough timbers, heavy, wet, and rotting, turned the dark crumbly tilth, sloped the ground, and seeded it. The next year's gardening would be done along the south and west sides of the house and in various pots and planters on the deck.

And then, on that summer evening, which could have been almost any summer evening, I looked out and saw the parsley, which was doing well notwithstanding the chubby woodchuck I had caught munching away a few days earlier, his proprietary front paws up on the pot and his greedy mouth at work like a fat man's at an all-you-can-scarf buffet. Woodchucks, at once as cocky as point guards and as nervous as whores in church, didn't often climb the steps to my back deck. This arrogant fatso did. When I chased him off I discovered a run under my deck. He'd tunneled into the bank and was helping himself to the loot. Bastard!

The oregano was likewise doing well, and the rosemary, the sage, and, of course, the sweet basil.

There was music on, I'm sure. There was always music on, and my youngest walked into the kitchen, eyes snapping. He dragged a stool from the bar-side of the counter, climbed up on it, and watched me. Before he even brought into focus what I was doing he said, "I smell tomatoes."

And so he did, for the tomatoes had finally come in, which meant that we were now, at long last, in the season of sweet basil, the long warm languid season of sweet basil, when a man could sing along to the *Confutatis* as he chopped fresh onions for sautéing in butter, ruffled the hair of a child underfoot, and suffered in that aromatic space the exquisite pleasures of longing that jabbed at his aching heart.

"Summertime, O Summertime! Pattern of life indelible," sang E.B. White, going once more to the lake. "O for the rapturous rebellious days of youth," said the immortal Binx on the cusp of his thirtieth birthday. "O the languor of youth," said Charles Ryder.

We had been eating the basil for some time, but I could never quite make myself believe that basil was doing its appointed job until the tomatoes were in. And then at last they were. They were in and ready to mingle concupiscently with the green and lusty basil. 'Twas the season—the season of sweet basil.

'Twas then and 'tis now as, once again, I stand above the cutting board.

Binx! I see you! I see you've sent down a pattern from above. My eye smarts with a tear of gratitude. This is almost like catching site of a splendid kneecap or that mysterious ridge that runs elegantly along the outer thigh between the knee and the hip when the thigh is crossed seductively over its companion. I'm tempted to believe in God—even though I already do.

Tonight the basil's appointed job is to grace a slightly toasted French baguette. The bread is in the oven. I chopped the fresh basil and the aromatic tomato as Alison Krauss sang about the steady pace that kept her steps between the cracks on Broadway. Her stride had already kept rhythm to the beat of home sweet home by the time I'd crushed the garlic.

The water is boiling because—did I mention?—the first of the sweet corn has come in too. I take a sip of Knob Creek and quiz Pugnacity on the foods in front of us. He answers passing well, spots the corn, and wants to husk it. Out the back he goes. There will be no woodchuck tonight if that noisy boy has any say in the matter. God bless the boy and damn the woodchuck.

Our parsley stars in the carbonara I can't seem to go very long without, especially if I can get the bacon to cook without burning on a hickory fire, and I put our sage in a blue-cheese cream sauce for pasta, a sauce that is the chief cause of my being on a statin right now. Not very sage of me, but wisdom seldom gets the better of pleasure. I like to sprinkle the rosemary on new potatoes, which I slice into discs and broil or grill in olive oil, salt, and pepper. I put the rosemary on right at the end, the last five minutes or so. It's especially good on purple potatoes done in this way exactly.

But tonight, because we're officially in the season of sweet basil, it's basil time, sweet-saint basil time, and the deep green pungent herb is going on my bread, which I now take from the oven, place on a cutting board, turn on its side, and slice lengthwise. In a tin bowl on the counter I've mixed the chopped basil, the chopped tomato, the crushed garlic, the salt and pepper, and the golden olive oil, all of which I now lavish on the bread turned flat-side up. I then slice the long pieces cross-wise, sprinkle on some shredded asagio cheese bought at the farmer's market from the family of uni-browed cheesemakers (blessed be they), and help myself to the first fruits, or what my dad at his grill used to call "chef's portion," which was never insubstantial.

God's body, this is good! The soft tomato against the crunchy bread, the hot garlic awash in olive oil, and there above it all, like an inverted pedal point or a faint obbligato, the delicate sweet basil, the sweet sweet basil.

There is nothing like it—okay, there's *one* thing like it—and so I toast the season with another hit of the bourbon. Down the lane like an ambrosial ribbon it flutters. These blessed days will last until the summer heat gives way to crisp fall days and the last tomatoes refuse to ripen. Not a problem. We'll fry them green and dying.

And now what is it that the Ozark Mountain Daredevils are singing? Thank you, Lord; you made it right?

It is; He did.

My son brings the corn in—it's inexpertly husked, so I help him finish the job—and into the boil it goes. The only things missing are the other two noisy children and a bronzed woman in a white summer dress. But lo! There she is, coming in from the back with a basket of green beans! How ripe and freshly picked she looks. I pour her a glass of a see-through wine that ought to be a kind of clothing—and which, if it were, I would touch. Do my eyes deceive me, or does she look as if she wants nothing more than to give me one of her long moist lascivious—and promissory—kisses?

She eyes the bourbon, walks past me, and begins washing the beans.

Not to worry. Everything's alive and throbbing. The Earth has brought forth her increase; we've had the salubrious seasons and the seasonable weather we've prayed for, and there's the bosky bite of Kentucky's noblest export to serenade it all!

Tonight we'll have a summer feast of vegetables and try our damnedest to be grateful for it—and for everything else, including the pesto we'll put by,

> summer's distillation left
> A lusty prisoner pent in walls of glass,

as Shakespeare almost put it. It isn't always easy to feel worthy of a meal that engages all your senses the way this one will—the light loamy smell of the fresh basil, the fragrant tomato and garlic, the sight of these vivid Christmassy colors mixed together in the bowl, the salty-sweet savor of the sweet corn dripping with salted butter, the feel of the glebe's own bounty as we wash and handle and prepare it, the sound of my knife on the cutting board and of Ms. Krause and the Ozark Mountain Daredevils and the gathering *Confutatis*.

But gratitude is what's called for, for soon the shadows will fall hard and touch the air with the chill of death—without which, of course, the season of sweet basil would lack all joy. Tonight it seems impossible that, come autumn, the exquisite pang of longing will smite me more thoroughly than all this, or that in winter it will smite more thoroughly still, but it will. I'm tempted to put on *Nine Lessons and Carols*. It's the most wonderful time of the year—for now, for this fleeting Now, this light and musical and airy Now, at once refulgent and weightlessly unbearable.

9

Turn the Turnip to Good Account

He had had much experience of physicians, and said "the only way to keep your health is to eat what you don't want, drink what you don't like, and do what you'd druther not."

—Mark Twain, *Pudd'nhead Wilson's New Calendar*

The turnip (*Brassica rapa*), though round and firm and white and beautifully suited to the hand, is not one of the jewels in the crown of creation. On this point you can even get dimwits, halfwits, dipshits, and other variations on the liberals and neocons to agree with you. Given the choice between turnips and new potatoes—especially at this time of year—most semi- to quasi-rational creatures will prefer new potatoes.

(Allowances must be made for shaved raw turnips added to salads and also for lightly salted raw thin turnip slices—both excellent so far as turnips go.)

I say nothing here of the turnip green, which is very good for you, as are almost all bitter and vile-tasting things the earth brings forth. Desperation may drive us to them, but for now I will maintain that God gave us the turnip green only to teach us how to shoot groundhogs.

(How? In the country, with a .22; in the city, where the discharging of firearms is somewhat frowned upon—because illegal—with an air rifle amply loaded with field pellets; or, lacking an air rifle, by bludgeoning: that is, with the back side of a shovel thunderously applied to the head—the groundhog's head. Be sure, however, whether in country or city, that the fat-bastard garden thief you've just plugged or clobbered isn't going to waddle off and die under a deck or a nearby shed or—God forbid!—the front porch. Putrefying flesh is unpleasant, especially when you can't get to it to remove it.)

And yet the turnip itself can be turned to good account, as is suggested by the sheer proliferation of turnip recipes proffered by Turnip Loyalists, who are well-meaning individuals, if slightly north-northwest in their orientation.

Why bother turning the turnip to good account? Because it is important to eat in season.

Why? Because soon enough everyone (everyone who's left) will *have* to eat in season, and turnips keep well in root cellars, as all the generations of make-do folk preceding my own generation of know-nothings knew well.

Why? Because transporting food long distances (in addition to being a mistake) is a luxury of the age of cheap oil, and that's an age that is all but over. So learn to localize and seasonalize. Resist those, beginning with your academic dean, who would globalize and internationalize. (A "global economy" is a contradiction in terms, which only a little acquaintance with Greek makes plain, and "global learning" is just plain nonsense.) Inhabit your *place*, not everyplace.

Now how to turn the turnip to good account: that's the sticking point. I'm going to suggest a way. I hope that doing so—am I masking the desperation well enough?—will encourage others to part with their own successes with the turnip and share them with their neighbors.

For the turnip, truth be told, though lovely, is like a student you don't hold out much hope for but who somehow manages to turn himself to good account. (*Him*self? Am I a sexist turnip-fed pig? No! It is more often a he than a she whom you don't hold out much hope for.)

Step One: Divert your attention from the fact that you're trying to turn a turnip to good account. Diversion is key, like when a colleague starts talking in a committee meeting and, to make the crucible bearable, you force yourself to think of something even *more* unpleasant, like chewing on tin foil or watching a Tom Cruise movie or reading Sylvia Plath.

So put on some contemporary "Christian" "music"—something by someone who was raised by wolves. Soon you'll long for the noise to end so that the chewing and swallowing may commence. (Christian rock, as everyone knows, doesn't make Christianity better; it only makes rock 'n roll worse.) Pour yourself a drink (never, except during liturgical fasts, deny yourself this), but make it unpleasant. Miller Lite will do if you can get your hands on some without actually having to part with money, gold, or favors. A dirty vodka "martini," which is blasphemy against the Holy Ghost, will also do.

Step Two: Instead of banishing the children to another room, lock them in the kitchen with you and let them fight like hell. The more children the better. If you don't have very many, grab your Espouséd Saint and run upstairs for a few minutes. You must lay up in store more screaming brats for turnip seasons to come.

Step Three: Bearing in mind the rule of simplicity (for you *do* have to eat this), melt some butter in a pan over low heat. If you think it will help, sing along with the "music." You can rinse the bad theology from your mind with a requiem mass later.

Step Four: Slice your turnip(s) into thin disks. Salt one side and, when the butter is melted, place the disks, salted-side down, in the pan. Salt the unsalted sides and crack a little black pepper over them.

Step Five: Smile at the children when they say all the words you ordinarily forbid them to say. (As always, local rules obtain. For my part I expect to hear "shut-up," "idiot," "stupid," and of course all the really bad ones.)

Step Six: Turn up the fire to "medium" and, when the turnips are a little soft (maybe after three or four minutes), flip them. Leave them for another three or four minutes and then remove them from the heat.

Step Seven (the final step: we're working here with a biblical number for good luck): Dress the disks variously. Sprinkle oregano on some, rosemary on others, nutmeg on a few more, and, on the remaining turnip disks, mustard or local honey or soy sauce or—hell, I don't know, make it a dash of talcum powder.

What I'm saying is, we're dealing here with an unpromising student. Try anything.

Now you're ready to eat. The turnips will all taste pretty good, I promise, for butter and salt and pepper, all of which are magical, have touched them.

But, as you can see, the question is, what finishes them best? That's where you have to get creative—and hope that the music and the beer haven't destroyed your imagination even though they have, without exception, successfully destroyed the imaginations of millions of Americans already.

Eat. Judge. Take notes. Imagine other possibilities. Apologize to no one. You're eating locally and in season. You're preparing for the real future, not the one colleges and universities and other advertising agencies are promising.

Now be good to yourself. Fast-forward to the clean-up. Put on Chicago XVI or XVII and pour yourself a really good Michigan IPA. I suggest Mad Hatter, Crooked Tree, and Huma-Lupa Licious. Norm's Raggedy-Ass IPA will do excellently as well, for, alas, High Seas is no longer available. Be prepared to make adjustments: other people might be turning the turnip to good account as well.

Banish everyone from the kitchen, even your Espouséd Saint, who is either pregnant or has done you the honors. Sing along loudly and take twice as much time as you normally would to clean up. Prepare for several more days of turnips. They make for an incomparable stew, you know—provided you've put up enough stock.

But that, loyal reader (I use the singular with steely but not despairing resignation), is grist for another mill.

10

The Lamb Shank Redemption

I walk through the door after a hard two hours at the office. Whew! That damn-near killed me. Good thing I had time to stop at the campus garden to harvest a little red romaine and arugula. And good thing I'm the faculty advisor to this great unremunerated, unknown, and unappreciated project: I get to help myself. Nothing like occupying an endowed chair *and* enjoying the same status as the groundhogs and rabbits.

And good thing I arrive at the garden in time. The heat later this week will render the arugula certainly, and the lettuce probably, too bitter even for the rabbits—well, maybe not for those fur-bearing varmints, as Yosemite Sam called them—but tonight these fine leaves will feed me and mine.

And what else will feed us?

Interesting you should ask. I see that the Little Missus has boiled some bowtie pasta. This means two things: that bowties were made for eating, not wearing, and that she wants a green & pasta combo salad tonight.

Happy to oblige! (She's upstairs painting. Long may she paint. That's work I dislike with the intensity of a million suns. I also feign incompetence well enough to have scored myself a court order: I'm not allowed to come within two-hundred feet of a roller or brush.)

So there will be a red-and-green-leaf starched salad with our local-famous (as opposed to world-famous) vinaigrette—olive oil, balsamic vinegar, strawberry freezer jam, Dijon mustard, salt, and pepper—plus a little feta cheese and maybe a few homemade croutons.

Me, I'm having a lamb shank. The goddess in scrubs upstairs, lathering a wall, doesn't eat *agnus*—another one of those great mysteries that marriage reveals—but I most decidedly *do* eat it. Lemmings aren't led astray, or brought like the sheep they are to the slaughter, only so that we can wear sweaters and itchy socks. If we're not supposed to eat these creatures, why are they made of such savory meat?

But my Sweet Precious, so sentimental about little lambs, isn't quite so watery when it comes to chickens, so it will be a stuffed chicken breast for her and the youngest urchin. (The other two have been shipped off to a camp. May God have mercy on the master and mistress of their cabins.)

No time to lose! Into the pan goes a drizzle of olive oil. I've got to brown the shank, lately o'erspread with salt, black pepper, and Italian seasoning. That done, I remove the shank and add to the pan—wait! There's no music!

Onto the hi-fi goes the music of the greatest rock band ever—just as the scrubbed, sweaty, and paint-bespecked goddess descends to retrieve a spackling knife. Though on the issue of the main course we've touched and gone our separate ways, there's still room for a little lovin' and squeezin'.

Or not. She's a woman on a mission, and I'm no pool boy with oiled pecs. I'm just the cook. ("Greatest rock band ever," it shouldn't need saying, is meant ironically. Maybe.)

"Just so you know," she says, "I hate this music. You play it all the time."

"You said the same thing about the choral music I was playing *for only the second time* last night."

"You play everything all the time."

"That's the Eagles, which I don't play all the time."

"Yes you do. You play everything all the time. Every time I come down here you're playing the same thing again."

"But this is different from what I was playing last night."

"No it isn't. It's the same different thing," she says and vanishes up the stairs. In the background I hear the emotionally stable Steve Perry thinking about the time someone walked out on him.

What a girl! There's no combination like beautiful and irrational! It makes my blood boil like an unwatched pot. "Son of a bitch," said Binx, "it is enough to bring tears to your eyes." I swear the back pocket on a pair of scrubs is the best-made thing in the world. I'd sacrifice a lamb to it if I could find one.

Lamb! How could I forget thee, even for the least division of an hour? Back to the kitchen! I add to the pan a diced *mirepoix* plus some chopped garlic and then, after a fine aroma fills the kitchen, about a cup of diced fresh tomatoes and a cup or so of red wine.

I sing along, a singer in a fragrant room, smell of wine and cheap legume. I think of my Dissenter's dissenting opinion. It's not like I'm listening to John Cougar Menstrualcramps, for God's sake!

I sprinkle in some rosemary and thyme and pour in some chicken stock. The juices reach three-quarters of the way up the shank. Perfect.

Cover and set at 200 for maybe two hours, though the Rule of Undercook obtains.

Time to go out back and clean the golf clubs I'm borrowing after a thief left me with aught but a hickory-shafted mashie, a niblick, and a baffing spoon.

About an hour and a half into the bake I place in the oven two chicken breasts, both having been cut open and stuffed with mushrooms, sun-dried tomatoes, and gournay cheese and then seasoned with salt, black pepper, and oregano. I'm husband of the year! When the lights go down in this city, who wouldn't want to be here?

A woman on a mission, apparently.

Downtime? Not for me! Time to wash the—wait! Where's the drinky-poo? Lordy, I'm slipping in my old age! Into a snifter goes a bottle of double IPA. Ah! Look at that! Almost as good as a back pocket on old scrubs!

Time to wash the greens, prepare the salad, and think about Binx—Binx!—who, at one of those moments when subtlety, apparently, wasn't called for, said plainly of Sharon Kincaid, "Her bottom is so beautiful that once as she crossed the room to the cooler I felt my eyes smart with tears of gratitude."

Out back a wren lights upon my bird feeder, eats, sings her song *nonpareil*, and darts off to the house I've made for her. Hopkins! Troubled Welsh bard! My heart stirs for this bird—the achieve of, the mastery of the thing! Too soon these trees will be the bare ruined choirs where late the sweet birds sang.

And you, Mr. Groundhog down below, enjoy your clover, you fat blind bastard, you! Soon you'll be groundhog stew. I don't raise tomatoes to fatten you, my big-toothed enemy-friend. You undermine my operation here.

But digging under my foundations is only one of your offenses, you cowardly ravenous ugly S.O.B. Did I not catch you in my parsley pot just the other day?

Parsley! I almost forgot the *gremolata!*

Zest a lemon, mince a clove of garlic, and chop up a few sprigs of parsley: *gremolata*. I'll sprinkle it on the lamb shank just before serving it—to myself. This is typically used on *ossobuco*, but I'm not cutting my shank crosswise to make a lambsteak. And tonight, notwithstanding the back pocket, I'm above riffing on the translation of *ossobuco*. No amount of double IPA can induce me to hit the fat slow curve of "bone with a hole."

Out of the oven with the shank, which I remove to a separate bowl and cover. Time to skim the grease and reduce the juices with a slurry.

This process requires corn starch, which behaves like flour and cream-of-wheat: badly. It lumps up like fat—the fat on the underside of an old thigh. So: a couple of table spoons of corn starch into a bowl, into which I add a couple spoons-full of the liquid from the pan. Stir. Stir some more. Add more liquid. Then, as the pan now boils and reduces over heat on the stove, I stir in the corn starch. This is one fine glaze—or will be once I add two tablespoons of butter—one for me and one for my cardiologist.

Ah, butter: These things I do . . . it's all because of you . . . all I wanted was to eat you. I *won't* be alright without you.

Onto the plate goes the shank, onto the shank the *gremolata*, and beside them both the glaze. Behold! A lamb of God, which taketh away the hunger of the day, which included two brutal hours in the office.

Mix the bowties, the greens, the feta, and the croutons, and pour on the dressing; uncork the shiraz, serve the chicken to the non-shankers. Not bad for a Tuesday.

But why lamb shank "redemption"? you ask.

Well, I was walking through the farmers' market on Saturday when I was accosted by a teen-age boy behind a table. "You, sir! You need a whole chicken!" he informed me.

So I stopped. "In fact I don't," I said, but, reading the board that advertised his goods, I noticed lamb shanks. "I suppose I could use a lamb shank," I admitted sheepishly.

This boy was pure huckster. "How do you prepare it?" he asked. "I've been hearing several interesting recipes today"—and paying attention to none, I wagered.

This smooth-talking silver-tongued schemer had me already. I bluffed my way through an answer, which he pretended to find interesting. Next thing I knew I was parting with $9 for a lamb shank.

Who's cryin' now?

Whereupon I called a pal whom I'll call "Garry," because that's his name. He's actually been to culinary school. I knew he'd be able to tell me what to do with a lamb shank.

Now both the Scriptures and *Henry IV* (Part One) would have us "redeem the time," and I'm no one to argue with God *or* Shakespeare, so I'll go ahead and consider this another chapter and meal redeemed—and own up, of course, to any errors that may be found herein.

But, now, time to lug my guts up the stairs to bed, where lies a goddess in the strong loving masculine arms of my great rival: he that goes by the name "Sleep."

11

Cioppino in the Heartland and the Cost of Misbehaving

Recently my oldest daughter had called, advising against ordering cioppino in Montana.

—Jim Harrison, *The Raw and the Cooked*

The best cioppino I've ever had was in a farm house in New Liberty, Iowa, two-thousand miles from what I'm told is its *locus originis* in San Francisco, give or take a hectare.

I have no reason to dispute San Fran's proprietary claim on this gustatory marvel, none except that every now and then I find myself listening unwillingly to an overly chauvinistic displaced Californian making far too many preposterous claims about his state's genius for starting things. That the terminus of the westward expansion should suddenly become the source and fountainhead of All Good Things seems dubious. "You know, the way we did that in California, where (of course) all this got started"—that's just the kind of sentence I don't usually stick around for the ending of.

I take no issue with you native Californians who have stayed put. I honor the patriotism that is proper to you. But you should know, if you don't know already, that some of your people have left California, and they are annoying the hell out of the rest of us.

Already I can feel the coastal food snobs pouncing: Your fish couldn't have been fresh! There's no way your crabs and clams and shrimp were fresh! (Like ours!) Etc., etc.

I'll grant these *haute cuisiners* a little credit for at least intuiting something about the general geographic location of a place they would never condescend to live in—which I'm sure the Iowans are fine with—but my answer is: You weren't there in Garry's kitchen.

And here's another thing: just because you live near an ocean doesn't mean you know more or are cooler than the rest of us.

The Garry of whom I speak, the Garry aforementioned in the previous chapter, actually lived in California for a while—a long while, as it turns out. But this noble denizen of Iowa doesn't go around acting like it. He lives where he lives and knows how to belong there without the apparent requisite snobbery. (A displaced "intellectual" writing out of Iowa City once referred to this lovely breadbasket state as "my laboratory." Pox *and* devil take that arrogant bastard!) And I promise you this: Garry could use ant bait for *amuse-bouche* or turn shark shit into charcuterie—all the while living by the unpretentious and unimpeachable Irving Cobb doctrine: "When you really have something to eat you don't need to worry trying to think up the French for napkin." If you doubt this, I'll arrange for you to consult with Garry's excellent wife—one lucky girl each evening at suppertime, if not at bedtime—who gives his cioppino the O Rating—the Big O, and for once I'm not talking about basketball.

You could almost be content to watch this genius in his kitchen, except that at some point your nose is going to tell your hands and mouth to seize what it just got a whiff of. With a hand motion more deft than the one Tom Buchanan used to break Myrtle Wilson's nose Garry can pull a *Hasenpfeffer* from a hat. And then *bam!* A pile of sliced *soucisson* that you scarcely noticed was there falls from his cupped hands into a bowl half-filled with something you've never heard of, fully stirred and ready for the herbs and the grated cheese. He wheels around to the stove, grabs the handle of a sauté pan, and with a manly kind of Jonsonian delicacy, back and forward and quickly back again, he scrambles a *brunoise* without spilling so much as a molecule of earth's increase. Stretched out on a floured cutting board lies in wait a loaf of his own homemade ciabatta, a sensuous mound of that essential thing we do not live alone by. As certainly as there's a roux on hand in his fridge and homemade pizza crusts on call in his freezer and the labor of his summer canning stockpiled in his basement, so just as certainly a crème brûlée loiters, poised, in this excellent Iowa kitchen. Near it, amid the orderly mess on the countertop, stands his go-to drinky-poo: a bourbon on the rocks, noble, stately, and glorious. You raise your Iowa swill (Templeton Rye, neat), take a sip, and vow to quit cooking altogether. This dude's out of your league.

As a sign of Garry's good sense I offer this: I once asked him to tell me what goes into *his* cioppino. He said, and I quote, "Garlic, onion, tomato, fennel, wine, clam juice/fish stock, hot pepper flakes, whitefish (halibut, cod, etc.), clams, shrimp, crab, mussels and whatever else sounds good."

You will note the primacy of garlic. Next comes onion and so on. This is the mark of a man of good sense. It follows that he's a fly-fisherman, a golfer, and an admirer of back pockets. Note also that he doesn't quibble about the fish: "whitefish (halibut, cod, etc.)," where "etc." means "you get the point," though I'm certain he would draw the line at tilapia, which he rightly regards as a fish of uncommitted flavor at best. And "whatever else sounds good" obviously means "use your judgment but don't be stupid."

You will also note his utter indifference, at least in his answer, to quantities. That's because he's not an assessment-mad administrator maniacal about measuring institutional shit—its official name is "outcomes"—in precise cubic centimeters. He knows the proof is in the pudding, not on the summary sheets presuming to report on "effectiveness."

"On a scale of one to five, five being the most and one the least, how effective was the cioppino in meeting its stated objectives?"

No. Garry is a sensible head chef, not an insensate associate dean. He knows the right questions to ask. Does this taste good? Does it or does it not get the O Rating?

At coordinates 42.6889° north and 84.2830° west I set out on my maiden voyage into the sea of cioppino. It was a cold January day, a day cold enough for the waters I set out on to be frozen, which they were, but not because of the weather. They were frozen because of the chilly blast issuing from a certain pair of eyes normally given to rolling but at this moment icy and still and not entirely pleased to have caught me using the wall for assistance in walking upright.

Mind you, I was bibulous but not sloppy, happy but not halfway to Concord. Not by half. Okay, maybe by half. But there was a little speed bump in the hallway runner, a wrinkle that caught my toe, so I reached out for the wall to keep from stumbling. And who just had to be looking down the hall from the kitchen at that precise moment? Talk about being in the wrong place at the wrong time. It was like I was in a committee meeting.

Truth be told, I *had* flirted a little with a daughter of Madame Jenever perhaps a bit more than befits a man pledged to another. The offending seductress, damn her, was Beefeater—or, as I have previously called her, Memoryeater. This happened while I was preparing a steak and lobster dinner during those festal days between Nativity and Theophany, when, it seems to me, a proper Christian ought to get tight a time or two. (You *know* the disciples got obliterated on Holy Saturday. That's the reason the women beat them to the tomb the next day.) But at the end of the meal, which was magnificent, things began to seem, ah, maleficent to Someone Else. I was decidedly not in the position Our Lord was in in the river Jordan. You could almost hear the voice of the Goddess: "This is my besotted husband in whom I am *most* displeased."

And get this: my great offense was that I dozed off during the Lions' play-off game. The *Lions!* They hadn't made the play-offs since Esau last fricasseed a rabbit for Isaac, and still they managed to make the game soporific. But apparently neither of these two glaring facts had anything to do with my somnambulant behavior. No! My falling asleep was attributed not to them but to an innocent stolen grope, a harmless mistletoe smooch I allowed that coquette Beefeatress (damn her) to give me!

Guilty or not, a man has to make amends. So I thought I'd see what cioppino could do to help me out.

The difficulty here, I realized almost at once, is that the displeased Goddess doesn't go for mollusks of any sort—a moral failure, in my opinion, though one she more than makes up for in ire and disapproval. I, on the other hand, will swallow mollusks whole, cooked or not. And although it's well-established that I can trespass like a Medici when it comes to sins of commission, the sins of omission do not appeal to me at all. So I decided from the start that there would be mussels.

And, of course, a libation. But not a clear one! Too soon for that. I'd go with a Manhattan—to help myself feel more charitable toward the coastal snobs out east. I like the word "Sazerac" better than "Manhattan" and the name "Old Fashioned" better still, but I thought it was time to honor my late father by using some of the sweet vermouth he left behind and that my sainted mother had no use for. A Manhattan, then. A west-coast meal and an east-coast drink in the Great White North.

So I began by making sure I had the ingredients prescribed by the Iowan master—and also those not prescribed, such as Angostura bitters. And since a quick glance into the cabinet revealed that the bitters were poised and ready, it was time to go fishing and shrimping.

Turns out I can get local shrimp. Not five miles from my house there's a modest inland shrimp "farm." The local shrimp are good. They're more expensive than the ones in the grocer's freezer, the shrimp that are "a product of"—and here the label lists several distant regions, all or some or one of which you can choose to believe your shrimp come from—but the local shrimp are worth the extra jingle in your pocket. And, at any rate, lacking shrimp that were swimming a few hours ago in the nitrogen-infused waters of the Gulf of Mexico, a man should spend his money as close to home as possible, whenever possible. (Next to Traverse City, Trinidad seems to be the nearest place for me to get my bitters from. Yes: I am a man who hates compromise but has compromised, as E.B. White once put it.) A man should also subscribe to the Joel Salatin doctrine: I see you're a person of quality. You pay top dollar for a nice car and fine clothing, which you don't put in your body; why wouldn't you pay top dollar for good food, which you *do* put in your body?

So I went shrimping about five miles from home. I also found some good-looking cod at a little unprepossessing seafood boutique. The fish bore with it the conflicted remembrance of Mark Kurlansky's *Cod*, a happy read chronicling an unhappy history. In exchanging money for my Midwestern cod I managed to swallow any remorse I might have indulged were I unfortunate enough to have been born a white sociologist working out of, say, Madison or Ann Arbor or anywhere else sociologists spread their delicate manufactured guilt for being born white and having access to cod.

I exclude the learned sociologist John Shelton Reed, whose *Barbecue* (UNC Press, 2016) is a kind of Glory Hallelujah in and of itself. He's what all those other sociologists in Birkenstocks ought to be.

"What can you tell me about this cod," I asked the cherubic skillet-faced youngster behind the counter.

"It come frash-fwozen," he said.

"From where?"

"Fwum ohshin."

The fish was on ice behind glass. It was from the ocean, all right, but I was a monkey's uncle if it had been flash-frozen. I wasn't about to go ice-fishing for something else, however. For starters, things were chilly enough at home; for another, men who go ice-fishing only think they're having fun.

Standing approximately equidistant between two great freshwater lakes, Michigan and Huron, I bought the cod. It was as local and as fresh as I was going to get. I procured the other necessary sea creatures, no less local or fresh, and a whole fennel—fennel! green herb for the service of men, as the Sweet Singer of Israel said in that beautiful Tudor English of his—and then I ventured home.

How cold was it at home? When I opened the door, a light came on. Time to warm things up, and that might even mean risking vasodilation.

My older boy, Jake the Fake—and here "fake" could refer either to an evading jab-step on the hardwood or an evasive answer concerning homework—eyed the wooden cutting board. On it was a lovely tableau in three piles: chopped garlic, chopped onion, and fennel—the bulb, not the leaves.

"What's for dinner?"

"You and I will like it. Jury's out on the others," I said as I cupped the onions and dropped them into the eight-quart copper-bottomed pot I inherited from my grandmother. Almost immediately one of the greatest smells on earth, onions sautéing in butter and olive oil, reached what Corporal Klinger, pointing to his impressive schnoz, called "the old factory." "Here," I said, handing my maddening but much-loved boy a wooden spatula. "Stir this and breathe it in."

To my surprise, he did. And although his doing this didn't involve a screen of any sort, he seemed to like it. My guess: I was about to be asked a favor. He wasn't just stirring. He was stirring up the courage to ask me to take him to the store—*if* he could stir up the courage to ask a certain girl to the upcoming dance. Poor kid, I thought. I remember the paralyzing fear. How does anyone ever survive those years, especially anyone strapped with a dad like me?

We added the garlic and fennel. I measured some salt in my hand and dumped it in. I then added more red pepper flakes than any sane person should add to anything.

"What is this called?"

"It's called 'helping me so I'll take you to get flowers.'" I stole a half-glance. There was no way he was going to look at me, much less tell me anything. "Also 'cioppino,'" I said.

"What's in it?"

"What you're looking at plus shrimp, fish, mussels, and this." I added the diced tomato-plus-juices, the stock (I went with half fish, half chicken), and the wine. "Be the good kid who needs money for flowers and stir that a little. Then turn up the heat a bit and cover it."

And, again to my surprise, he did.

"So when can we, you know, go do that?" he asked.

"How about tomorrow."

"Okay. Are we done yet?" Teenaged boys think that every chore takes about three minutes. That includes such chores as mowing ten acres.

"For now, yeah. Come back and help later if you're not taking a nap." It was a Saturday, and he must certainly have been tired from being awake for four hours. Did I mention that it's hard to be cross with a kid when your abiding image of him is a metonymic pair of newly foliated motionless shins sticking out from under a comforter, feet like Bob Lanier's pushing top and bottom sheets alike to the nether corner of the bed? For who, after all, needs sheets when there's a mattress pad and a comforter and parents to follow you around, cleaning up after you and turning off lights?

I reduced the heat and made my Manhattan. I went to the hi-fi and put on a Don Henley post-Eagles / pre-*Hell Freezes Over* mix. At the kitchen island I sang along—I too bade goodbye to a river—and then bade goodbye to the first hit of my concoction. There's no such thing as one Manhattan, I thought to myself, except for men in my position. So I vowed to nurse it.

After about twenty minutes I added the mussels and then, after another five or so, the local shrimp and frash-fwozen cod.

Garry had said "whatever else sounds good." I decided to dump some dried oregano in. I quickly chopped up the fennel stalks and dumped them in. The leaves I'd sprinkle over the soup, once ladled into the bowls.

Speaking of: we'd need a bowl for the discarded mussel shells. I put one in the center of the table. A minute later the C.E.O. walked in, picked it up, and went to put it away.

"What are you doing?

"Putting this away."

"Put it back."

"Put it back why?"

I suppressed an urge to make a bad joke about how this conversation usually plays out differently and told her plainly that we needed it for the discarded mussel shells. To my surprise she allowed that an idea not hers was actually a good one—my first since donning the padlocked hymeneal chain.

It is customary to serve cioppino with sourdough bread. I've heard of folks putting it over a little pasta or rice. I decided against the pasta and rice and used the French bread that I had on hand. I served the soup at the stove and sent everyone, each with his or her plate and bowl in hand, to the table. Four of us sat down, Pergolesi's *Stabat Mater* now coming from the speakers, and I steeled myself against the usual abuse, which I began almost immediately to suffer: inexplicable dissent from Eeyore, the doleful younger boy, which I get whenever I serve seafood, and abuse from the eye-roller concerning the quantity of "alcohol" in my glass, as if I'd just snatched a quart mug from some bosomy Hofbrau Frau, groped her fine Teutonic rump, and filled the mug to the brim with Sauvignon blanc.

"It's a *wine* glass," I protested. "It's a glass of *wine*."

"Uh-huh." She pronounced this as if it were a trochaic foot pitched in a mid-range member-shriveling alto. She was having water—for the sake of contrast, I thought—because the vital ingredients in the pomegranate "martini" I made her, which she didn't finish, had already collided with that inscrutable gray matter behind her disapproving and yet unrivalled eyes.

I took my first spoonful and got perhaps three-quarters of the red pepper flakes that I had dumped in. Immediately I went into a coughing fit, behavior that Eeyore took as unbefitting an adult and certainly proof that sea creatures aren't made to be eaten.

After that things calmed down. Jake the Fake said, "this is actually pretty good," and he didn't seem to be faking it, even though he needed money for flowers. I looked up and saw Madame Censorious putting a mussel shell into the bowl provided.

"Did you just eat one of those?" I asked in the kind of transparent astonishment I try never to show.

"Uh-huh." This "uh-huh" was iambic. She said it in that cheerful soprano of hers. My heart began to stir. "It was good." An anapest! In the treble clef! Trouser tousling commenced, like in the limerick.

> (A pious young lady of Chichester
> Made all of the saints in their niches stir.
> One morning at matins
> Her melons in satins
> Made the Bishop of Chichester's britches stir.)

By meal's end my Disapprover would have eaten four. *Four!* Notwithstanding the mulish insolence I was getting from the donkey, who I could tell was already plotting how to sneak an alternate supper of ice-cream later on, this was turning out better than I thought it would. Next time I would add crab, clams, and a little lobster. I'd go whole hog.

During the clean-up I felt an arm fall across my shoulders, not exactly the arm I was hoping for but not an unwelcome arm, an arm that constitutes one side of a six-foot-four-inch wingspan.

"So, Dad. About those flowers."

"What about them?"

"I'll need a box of chocolates too."

"Who are these for?"

I'd have to cut it out of him. He excels at sleeping and being evasive.

"Someone."

"Someone who?"

"Just someone."

"Not someone who just moved here from California, I hope."

His reply was delayed just long enough to give me a scare, but then my fears were put to rest. It's not that he was thinking about it. It's that he simply wasn't going to answer—or help with the dishes, which would take more than three minutes.

III
High Summer 1

Summertime, oh summertime, pattern of life indelible, the fade-proof lake, the woods unshatterable, the pasture with the sweetfern and the juniper forever and ever, summer without end.

—E.B. White, "Once More to the Lake"

12

Hungry for Meatless

The high summer day slides languorously toward evening as the cicadas grind out their metallic song. Your gastric longings peak at a level that can almost be described as libidinous.

Your teeth and taste buds crave something substantial, like flesh, yet lighter, like farfel bathed sparingly in cream sauce. They want something savory and assertive, something that will hang on the tongue but not in the belly.

Your conscience, which always sits down to dine with you whether you know it or not, requires something seasonal and local, and your damned imagination interrupts with talk of color and texture. "Show me a palate," it says. "Give me something soft yet crunchy, warm yet cold."

In this season of oxymorons and paradoxes that would please even that tent-making proto-Puritan ("as sorrowful, yet alway rejoicing; as poor, yet making many rich; as having nothing, and yet possessing all things") let not your hearts be troubled; neither let them be confused. The most perfectest and yet most simplest meal awaits you. It's more simpler than well grammar.

So for the moment I disregard what an English wag once said about his neighbors to the southeast ("nice place, France; pity about the French") and pull a nice big French baguette out of the freezer—one of those prepared numbers that, once defrosted, needs only a short visit to the oven. The ones I get require about eight minutes at 375. (You can make your own, it is true. But remember that the day is already slipping into evening.)

Set the baguette down on a counter top cleared of all clutter. Remember: the *mise en place* is part of the experience.

But so too is everything. The fullness of man is the incarnate condition. So choose your music wisely. For the dish I am about to describe, I recommend something refined: Bach's concerto for violin and oboe in D minor for your *L'Allegro* mood, or, if *Il Penseroso* be your portion, Elgar's sonata for violin and piano in E minor.

Or crank up some Skynyrd—or the DBTs on that rare occasion when no one is around to roll her eyes at you. But be sure your amp goes to eleven.

You'll be having wine with this meal, but that doesn't mean you shouldn't have a little drinky-poo while you work. God would not have you treating with contempt or disdain the bounties of this refulgent world.

Most authorities I have consulted on the matter say that Skynyrd requires a cold beer as see-through as intimate apparel, Bach a martini with a lemon twist and only an accusation of vermouth, and Elgar a finger or six of Laphroaig, opened to the nose with no more than two or three drops of hard water. If you are caught putting ice in your peaty Islay malt, you will be hunted down and, in the spirit of oxymorons, killed to within an inch of your life.

If the children are around and want to help, by all means let them. Suffer the little children to come unto you. (For their own dinner they'll require more than what you're currently preparing—which is why this is such a great meal to make when you're home alone—but whatever else you're going to have to feed them is your problem.) Cheese will need grating, garlic pressing, oil drizzling, tomatoes and green herbs chopping. All of these they can do or help with. Teach the children well, especially if you're going your own way and listening to CS&N, which I would certainly allow.

On a large wooden cutting board place about five cloves of garlic, maybe more, for garlic, as I have already said, is like irony and thigh (provided the thigh's a good one). Also place thereon a brick of hard cheese, preferably asiago.

Put a ripe sensuous tomato next to the cheese. An aromatic heirloom such as a Brandywine (thou name doubly blessed!) will do nicely. Next to it place the leaves of your favorite green herb. For this most exquisite of meals I generally prefer sweet basil first, oregano next, and sage after that, but I will in no wise commit an act of culinary imperialism here. Choose ye this day which herb ye shall eat. There's no disputing taste, as the ancients said. (They said this not because you can't in fact dispute taste, but because people with bad taste—soccer fans, for example—can't be argued with.)

Lovingly place the bread along the back edge of the cutting board. Be sure that behind it all stand your olive oil, your favorite salt dispenser (mine's stainless and has a handle), and a pepper grinder. Now look at the tableau before you. Look for a long time. Sip your drink and look again. The foods here assembled, when combined, are going to throw your tongue into spasms of pleasure that test the boundaries of analogy. You will seek far and wide, high and low, for the proper comparisons. Do not be surprised if your imagination hastens toward the bed ere you reach it at day's end.

Behold the wild civility of the basil! The erotic plumpness of the tomato! The solidity—nay, the native unity—of that *cosmo cosmema:* cheese! Behold the garlic cloves on their sides, inclining in love and affection toward one ingredient or another, the stately and solemn olive oil, erect and ready behind it all! Lord have mercy but the heart cracks!

Grab the bread. Slice it down the middle lengthwise but keep the two pieces together, cap on bottom, when you place it in the oven. Close the oven door, set the timer to the appropriate number—your mileage may vary—and reach for the Laphroaig.

Peel the garlic as you hum or sing along to the music. Set the peeled garlic aside. Sharpen your knife. Knives are like undergraduates: the only thing more dangerous than a sharp one is a dull one, especially in the business college. Slice your tomato and chop it into small cubes according to local preferences. Pay no attention to what chefs on national cooking shows do. Indeed, avoid TV like the plague and other clichés.

Chop your herb of choice. Press the garlic.

Place all of this in a bowl. Sprinkle it with salt and grind in some black pepper to taste. Open the spigot to the olive oil. Stir. Stir slowly at first. Stir rhythmically. Behold the concupiscent mixing of colors. Moan a little if you must.

Now for the cheese. This is a matter of some debate. The widely accepted practice is to grate the cheese and apply it to the dish last. I'll allow this method because "I'm open to all truth," as I once said to a bartender who asked, "what'll it be?"

So consider this: the bread you are warming (or baking) is going to have chopped tomatoes, a chopped herb, crushed garlic, salt, pepper, and olive oil on it. It is likely to be served not as a sandwich (though I'm open to all truth) but open-faced—that is, bread down and colors up. So you have to ask yourself: where do I want the cheese? As I said, conventional wisdom says you put the grated cheese on last. I'm ecumenical enough on this matter to give conventional wisdom its due.

But here are some other options:

You can prepare thin slices that are as long as the brick of cheese itself, and you can place them first or last on the bread. If first, the cheese melts a little and sticks. If last it neither melts nor sticks. You can also grate it and place it first or last on the bread, with the same results. You can also place it last and then re-heat the whole concoction so that the cheese melts and holds everything else in place.

But this, I must insist, is a mistake—notwithstanding *de gustibus* and notwithstanding my avowed openness to all truth. You will have a cleaner plate when you are done, but you will also have ruined the cool freshness of the tomato. As with most things that grow from the ground, so with the tomato: it is better uncooked.

Here, for what it's worth, is my method: take another drink. Remove the bread from the oven at the appropriate time. Lace it with grated cheese and let the cheese melt a little. After you've stirred the bowl in which the other ingredients mingle, spoon these same ingredients on the cheese-besprinkled bread.

Your conscience does not bother you. For the moment disregard what you've learned about Italians—that for them a broken arm is a speech impediment—and thank them for the general concept of Bruschetta. What you're about to eat is a variation thereon.

Now, as I said, there will be wine with this meal. And it *is* a meal. You've been moderate with the libations during your prep time, and that's good, for too much foreplay will ruin the getting-down-to-business of eating your bread. But now you must choose a wine.

Holy Writ is silent on the matter, and, so far as I can discern, so is Holy Tradition. I therefore recommend a white sauvignon if the day remains clear and sunny. This wine is light and fruity enough and will not make you think that you ate a box of Grape Nuts for supper. But should the storm clouds of summer move in suddenly, as they are sometimes wont to do, an inky red wine will answer to this simple meal of bread, tomatoes, garlic, basil, cheese, salt, pepper, and olive oil. Merlot I would shy away from. It is a grape meant to be blended sparingly with its superiors. Also avoid Pinot Noir. Get something thick and assertive, something you can write your name with, especially if your name has about thirteen syllables, like Wilhelmina Margareta Van Overloopen.

Now where to eat. If your kitchen has a countertop area that opens onto another room with bar stools on the other side, this is the place for you—especially if there are speakers behind you, as there are in my kitchen.

All your senses will be assaulted on such a stool. This is what we call a Christian Space. Properly understood and practiced, Christianity addresses the whole person, not the chimerical shade-like soul putatively separable from the somatic mass. If you want Platonism you can have it, but good luck eating your ideal forms.

If your kitchen does not afford you such a spot, seat yourself in a place that will allow you to hear the music and relish the work put into this simple meal. If you're in the dining room, choose a chair that gives you a glimpse of the kitchen. If no glimpse is available, make sure your imagination has been properly trained by early nineteenth-century British poetry to conjure the glimpse. "This Lime Tree Bower My Prison" is a good tutor.

And eat slowly—the way you read poetry if you know how to read poetry—and imagine writing something titled "This Lime-Wedge Drink My Prison." Let the oil, like words, dribble out of your mouth and onto your hands. Let the rogue tomato chunks spill onto the plate, the excess cheese slivers joining them. For what, I ask, did God invent spoons? Your job—is it not?—is to taste and see that the Lord is good, or at least that the food is. For at this point—remembering the fullness of your condition—you should be savoring whatever the five senses tell you to savor.

You should *see*, if you can, the place where you did the work. You should also see the varied colors of your work. You're going to *smell* it—I guarantee you will—for you're using an anti-social amount of garlic (and this in some measure is always the point of careful food preparation). You're going to *feel* the various textures in your mouth. And you're going to *hear* the music of your choice turned up to eleven. You're listening to something that will really get your dog on. I once tried Mozart's requiem mass—Martin Pearlman and the Boston Baroque (Telarc)—and nearly had an accident.

Now, for those of you with rapacious appetites, there's an addition to this meal:

Prepare some sweet corn (O sweet corn! My spirit hath rejoiced in thee!) to accompany the bread. Boil if you can't grill it and then load it with butter and salt. Sweet corn is part-delivery system for butter and salt, a vehicle of the grace we're saved by. Trust me.

After dinner, clean up. This is bliss itself. If you are not home alone, it is especial bliss, for your Sweet Precious or someone else is putting the children (or the children are putting themselves) to bed. But even if you are home alone, you are in the kitchen working to chord sequences turned up to eleven. What more do you want?

Clean up, finish your potable, and grab a book—the one you're holding right now, for example, the one you've bought no fewer than ten extra copies of to give as gifts to your favorite lusty, thieving, God-fearing friends.

13

She's Headed for the Pollo Side of Town

When the C.E.O. announces her preference for Pollo Piccata tonight and then vanishes, I can't help but wonder whether she read the draft of an essay on marital jokes I accidentally left sitting out in plain view. (Samples: What food reduces a woman's sex drive by 95%? Wedding cake. Where can you count on a man to complete a task ahead of schedule? In bed.)

No matter. This is a dish as popular at the table as in the kitchen—always a pleasure and not in the least bit difficult, especially if you're cooking through the first disc of the Very Best of the Eagles and planning to eat through the second one, which I determine at once I am. I know what the queen of hearts is.

The chicken comes from a good old boy down at the Saturday farmers' market who sells me eggs and whole fryers and who can really flirt with the women, especially the ones with the moon in their eyes. His birds put the *suck* in *succulent* and take the *Lent* right out of it. Even the restaurant chefs up and down the river know enough to buy from him.

Rather than pound the chicken breasts into airy thinness, as some culinary spastics do, I prefer to slice them in half lengthwise into thin botulismic slabs of future energy. I then dry them with paper towel, salt them like there's no tomorrow, besmirch them with paprika, bespeckle them with black pepper (freshly ground), and roll them in flour. Meantime, two pots of water heat up, one for the sweet corn and one for the fettuccine, while in a small sauce pan chopped garlic and pine nuts improve the aroma in the kitchen in their slow self-sacrificial effort to soften themselves in butter for my dining pleasure. Behind them, in a large sauce pan, a cube of butter rides on its own melting and becomes one flesh with a small puddle of olive oil. This concupiscence is what I'll sauté the sliced chicken in while thinking uncharitable thoughts about Hippolyte Mège-Mouriès, the French maniac who at the diabolical insistence of Napoleon III invented margarine.

Is the olive oil local? No. The olive oil isn't local. But I found out a long time ago what olive oil can do to your soul.

On the cutting board sun-dried tomatoes and fresh oregano from the herb garden await chopping. Some fairly skilled local farmers dry their own tomatoes and sell them at the market, but if you want them you either have to place an order ahead of time or get to the Saturday market at dawn's early crack. Otherwise, they're already gone. I myself prefer early arrival. Saves talking on the phone or using that accursed email.

We're not in a fast, obviously, so there's also a libation going: tonight a Bombay Sapphire martini with a lemon twist—in devout observance of the David Brower rule concerning olives.

The chicken goes in a little ahead of the corn and pasta, which take about the same amount of time. I'll need a little extra time once the fowl is done to make the glaze. So in goes the chicken. About the time I turn it, in go the corn and fettuccine in their respective pots.

When the chicken is done—but first another sip; ah, that's glorious!—I put it on a plate in the oven to keep it warm. That noise you hear is a half-cup of white wine—real cheap stuff—sizzling in the large sauce pan and going to work on the bits of chicken and flour, now good and stuck to the pan. I scrape them loose with a spatula and pour in the juice squeezed not one minute ago from a lemon, also, alas, not local. Then, as the glaze thickens, another cube of butter miraculously appears in the pan. (The butter is frozen, to decrease its chance of separating because of culinary dumbassery.) I'm taking this sauce to the limit—one more time. When I'm satisfied with its viscosity I'll drizzle it over the chicken, by then sprinkled with capers.

The timer announces that the boils are done. The corn goes into a covered serving dish. The pasta goes first to the colander and then to another serving dish, there to mingle promiscuously with the sun-dried tomatoes, oregano, garlic, pine nuts, and grated parmesan.

Behold! A certain someone has heard the timer and reappeared. Damn me but she's a moving violation! To paraphrase Glenn Frey on the topic of city girls, she discovered early what a smile can open.

The salad, having been prepared ahead of time, waits patiently. I put everything on the table, also prepped ahead of time, call Recalcitrance, Mendacity, and Belligerence, and we listen to them fight over who gets to call down the blessing from above. Fighting over prayer! No wonder the right words never come.

Even She Who Must Be Obeyed allows that the food is good. If I am not deceived, all's forgiven for that essay about marital jokes. No lyin' eyes, hers. She may get the worst but she also gets the very best of my love. And lo! I seem to detect up ahead in the distance a blinking—no!—a *shimmering* light! A midnight flyer! Only time and the fatigue of The Three Incorrigibles will tell. O let it be fatigue in earnest—not one of these nights but *this* night, this night of oil and garlic and textures *al dente* and the unparalleled sapphiric botanicals penetrating the splendid nuance of the noble juniper berry.

And outside the kitchen window, another Jenever moonrise.

14

How to Cheat on Your Wife in the Kitchen

You know you're a lucky man if, on a Saturday morning in May, shortly after you've left coffee and the morning paper on the bed stand next to an awakening goddess, you hear a creaky voice calling out and asking, "do we have any mint?"

Sleepy-Pie has roused herself; she's reading about the Kentucky Derby, and all at once your day is taken care of. You almost feel a string's pluck of guilt about the fact that, later on, you're going to cheat on her in the kitchen. You almost feel it, but not quite. For cheating is now your plan—in strict accordance with how sin works. Ask Young Goodman Brown. And isn't it entirely to your advantage that for once she is the one to register the day's first thought about the afternoon's first drink?

And how!

Now tomorrow is Mother's Day—a poor excuse for picking a man's pocket, but we'll leave that be for the moment—and you're sure The Mother will opt for your famous barbecued chicken on the grill, real garlic bread, which is to say bread toasted on the grill and brushed with melted butter in which swims an entire island population of chopped garlic bits, a leaf salad (the spinach is going nuts right now) with your vinaigrette, her spicy toasted walnuts (crushed), Hellas's own feta cheese, and on the side rosemary potatoes and a little tiny splash of cold cold chardonnay.

So tomorrow, which as the Good Book says has its own worries, is worry-free. All you have to do is buy all the cards, flowers, and presents, and do all those other things you've left undone, and do it all in half a day, which happens to be the same day on which you're going to cheat and get away with it—indeed, be adored and loved all the more for it.

(In some cases today may be trickier: you may have agreed to plant the impatiens and to hang those beautiful cedar birdhouses you've been building with your son. But take courage and be of good cheer: you'll be cheered up good and plenty by the singing of "My Old Kentucky Home," which, face it, is a right proper song. And although you'll catch a little hell for the fact that no one can distinguish a horse from a hambone on your ancient TV with its government-issued digital converter box, you've proven o'er and o'er that you're not going to spend a dime on a TV, so don't worry.)

Think back now to the first paragraph. You've been called to the bedroom—always a good sign—and the question at hand is: will you make me a mint julep later on? You race to the stairs; you take them two at a time. In an instant you stand heroically at the foot of the bed. Ah, and there she is: hair disheveled, cotton jammies wantonly askew.

> Robes loosely flowing; hair as free:
> Such sweet neglect more taketh me
> Than all the adulteries of art;
> They strike mine eyes, but not my heart.

In her hands is the hot milkshake she calls "coffee" (a mug of flavored sweetened creamer *and* sugar infused with a small trace of hot water that has been filtered through ground coffee beans). On her lap: the paper. O, lucky morning paper! (Binx, you old devil! Now I understand the conceits of the poets, too!) O, thou sports section! Would that I were thou, box scores!

"I'm sorry?" you say. You know full well what she's asked, you lecher. You're the day's hero, and tomorrow's hero too (assuming you can sneak out later on and do what you should have done on any one of the 364 days allotted to you for performing the basic tasks of surviving Mother's Day). There's a slight grin on her face, harbinger of a glorious sunny Saturday in May with all its darling buds attending, and the question again, which itself could send a man into orbit: "Do we have any mint?"

"We do. And speaking of dinner," which you weren't, "how about my famous shrimp and pasta?"

"I don't like my shrimp cold, you know." It's an old issue, mildly contentious, and you feel the blood cool a little. But you remember that you could fail miserably this weekend, so now is no time to fight over the temperature of little pink sea creatures.

"I'll serve it warm," you say. "You enjoy your hot milkshake. Call me if there's anything else you need a man for."

And you're off (not expecting to be called) but brimming with the words of the incomparable Robert Capon: "The graces of the world are the looks of a woman in love; without the woman they could not be there at all; but without her lover"—that's you and me!—"they would not quicken into loveliness."

[Cut to late afternoon. The Mother's Day pickpockets have picked your pockets—and she's not even your mother!—but: Mission Accomplished. You've put four trays of impatiens in the ground, hung six more beautiful cedar bird houses, each one an original design, and purchased the required purchasables that will get you through tomorrow successfully.]

The horse race is about to begin, so you present your Espoused Saint (whom you're about to betray) with a mint julep prepared according to Uncle Will's specifications in *Signposts From a Strange Land*. "Thank you," she says, and the morning grin returns.

Binx, you were right! It is a stitch in the side! It is a sword in the heart!

Off to the kitchen you bound. You've got several large cooked shrimp (from the local shrimp farm) ready to be literally detailed. So you detail them. You could skewer and grill them yourself, and doing so is great fun, but if you're going to cheat on your wife in the kitchen, you might as well *cheat*. So you cook them quickly on the stove top in olive oil or butter or both. Then into a tin mixing bowl they go.

Next you press a ton of garlic into the bowl. This raw garlic will serve you well tomorrow at "coffee hour": no one will want to talk to you, which is about all you can ask for after a bad Mother's Day sermon, especially if there's no mention of the Mother of God. (Walter Savage Landor called the epitaph to Gray's "Elegy" a tin kettle tied to the tail of a noble dog. That's about what coffee hour is to Mass or the Divine Liturgy. Pray, commune, scoot.)

Drizzle God's Own Plenty of olive oil over the pressed garlic and shrimp. Sprinkle in some dried oregano. If you've got some from Mt. Athos—and I seem to have it in abundance—use it. Remember: you're about to cheat. Athonite oregano can't hurt.

And now for the cheating: don't chop up any peppers. Don't rub anything. Don't cry over anything live and combustible. Reach into the spice cabinet, yawn, check the American League scores, grab a can of Konriko's Jalapeño All-Purpose Seasoning, and sprinkle a healthy dose of it on the shrimp. (You folks at Konriko's are welcome to send me a case of this stuff in exchange for the free advertising.)

My friends, I know there are many seasonings and rubs out there. And many of them are very good, including the ones you yourself have made. But think of the mere mileage you'll get out of Konriko's Jalapeño Seasoning. I mean, it's Mother's Day weekend, and your life is bad enough as it is. Once in a while you've got to go easy on yourself.

Toss it. Mix it all together. Sneak a shrimp or two. Cheating never tasted so good, for

> O love's best habit is in seeming trust,
> And rub on shrimp loves not to have rub told.

Into the boil goes angel hair pasta. Shred some hard cheese—asiago, parmesan, I don't care. (Just avoid the knock-off foot powder Kraft sells). Either of these will answer, and one or the other is necessary, because the last thing you're going to do, after you've tossed the pasta and the shrimp together, is adorn it with a hard cheese—unless you're also going to sprinkle it with capers.

On the side you've got a small saucepan in which a little chopped garlic and pine nuts soften in olive oil. You don't need more garlic in this dish, but you do want the smell of garlic softening in olive oil to fill your kitchen, so you soften a little garlic. You'll add it to the angel hair (boiled in salted and well-oiled water for about five minutes).

Damnation! You almost forgot that you yourself have a mint julep going. Just be sure you've used middling bourbon, because you don't want to waste the good stuff on added sugar, crushed ice, and mint. The good stuff you take God's way as prescribed by Levitical law: neat.

You hear yelling. The race is apparently on. You don't care, but you must persuade the little world you've made cunningly that you do. You rush to the old TV. It's all snow, but a voice is there to make sense of it all. Apparently one horse leads all the others at the end and is therefore accounted the winner. Amazing, you agree, and race back to your infidelity.

Now the best way to serve this dish, unless you are governed by the opinions of the one you're cheating on, is with chilled shrimp on hot pasta. But this weekend belongs to The Mother, and you're no match for her, not now, not ever, as that man among men Sully put it, so you put the shrimp into an oven set to "warm." In goes a baguette as well. And what's this? Green beans? Someone other than you went a-harvesting. Clean and snip them and put them into the steamer. Seven minutes of steam and they won't be mushy enough for a basement potluck at First Baptist but they'll still be crispy enough for you.

Sneak another mint julep during the replay. Oh lord that's good! Binx! Kate! Aunt Emily! Where are you? We're serving shrimp sprinkled with Konriko Jalapeño Seasoning—from Louisana, for God's sake!

I'm an unreconstructed sports nut, but I'm here to tell you that there's nothing in the NBA, PGA, or MLB to arouse a man's interest when there's a shimmering woman in close proximity sipping an Uncle-Will mint julep and thinking of horses.

And now your crew empties itself into the kitchen. "Was the winner a horse with a weird name?" you ask. Of course it was, says the crew. It always is. You hope that someday "Tom" will win the derby. Tom will be a scraggly-looking nag owned by Sally and Ned Jenkins of Newcastle, Kentucky.

"Wash up," you say, and soon clean people appear at your table. They're getting a fine shrimp dinner, plus beans plus pasta plus bread plus cold cold chardonnay or milk, depending on their ages, all for minimal labor.

You're not in *favor* of minimal labor, mind. You're for spending as much time at the kitchen window looking out at your bird houses as you can spend. You're for smelling all the smells you can smell and sucking down all the mint juleps you can suck down—I mean get away with. But it's Mother's Day weekend, and every man could use a little help, a little something on the side.

N.B. In other chapters, O Theophilus, I sing the praises of local beer. A very fine brewer in Kansas, grateful for what I had once written on behalf of his industry, sent me a sample of his work. And what fine work it was! I only wish more of his fellow brewers understood what a *wide* readership my book has, and how much I could reward their labors if only my own labors were more widely rewarded.

So if Konriko wants to send me a lifetime supply of Jalapeño Seasoning in appreciation for this selfless plug, well, may God bless Konriko, too, for God knows Konriko has blessed me and mine. (Use it on fish too.)

15

Chicken Erotica and the Venus Transit

Before the chicken breasts, a little trip down mammary lane.

It was five-o-five, June 5, 2012, and I was looking directly at the sun. Why? Because I also run with scissors? No, although I do that too. (No fate has yet tempted me to lick an aluminum fence post in January.) I was looking directly at the sun—through my son's "Eclipse Glasses" ("safe for direct solar viewing," said the label)—because on that day Venus was making a pass between us and Old Sol and wouldn't do so again until I and my children had given ourselves to the family mould. The next time this would happen—December 11, 2117—a new kind of reader would be lifting this fine book from the remainder bin before rejecting it in favor of Italian cleavage.

We had witnessed a Venus transit in 2004. The Venus transit occurs in pairs, each pair consisting of occurrences separated by eight years and each *paired* occurrence separated by 105 five years. The next pair of transits will occur in 2117 and 2125, so unless I live to be 154, I'll not witness another. It's fairly certain, given my cholesterol and other cards I've been dealt, that I've seen my last Venus transit.

Which is why on that day, June 5, 2012, I was looking directly at the sun. This planetary event was about to take its 105-year hiatus.

But because history is bunk, as that idiot-savant Henry Ford assured us, let's give *Eros* the immediacy it deserves. Let's fast-forward to the here-and-now, for, as smoke ariseth from the coals yonder, I'm also preparing

Chicken Erotica, just as I did on that day in June of 2012, when last I looked directly at the sun.

You readers in Henderson, Nevada, might wish to pour yourselves a snifter of Joseph James Hop Box IPA. For some reason a can of this imperial Foxbrew has appeared before me here in the Midwest, and, because I honor all things local, I honor those of you in Henderson. (You keepers of the Foxbrews may wish to send me a case of your Imperial IPA. As I said in the last chapter, I'm not above being treated well for the free advertising I provide, though I wish to make plain to my millions of readers that, whatever remuneration or neglect I elicit, Hop Box is A-1 prime stuff. Well done, my friends in Henderson. Love your place and drink your local beer.)

Damn it! I should be singing along to something, but the house is as silent as a tomb. How about a little Alison Krauss? Excellent choice. Now that I've found this marinade, I'll wrap my world around it.

(Our daughter called home not long ago and said, "you're grilling chicken, aren't you?" I said, "How did you know?" She said, "I hear Alison Krauss in the background. You always play Alison Krauss when you're grilling chicken." God bless the girl and Alison Krauss & Union Station too!)

I'm pretty sure this marinade descends from an issue of *Gourmet* published in the latter decades of the twentieth century. A buddy from grad school had—and still has—a wife who served this under the title (if the plagiarist remembers correctly) "Chicken Lipscomb." The present thief has tinkered with it over the years and renamed it "Chicken Erotica" (guaranteed to get you . . . well, just try it).

What you do is pretty simple: you combine dry sherry, olive oil, salt, pepper, red pepper flakes, oregano, rosemary, chopped onion and garlic (n.b. *chopped* garlic in this case, not pressed), and then you plop a few pieces of chicken into the marinade. Wisdom of the general sort would have you drop chicken breasts into the marinade. I'm here to tell you that thighs work well too, for I'm also a leg man and I agree with Jim Harrison that the chicken breast is overrated. My view, for what it's worth, is that you should never treat the dark meat of any bird with contempt, if for no other reason than that sooner or later a sociologist specializing in blah-blah-blah will tell you that your preference is a sign of a deep-seated racial bias. (Likewise, eating hens instead of roosters is a gender-based micro-aggression—and will get the micro-apology it deserves: aggressions you can't see warrant apologies you can't hear.) But let whatever cut you choose soak overnight and then grill it over low heat slowly. Serve with whatever you fancy. I usually fancy pasta and a cream sauce with black pepper and nutmeg and maybe a little lemon juice, freshly squeezed from local lemons.

Tonight we're also having a mixed green salad. I've patronized two local farmers in the making of this fine mix, not to mention a fromagister who, together with his goats, produces a very fine ricotta.

O that the little missus were here tonight! But, alas, she's in the cardiac unit, treating people who have hydraulic cement in their arteries because they eat like I do. Thus does she keep me in statin money. What a girl!

I lug my shitty genetics out to the grill and sneak an oblique glance at the sun. We're in the 105-year hiatus. There is no goddess of love moving across the all-seeing eye of heaven—nor none beside me. It appears that for once my marinade will fail of its final effect.

But not of its mediate effect. This will be good. I turn the chicken and spoon residual marinade across it. O, my darling! If only you weren't feeding catheters into the urethras of other men tonight!

IV
That's Some Pig!

---

let this day begin again in the change of hogs into people,
    not the other way around,
for today we celebrate again our lives' wedding with the world,
for by our hunger, by this provisioning, we renew the bond.
    —Wendell Berry, "For the Hog Killing"

16

Carbonara-Based Life[*]

There's a story, if memory serves, about a little spat that affected the greatest and best-dressed rock band ever. (I never know, given the mendacity of consciousness, whether I'm being ironic or sincere.) During a rehearsal or a sound check or something, Neal Schon was wailing away on his guitar, as was (and is) his wont—and *long* may he wail—when the ever-humble and psychologically stable Steve Perry came over and turned Schon's amp down. "They want to hear the voice," Perry said, pointing to himself. "The *voice*."

Separate ways were inevitable, and eventually came, and I, like many whose musical tastes are impeccable, regretted it. But still there are days when, standing in my kitchen, inching toward the vital late-afternoon decision as the lights go down in the city, I want to hear both the wailing guitar and the soaring pinched voice. And that can mean only one thing: I've decided to feed the troops some carbonara.

That this culinary delight is not on the lips of more people is a mystery, given how good it tastes and how simple it is to make. Of course you can make it more complicated if you want to, and that's okay by me (first rule of cooking to music: more time in the kitchen is better than less; you could

---

[*] Those science-mad humanoids whose bizarre intellectual habit is to break the universe down into smaller and smaller things—and then assure us sane people that the smallest things are the realest—argue about the essentiality to life of carbon. Those who defend this view are sometimes accused of "carbon chauvinism." But in more humane endeavors than science, endeavors wherein the whole is greater than the sum of its constituent parts, we talk about verities, such as Carbonara Chauvinism.

do worse than to grab a bottle of sherry and tell yourself, twice, to hold on). Just be aware: something about carbonara will bring out the 1980s in you, and that, maybe, is not an absolute good.

Carbonara makes use of two important staples that should be food groups unto themselves: bacon and eggs. Bacon! Is there anything it can't do? And, O, thou egg! How noble in design, how infinite in flavor! In form and moving how express and admirable!

Friendly reader—and even you, my enemy—hear the words of the greatest and best-dressed rock band ever: be good to yourself. Make a move across that Rubicon. Get a pound of bacon. I'm partial to dead pig smoked with apple wood but I don't think ill of hickory or maple or any other hard fiber set aflame. Just get some damned bacon.

Make sure that if your eight-track player isn't working you've got a selection of late-seventies / early-eighties songs on a cassette tape or CD, and by "selection" I mean your own Greatest Hits. Every band produced more plaque than platinum, so high-tech your way to a reasonable mix to protect your divine soul. Then put your selected mix on the hi-fi, check your mullet in the mirror, and pull out your favorite skillet.

If you prefer to do bacon in the microwave, you can put this book down right now and pound arsenic. You can return to your tartarus whence you came. The microwave is an abomination, and "microwave cooking" is oxymoronic, like "academic freedom." No. Spread your bacon strips on the skillet or, if for some strange reason you want to spend *less* time cooking, chop the bacon into small chunks *before* frying it and then dump the chunks into a pan. But for the love of God and Christ Jesus our Lord, give yourself the chance to stand over some sizzling bacon. Give yourself the chance to watch and smell the heat convert it from trichinosis into food.

When it's done—cooked but not crisp—put it on some paper towel and draw off the grease. (Save some of the grease in a cup so that, once it's cooled, you have something to drink later when you're swallowing your statin.)

Put some water in a pot, salt it generously, drizzle in some olive oil, and turn up the heat.

On a wooden cutting board chop up some parsley. Italian parsley is greatly to be preferred, but I'm no fundamentalist on this score. Put it in a bowl. Chop up the bacon, eating a few pieces or strips as you go, and add it to the bowl.

Tell your foolish heart to sing along. So what if you've been wrong before?

Take a sip of whatever it is you've poured to lubricate the process. I'll tell you who's not cryin' now. You, my friend.

Crack no fewer than two—allow yourself as many as four—eggs. Not those impious white store-bought eggs with the highlighter-yellow yolks. Be sure you're using Farmer Jim's eggs, newly squeezed from the hind-ends of chickens who enjoy the freedom to peck at bugs and worry about coyotes. Pour each egg back and forth from one half-shell to the other until you have discarded the whites; beat the yolks in a little tin bowl.

When the water is boiling, throw in about a pound of linguini or fettuccini. I don't care which. This is no time for dogmatism. Give it nine minutes in the boil, strain it, and dump it in a serving bowl.

Some benighted souls will tell you to add the egg yolks immediately. This is a mistake. It is true that you want the hot noodles to cook the eggs, but you don't want scrambled eggs. You don't want eggs that look as if they're curdled. So wait forty seconds, certainly no more than sixty, and then pour in the beaten eggs. Stir. Then dump in the parsley and bacon. Stir some more and cover.

You've made Carbonara.

Serve it with a deep assertive red wine. A good salice won't disappoint you. If you're richer than I am, get a good amarone.

Both Scripture and Tradition allow that hard cheese may be sprinkled atop the carbonara. Just don't use the ground goat bones that Kraft sells.

Then experiment with Carbonara. It's great with fresh sweet peas. It's great with chopped garlic, or chopped onions, or capers, or sun-dried tomatoes, but probably not with all of these, because it's in the nature of carbonara to be simple. Try it with several different combinations, not exceeding two or three on top of the basic ingredients I've suggested here.

You won't be alright without it. There isn't something else, so don't keep telling yourself. But mayhap you'll be greeted for your labors later on by open arms.

Once when I made this my younger boy presented me with a Hershey's kiss the next morning. "What's this for?" I asked. "For the best dinner *ever* last night," said my little baconator.

17

Carbonara *Redux En Toto* in the '80s Kitchen

Home in my driveway, tailgate of the pick-up down and serving as a workbench, I put the finishing touches on a child's bike that needs fixing. I'm not a bike mechanic, but I can play that role. And in short order, though I don't know it yet, I'll need children whose bikes are reliably working.

But soft you now! There are mouths to feed. Into the empty domicile I go, wash my greasy hands, and pull out a pound of bacon. Why? Because the parsley is in, of course.

Lick a finger and hold it up to the breeze to get the general drift of things. Weather forecast says sunny all day with increasing carbonara toward evening. This time we'll do it with eggs *and* cream and suggest two new uses for bacon grease beyond using it to swallow your Lipitor.

Check the fridge. Doh! No heavy whipping cream, and damned if I've got no milk cow or goat out back. Time to do something about that.

But for now, search for wallet. Wallet, as usual, is nowhere to be found, not even in the unlocked and wide-open beautiful ugly brown '83 Dodge pick-up truck, a.k.a The Babe Magnet, where, for days on end, along with keys securely dangling from the ignition, I usually keep it.

Must've left it at the office.

Summon the two older children. "Look under all the cushions. I need two bucks."

The game works: they disperse. I promise two more bucks to the one who bikes to the store to get me some heavy cream.

They find two bucks' worth of pennies, nickels, dimes, and quarters. Off they go! I'm a genius, though penniless.

But wait! It's as quiet as a morgue in here, quieter than libraries back before they became Information Retrieval Centers. This kitchen needs tunes.

Into the tray goes Toto *Past to Present* 1977–1990. Let that troubled and storied band serenade the studio session in the kitchen. I'll sing harmony, play air guitar to the memory of drummer Jeff Porcaro, and think about growing a mullet this summer.

Last time I browned the bacon and then crumbled it up. Not this time. Not this pig. Sometimes you just want to get there by means of a different route. So I slice the bacon into little bits on a cutting board and send it into a sauce pan. Medium heat brings the room into a state of solemn yet joyous baconation. I'll bless the pigs down in Africa if there are any. Behold how the bacon changes slowly.

To the sink to wash enough lettuce for four salads. This is excellent lettuce raised by a former student who is paying off his inordinate college debts one dime per year by doing something good and useful: growing food. He's Andy, the "One Acre" farmer, keeping honest and decent people in honest and decent vegetables.

Wash, spin, and distribute the lettuce into four bowls. Would that the Goddess Excellently Bright were here. But, alas, she's at work, keeping cornfed Americans alive and me in poker money. Did I say that aloud or just think it? No matter. She's not here, the downside of which is that there's no one to bump into in the kitchen. Thus deprived, I pull out a can of "Modus Hoperandi," an IPA that will change your life. Plus it's local (if you live in Durango, Colorado). What a great find. It's no shimmering goddess in a white cotton summer dress, but it will do in a pinch.

I move the bits of pig around and tell them it's gonna take a lot to drag me away from them. I turn the heat down a bit and crack four eggs into a cup. Some carbonarying folk will tell you to use only the yolks. I'm one of them. I whisk the yolks and lay them by.

I hear the thud of a basketball. The older boy's out shooting around. I step outside and give him a move to work on. It's a great one if you've got the feet to pull it off: left side, dribbling right-handed toward the top of the key, then a sudden change of direction with a behind the back dribble. Don't turn your back to the basket, I tell him. Sell it. Just look your defender in the eye, take him to his left, and then with one deft move off your right foot leave him standing there with nothing to do but pull his jockstrap back up around his pathetic giblets.

Wait! Parsley! Out back to the parsley. Ah, fresh herbs. Cut a few sprigs and bring them in for chopping. Chop them and lay them by.

After Gorgy Porgy I sing out, in advance of the next track, about how some people live their dreams. Damn! I miss by about a half-pitch. Who gave me these imperfect ears anyway?

Stir the bacon bits. They're ready. Scoop them with a slotted spatula onto some paper towel, where they'll remain until they're needed.

Now comes decision time. This is one of those famous Yogi-Berra-style forks in the road that, when you come to it, you have to take. You could (A) dab the bacon grease out of the pan and boil your pasta in said pan, thereby infusing your pasta with the great taste of bacon, or you could (B) dab the bacon grease, add your cream to the pan, and infuse *that* with the great taste of bacon. Either option is good; neither imperils your manhood. And I'm not too systematic. It's just that I'm an addict for this fatty lovely bacon grease.

I choose B because I like the look of the white cream against the brown grease. So I start boiling water for the pasta in another pan and pour the heavy whipping cream—for my servants, whose bikes are in working order, have returned from the store with it—into the residual bacon grease. Then I add a dab of butter, dub it "Pamela," and tell it not to stop this heart of mine. The water comes to a boil even as the cream thickens. I take the cream off the heat and add the pasta. Seven or eight minutes until straining time. If it's true that you are what you eat, then as soon as forever is through, I'll be bacon too.

At length the timer sounds and I strain the pasta. After about forty seconds I add the eggs and stir. True enough, as Toto says, love isn't always on time, but when it comes to carbonara your eggs had better be, as I said in the previous chapter. Add the bacon and stir. Add the parsley and stir. By now the cream has cooled a little, so add it and stir. I don't have scrambled eggs. Perfect.

You know I love you, ninety-nine, which is my average total cholesterol—if you've divided it by four.

The table is set, the milk poured. Call the children. Call them again. Call them again. Call them again. Call them again. Call them again. Call them again. Call them again. Call them again. Call them again. Call them again. Call them again. Call them again. Call them again. Call them again. Call them again. Call them again.

At long last we're assembled. My argumentative youngest, the junior lawyer in this firm, wants to pronounce the blessing. The tell-tale oldest takes this opportunity to ask about that time he, the youngest, was sent to the principal's office. It turns out (I learn after considerable prodding) that he said to his teacher, and I quote, "You are *not* the boss of me!"

I should be alarmed and outraged but I'm laughing my fool head off. And then the boy inhales a plate of carbonara before I'm done serving everyone. He'll polish off three plates before the supper's done. And I know exactly why. There's nothing like using pasta as a delivery system for bacon and eggs. Wanting every part of it is not a crime.

As for me, I know to do what's right—sure as Kilimanjaro, like Olympus, rises above the Serengeti. So on my own pile of savory arterial concrete mix I sprinkle a few capers. Now would be the time to call out to Pamela one last time: don't stop this heart of mine. It is true, as Jim Harrison has said, that "the idea is to eat well and not die from it—for the simple reason that that would be the end of your eating." But he also said, "One of the main causes of death is fretting about your diet." Some live their dreams. Some close their eyes.

From all of which I conclude: eat carbonara. Tight jeans and mullet optional.

18

Carpe Bacon

My elder boy—what a pick-six in the Parks & Rec game last night! what wheels he has!—my elder boy tells me he wants a haircut, which is an excuse for some quality father-son time in a men-only zone. So Wheels and I walk to the local barber shop for tonsorial improvement and a little male banter. ("You want a shave too, young feller, or do the girls *like* you that way?")

But then I leave him in the queue there briefly and duck across the street to the hardware. Today, on the back deck, I'll be re-wiring the Neighborhood-Famous Home-Designed Patent-Pending Daylight-"Saving"-Time Grilling-Light-With-Deck-Rail-Attachment, commonly known by its abbreviation: NFHDPPDSTGLWDRA. The time-change that's a few months off but coming soon enough defies the faultiest logic, and it makes late autumnal grilling even at five o'clock damn-near impossible, but I'll roll with it. I'm not going to take on Daylight Losing Time, because already things are going my way. (Witness the boy in the barber's chair, the banter with the hardware guys and the feisty girl at the checkout, who can give it right back. Every time I hand over money she sharpens her ferric wit on the iron of mine, and good for her! So we practice the arts of placed habitation.)

Back to the barber shop with my Romex to see Wheels aloft in the chair. How he loves the hum of the clippers on his head! How his grin betrays him! Yes, what a boy. The heart cracks, does it not?

Home to the electrical project and all the others I can dream up for myself on this glorious day. And to think that some men don't like yard work or home-improvement projects! They're computer junkies, TV addicts, daylight readers, as if books weren't made for the morning darkness and coffee or the fireside darkness and candlelight and the soft company of scotch whiskey, neat, in a thick tumbler.

Home, too, let us not forget, to the hope of splendid back pockets. The briefest glimpse of them will suffice (until I get the briefest glimpse of them). Do my eyes deceive me? They do not! A brief flash of denim across the deadlight window in front. And was that not the pink t-shirt, the one with the v-neck? It was!

I piggy-back on an existing outdoor receptacle and run my wire under the deck to a hole pre-drilled near a rail post. I run the wire up the hole and through conduit and then wire in my new receptacle newly screwed to the deck post.

Hit the breaker. Test it for power. Good. Mount my NFHDPPDST-GLWDRA in its new position. Mission accomplished.

To the garage. And what's this? IPA in the keg? This *is* my day. Time for a little break in the action. The pint glass fills. All indicators point to evidence not even instant replay can overturn: it's time for my Bacon Bomb, a.k.a. Hog-in-a-Pig Pig-Out, the Pork à la Bacon Baconplatter, the How Now Ground Sow Event, the Sine-Porcine Tangent, the Feast of St. Hoggustine, The Swining, The Pig Bang.

I'm sorry, *what*? a reader may ask.

You've heard of pig-in-a-blanket? This is pig-in-a-pig-blanket. This is the pig dish for my best pigskin soul.

The missus flashes before me, back pockets and pink t-shirt shouting instructions at me like a game-show audience. Above the noise I hear her ask, "What shall we do for dinner?" and I see by the way she's looking at me, a look caused by the way I'm looking at *her*, that she's expecting an answer not at all to the purpose. I can see that she's preparing to roll her eyes—to walk away if necessary, to gather up every syllable of body language in the service of saying, "For the love of God! It's the middle of the day!"

But all my eros is now turned pigward. All I can do is make blubbering comments about pork and bacon. The blubbering she's used to. But now it's different. And she's relieved, for she knows that every now and again my incoherence isn't pocket-induced. It isn't about Binx Bolling and the sword in the heart, the stitch in the side. She can tell that the pigskin stars are in a row. Jupiter is aligned with Mars, and she's a free woman. I might pat those pockets. I might even take a loving swipe at them. But she knows I'm going to leave her alone. This is the dawning of the age of Porcinius. Pork will guide planets, and lard will fill the stars, but none of it concerns her. I'm already out starting the charcoal grill, oblivious of all else, and she's inside, saved by dead pig.

Is that my lovely first born yonder in the sunlight? It is. I summon her.

"Quick. I simply must hear that poem about Cunningham." Once, during poetry month, she needed a poem to memorize, so I wrote one. Heck with Yeats and Ferlingetti.

She smiles—nay, beams—and commences:

> I met a man in Birmingham
> Who said his name was Cunningham.
> His porcine skin and double chin
> Suggested he was far from thin.
> His snout-like nose and dirty clothes
> Were all I needed to suppose
> That bacon fat and gristle spat
> Were favorites of a man like that.
> Did he eat those deep fried pig's feet?
> Was country ham his favorite treat?
> Did he say he loved to play
> In mud and filth and dirt all day?
> No, not this man from Birmingham
> Who said his name was Cunningham.
> "I'm way too proud, too proud, too proud!"
> But, as he left, he oinked out loud.

What a girl! What a dam she has—and what a sire!

Onto the cutting board—wait! Refill the pint glass at the garage keg—onto the cutting board go a large onion, a whole garlic bulb, mushrooms, and one green thing of my choice. A green pepper will do but a hotter pepper will do better. I chop them. Exuberantly I chop them, then I grate some sharp cheddar cheese. I make sure I have near me (1) my favorite pork rub and (2) my favorite barbecue sauce.

Onto another surface I dump no less than two pounds of ground pork—three if I've got more to feed than the Bar Jester Five—and I form the ground pork into a rectangular shingle about a half-inch thick. The thickness helps determine the dimensions. I don't get my boxers in a wad over the dimensions.

Onto a third surface I make a bacon weave. This requires a pound and a half, maybe two pounds, of bacon. I lay about eight strips out in one direction, then fold every other one in half and lay a cross-strip right at the fold. I re-straighten the folded strips and then fold the others, also in the every-other-one pattern, and lay a second cross strip. I repeat this pattern until I've reached the top. Then I start again from the middle until I've formed the same pattern all the way to the bottom.

What I have now is a beautiful and elaborate piece of lattice-work, such as you see beneath decking or porches—front porches, even. It's a bacon weave or, as the guys I stole this idea from call it, "bacon bark." I will use it momentarily.

Back to the ground pork. I sprinkle my rub and pour my barbecue sauce over it. I spread across it my onion, then my garlic, then my mushroom, then my pepper. After all that is done, I top it off with my shredded sharp cheddar.

Now the difficult part: I have to roll this fat concoction into a pork log.

Once I've done that, I set the pork log on the bacon lattice, because now I'm going to wrap the lattice around the log.

I sprinkle the finished sculpture with my rub. Then I rub the rub in. Then I drizzle my barbecue sauce over it. Verily, I paint it with barbecue sauce.

When my coals are ready, I push them to one side of the grill and place the Pig Bang on the other side of the grill. I want indirect heat. I make sure my coals are good and white and then add a few extra pieces of charcoal plus some wood for smoking. I cover the grill, leaving the top and bottom vents open. Fire, you know, likes oxygen.

If my heat reaches 300 degrees or more, I don't allot any more than 1 ½ hours for grilling this Pignificant Porksterpiece (though I might need more time on a very cold winter's day). I'll open the grill lid and turn the dead swine half-way through the grilling, usually stirring the coals and adding more wood at that time as well, even though doing so lowers the ambient temperature for a while.

When the grilling is done, this thing that was so hard to make hang together when I was rolling it, and then rolling it again, holds together beautifully. The bacon works like packaging twine and proves once again that there's nothing bacon can't do.

I put this beautiful hogroll on a platter and cut it as I would a loaf of bread: in big thick slices. I serve it with sweet corn or whatever suits my fancy.

And if this is good in the summer, imagine how well it will feed my pigskin soul and body in the fall when at long last I'll need the

NFHDPPDSTGLWDRA that I had the good sense to install well in advance of football Saturdays, when the painted tribes of November swirl in the breath of Autumn's being. Not yet but soon I'll intone: O wild west wind,

> Scatter, as from an unextinguish'd hearth
> Ashes and sparks, my words among mankind!
> Be through my lips to unawaken'd earth
> The trumpet of a prophecy! O Wind,
> If Ohio State and Minnesota lose, can the University of
>   Michigan be far behind?

19

Baconation on a Theme

Misery, misery, sonofabitch of all miseries! So said Binx Bolling on his way to Chicago, the city with no genie soul. And who could blame old Binx, what with the scolding he had waiting for him from Aunt Emily upon his return?

But what would Binx say had he the motive and the cue for passion that I have—I, who have my heart set on another Bacon Bomb but can find no ground pork in the house?

No worries. I'll try a variation on that theme. This time I'll use ground beef rather than ground pork. I'll use a shallot rather than an onion. I'll forgo the green pepper and mushroom. I'll double the garlic, and I'll use sharp cheddar and mozzarella instead of cheddar only.

First, to the hi-fi I go to put on a little Nora Jones, who can't help herself: she's got to see me again. Who can blame her? No, wait. How about, for this occasion, some Vaughan Williams and a few of *his* variations? *Dives and Lazarus* it is. Then to the fridge. I spy an Ethos IPA from my good friends at the Tallgrass brewing company at 5960 Dry Hop Circle in Manhattan, Kansas (tel. 785-537-1131), but I ain't in the mood. Inexplicable but true. How about an inch of grapefruit juice and a can of Coke on top of it? Yes. How about it. Best damned non-alcoholic drink in the world and just what the soul longs for when the flesh craves dead pig wrapped around dead cow.

Next I make the weave as described in the previous chapter and then pound out a slab of ground beef, this time right on top of the lattice work so I can roll everything all at once. What I'll have before the rolling is this: a weave of bacon covered by a slab of ground beef covered with chopped shallots and garlic covered with a sharp cheddar-mozzarella mix covered with blackened rub sprinkled with salt and pepper and doused with barbecue sauce. Then I'll roll it all into a log—of sorts.

When that is done, I'll put it on the grill: indirect heat—approximately 300 degrees—complete with hickory chips. An hour to ninety minutes will do.

Binx, old pal, you're not the only one who's on to something.

20

The Blouse, the Pig, and the Fox

In the slanting sun a boy and his dog wrestle for a toy. Is there any sound more pleasant to the ear—I mean not counting Mozart or the Ozark Mountain Daredevils or a farm animal munching at the grain trough—than the unselfconscious laughter of a child at play?

There isn't. But, having heard it, and having sat here in my Adirondack chair and watched and listened for a good half hour, I am ready for the sound of a Michigan IPA filling a glass. I'm ready for the sound of a pork tenderloin responding to the heat of a charcoal grill.

My coals are ready but I am not, so to the garage fridge I go with a pint glass in hand. Into it I pour a freshly cracked Huma Lupa Licious IPA from the Michigan-only / Michigan-forever / power-of-smallness Short's Brewing Company north of here. (The "Michigan only" part didn't last, sort of like the C in YMCA. Short's now sells out of state.) Beautifully it fills the glass with its coppery ambrosial goodness, and once again I think to myself that north is the only direction on the compass worth attending to, that the north country is what the inner man naturally longs for, northernness his native disposition.

Is it possible that I can sneak this one by the Counter of Cocktails and that when I crack my second she'll look at me disapprovingly and say, "That's *one*," which will magically turn the third into the second? Distaffal disapproval, I've learned, is worse than the general good of flying high. Plus, when she walks by me in that bewitching white summer blouse of hers, uncorks a bottle of cheap chardonnay at serving time, and then pours herself a mere taste (who ever heard of having a mere taste?), I'll shake off the enchantment of her sartorial ensemble and allow myself a small glass of her wine, probably without remonstrance, and later enjoy a peaceful slumber.

I've given up trying to understand what does and what doesn't count for acceptable bibulous behavior. It's all unacceptable. But I haven't given up trying to reclaim our strawberries. Weeding them is not what I would call gratifying work. The labor/reward ratio is way out of whack, but what I've been doing is weeding them nonetheless—plus weeding the brussel sprouts, plus the potatoes, plus the onions, plus the peppers, which, for reasons I can't account for, currently bear nothing—except for my jalapeño plant, which is the Speedy Gonzalez of all my peppers, except I doubt it knows everybody's seester.

And now, wearied by weeding and made glad by the sound of a boy's unselfconscious laughter, I'm ready to stretch out upon the hot coals a long pork tenderloin, which this same Counter of mine, this Goddess in a fetching summer blouse, has marinated in a concoction that includes (among other ingredients) a chopped jalapeño recently harvested from my now-weeded garden, soy sauce, ginger, garlic, and coffee grounds. There's other magic involved, but I haven't attempted to plumb its depths. I've been too busy working on my joke about the tenderloin, sure to elicit the hoped-for eye-rolling. Nothing says "I love you, baby!" like a woman rolling her eyes and walking away from a man with a predictable joke on his lips.

Looking for something I know not what, I open a wrong cupboard and see my shot glasses. They remind me that when I'm grilling dead pig, no matter the cut, I inexplicably desire the taste of bourbon. I snatch a shot glass from the cupboard and fill it almost to the rim with a little Buffalo Trace, knock it back, and place the shot glass in the sink.

Later, when the Counter sees it, she'll ask me why it's out. I'll look her in the eyes and tell her the truth: "It leapt into my hand without any warning. I just barely kept it from crashing to the floor."

Whereupon . . . wait for it . . . *they'll roll!*

I take from the fridge a platter on which a pork tenderloin soaks in a locking bag all a-slosh with my best gal's marinade. To the grill we go, my pig and I—that's *some* pig—and with a pair of long wooden-handled tongs I place the meat over the coals. This is a grill, not a griddle, so the searing won't be as impressive, but I'll give to each of the four sides of this loin a few initial minutes—to crisp the beast all around. Then, at longer uniform intervals, I'll grill it until it at its thickest part it registers a solid 145 on my meat thermometer, maybe a little less, at which time it will be ready for the knife.

We've got summer sweet corn. My Eye-Roller is in charge of it. O butter! O salt! O sweet corn! O Eye-Roller! And I've dug a few of my blue potatoes, which I've sliced into disks, adorned with olive oil, salt, and pepper, and put in the oven. Toward the end I'll shower them with rosemary fresh from the herb garden.

Our kale forest has provided us with many-a salad this summer, but the tomatoes have convinced us to go swarthy: chopped tomatoes, chopped cukes, chopped red onion, oregano from the herb garden, feta cheese, pressed garlic (also from the garden), salt, black pepper, and olive oil. (The Counter will want balsamic vinegar on hers, but I prefer this as I prefer most of life: without astringency.)

When at last we sit down to this summer repast, when the urchins have been gathered from the four corners of Dumb-Ass Acres, the dog makes a show of being put out: why should all of us be allowed a seat on the screened-in porch and he be restricted to the out-of-doors? When the boys let him in (they're under strict orders not to feed him from the table), I relate the story of his impressive bravery early this morning:

He and I were headed toward the woods. I made a turn at the intersection of two paths and saw, astride the second one, a gray fox standing as still as if he'd been taxidermied there. I too stood still, and then at length the dog saw old Reynard. He also stopped to stare, and now we had a tableau. Out of the corner of my eye I could see the dog look up at me. (I can't lead a fast break any more, but I can still see sideways.) He went into his wonted Chief Brody mode: "How do we handle this?" he seemed to be saying. He looked again at the fox and then up at me. "How do we handle this?" he repeated.

The children are laughing unselfconsciously. They love stories about their dog. They're like a first-time mother demanding of the babysitter detailed accounts of what cute things her baby did while she was away buying work-out clothes that don't fit her. And the kids get my *Jaws* references.

I remained motionless. After about thirty seconds the dog looked up at me as if to opine that we would need a bigger boat. I include this detail in my telling, and the children laugh even louder.

And then, brave puppy that he is, he released a timid and unimpressive—an almost feline—muted "woof," which carried him backwards a step behind the armature of my legs, whereupon the fox leapt twice and was gone.

We walked to where we'd seen him last. The dog was interested but not much. He sniffed the ground but stayed close to me. He made no great show of courage, not even in the fox's absence, not even as if to say "and *stay* out!" Not even as if to announce to an unarmed and almost empty concentration camp, "Zee Rohssian army eez here to leeberate you!"

My clan laughs and rejoices to hear this tale, embellished as only a man with two Huma Lupa Licious IPAs in him (plus one shot of Kentucky's finest export) can embellish it. Count them if you will, I think to myself. Second to the unselfconscious laughter of a boy at play with his dog is a man at his table, a tale on his lips, and about him a laughing brood and their disapproving dam—whose million-dollar smile belies her disapproval.

O, thou Psalmist, thou sweet singer of Israel! Thou saidst true: Zeal for thy blouse shall consume me!

21

She Don't Lie, She Don't Lie, She Don't Lie . . . Propane!

This radio station—"Classic Hits All the Time"—claims to have been fulfilling its mission in these parts for over thirty years, but I have my doubts. I'm pretty sure some of the hits lack thirty winters on their heads and that many others are not hits at all but swings and misses. Whiffs. Case in point: "Hot Blooded." Don't check it and see.

Nevertheless, I'm on a big ol' jet air-a-liner. I'm takin' it to the limit. I'm smokin' in the boys' room.

Actually, I'm on a mission. In the bed of the Babe Magnet there's a propane tank with an illegal spring-loaded quick-couple brass fitting on it. It's a little tank that holds about seven pounds of propane designed to fuel the gas starter on my charcoal grill. I'm a charcoal and hardwood man. I'm on the side of the angels. The phrase "now we're cooking with gas" does not impress me unless I'm indoors, where gas is an improvement over electricity. In fact, the Weber charcoal tower I use for back-up is really my preferred means of setting the charcoal on fire: it's faster and fussier, and I prefer fussier.

But I also like getting away with using a perfectly good tank that happens now to be illegal because some Regulator doesn't like its regulator. And I like convincing my local propane guy to keep refilling it even though he isn't supposed to. What good is a law if there's no one willing to break it?

Now there's a pretty phrase: my local propane guy "isn't supposed to." But "supposed" by whom? Where's the agency in this wretched passive construction? I smell legislators and lawyers, who have pretty much ruined our lives. They've decided that the best posture for a creature made to walk upright and contemplate the heavens is that of a man looking over his shoulder, scared. They've decided that, because lawyers start all conversations with "what are the risks?" instead of "what are the benefits?" (as any sane person would do), the rest of us should also therefore inhabit a suspicious and litigious world—a world of retribution, ill-will, and greed.

The more I think about it, old Willy was right: kill all the lawyers. So said Nikon Don—*almost*. I've made a couple of slight changes to avoid action from any litigious prick who might 'scape whipping and come after my royalties.

Nikon Don! The most famous English major not counting the Culinary Plagiarist and the Bard of Port Royal!

I pass an ugly cage with Blue Rhino propane tanks poised for exchange—big clunky things for heathen gas grillers. I see a man open the cage to make a swap.

Carry on, wayward son. There'll be war when you are done.

To the local butcher I go for some local butterfly chops. I love my butcher, not because he's especially good at carving up those intricate delivery systems known as pigs, cows, chickens, and fish, though he is. I love him because he's fat.

You want your butcher to be fat. Your priest you want a bit less fleshy—gaunt, in fact, if possible, like your politician, because no one can trust the politics of a fat man. But your butcher, whose politics you needn't give a damn about, you want to be fat. Four, five, six chins are good, as is a distinct waddle in his gate and some wheezing in his chest. Fat-bottom butchers make the Betty Crockin' world go round.

"What'll it be today?" he asks breathlessly, like someone who's just set a PR in the 800, his several chins jiggling to the sound of his carnivorous baritone.

"You know what, Tad?" I say, thinking that "Tad" is the perfect name for a fat butcher. "I think I'll take five of those butterfly chops—the thicker ones, not these skinny ones cut for lawyers and league bowlers."

"You got dark beer at home?" Tad asks.

I also like it that my fat butcher isn't curious about my antipathy to lawyers and league bowlers. In this respect he resembles the rest of the world.

"Not if I can help it. I try to keep the bottles empty."

"Put 'em in dark beer and brown sugar. Chop up a little ginger. Let 'em sit overnight."

"Sounds good," I say, and it is: I've tried it. "But these are for tonight. I've got a rub that drives the missus wild."

In my periphery I see another customer, a man with much shorter hair than mine. His hair has "product" in it, which I have a fierce but perfectly reasonable prejudice against—a prejudice, I should add, validated by no less an authority than Bill Bryson. If you doubt me, read *The Road to Little Dribbling*. ("Now I have to say right here," writes Bryson, "that I did not like this young man already because he had a vaguely insolent air. Also, he had a lot of gel in his hair. My family tell me that you can't dislike people just because they have gel in their hair, but I think it is as good a reason as any.")

"Once the rub soaks in," I continue, "I bathe the dead pig in soy or teriyaki. This does the trick"—and here I look intently at my fat friend—"I *assure* you."

Gel-boy next to me looks my way and smiles knowingly. Get him out on the floor, and odds are he'll shuffle his feet away.

"You're going to grill them, I hope," says fatso.

"Over charcoal and apple wood, by God! Do I look like a gas-grilling gel-haired sissy lawyer?"

"Excellent!" says Tad, even as the brown-flip-flop-shod Night Owl beside me straightens.

"*I* have a gas grill," he says.

Seems I've stepped into it once again—on purpose, clearly.

"But you're no lawyer, I hope."

"In fact I am," he says. And, as I've said, there's another problem: he's got gel in his hair.

"I see," I say and smile. "You know, there are people out there who can help you." I reach out my hand. He takes it, and we shake. "I'm—" and here I give him the name of a colleague I don't like.

Tad knows a lie when he hears one and backs away. His assistant, Willem, steps up.

"What do *you* do?" asks the crisp-haired litigious ex-fratboy in brown flip-flops, cargo shorts, and a designer crew-neck shirt, implying by his question that whatever I do isn't as glamorous or lucrative as drawing up contracts all day long. A hundred bucks says he hasn't read a book in ten years and has an ugly golf swing. Obviously he hasn't read *Barbecue*, by the incomparable John Shelton Reed, who reminds us not to confuse the sacred and propane.

"What do I do?" I smile and say, "I grill over charcoal. I also teach feminist theory."

It occurs to me that the colleague whose name I have assumed is making me look bad.

"And what is feminist theory?" asks gel-boy.

"Well, it's not really a theory. It's just a way of talking. Like Pig Latin. You learn how it works and then start talking and never shut up."

I realize now that I'm giving my colleague way too much improv credit and think about backing off. But at the butcher's counter the stable world of laws and ordinances is suddenly of no use to this man. I smell lawyer blood, so I hold my smile and stare him down.

"I'm in sociology. It's more complex than what everyone else does, even lawyers. We 'interrogate' the 'socially constructed' and identify 'the Other.' Capital O Other. We object to Otherizing. We identify social problems that don't exist—sort of like those literary theorists who can find a phallus behind every bush."

If I am not mistaken, the lawyer-brain of this propaner of meats, this fratboy voted least likely to shoot par, is starting to short-circuit—as well it should at this socio-babble. It helps that I'm a good four inches taller than he. I tell myself not to look back. It's been *way* too long since I felt this way.

Out to the Dodge and classic hits with my chops, then home to the grill. I snap the starter tank in place, light the charcoal, and head in to soak some apple wood shaved from one of my apple trees. But first I click on the hi-fi and catch the end of some Bachman-Turner Overdrive.

Onto the chops goes the rub. The meat will draw it in while I'm taking care of business, which means pouring a couple of fingers—bulbous fingers, Meyer-Wolfsheim fingers—of bourbon.

Whereupon (wouldn't you know it?) My Lady Scrutiny, right on cue, and as oblivious as a spatula that Overdrive has now given way to Styx, enters the kitchen.

"Harrumpf!"

"I'm sailing away!" I croon in a tenor that ain't what it used to be—if it ever was anything to begin with.

"That's what I'm afraid of." The eyes roll. They imply that bourbon is like an accelerant to a house fire.

Now would have been a good time for a different alignment of the stars. For example, why couldn't I have decided to honor The King with an Old Latrobe just as serendipity was providing me with a little Jagger: "I know," I might have wailed, "it's only Rolling Rock but I like it."

But I've been caught bourbon-handed—and "free" to face the wife that's ahead of me.

"Nonsense!" I apparently say aloud, meaning only to think it—this after assuming, completely without justification, that she did in fact compare bourbon to an accelerant at a house fire, which she didn't.

"Nonsense?"

Which settles the matter. It appears I did in fact say, out loud and unprovoked, "nonsense."

"That is, '*on the fence*,'" I say. "I'm *on the fence* about whether to serve a salad or grilled asparagus."

The eyes roll. "Asparagus. And make it good—if you mean to sleep in clean sheets."

Kentucky's finest export, I want to say, doesn't accelerate anything. It brings out the true personality that sobriety merely restrains—like Major Tom set free to merge with the cosmos.

Time for Ground Control to get the asparagus going.

Cut the tips, then halve the stalks. Dump the fat bottoms into the compost bucket. But the rest of this stuff came fresh out of the ground earlier today. It's as fresh as . . .

Lordy, where's my freshened tumbler?

Freshened? I'm ahead of myself! Where's the Counter when I need her to see me ahead of myself!

I instruct the oldest of my lazy offspring to chop some garlic. She takes this as a sign to switch off the radio and put on a CD. It had better be "classic," in keeping with the promises of the radio station.

Ah! Good girl. She's making for the trades on the inside. What a sire she must have, and her dam incomparable! The bread is up to her. My love is an anchor chained to her, chained by a silver tie.

Onto the coals goes the soaked apple wood; then onto the grill go the chops. I drizzle the residual soy sauce as I turn the dead pig lovingly and quickly. Before it's done it goes off direct heat, and on goes the asparagus—first the thicker pieces then the thinner ones. They're drenched in olive oil, and the coals come alive. I turn the stalks, sprinkle them with salt and pepper, then brush them with maple syrup.

Off the grill with all of it and onto a covered platter. My daughter has timed the bread perfectly. We call the others to dinner.

There will be good eating tonight. But, more importantly:

I've insulted all propane grillers. I've masqueraded as someone I dislike and reduced a certain reductive academic *ism* to its essential characteristic. I've expressed my preference for gaunt priests and fat butchers. I've heard a mix of classic hits and classic shits. I've seen eyes roll and cocktails counted (one by my count, but I'm not the official score keeper). I've screwed with a local lawyer who, much to his discredit, wears brown flip-flops and designer crew-neck shirts, owns a gas grill, and puts *gel* in his hair. I've broken a propane law and convinced my LP guy to break another.

Not bad for a Tuesday in June, given that the peripatetic NBA still pollutes our world with its pretense to sport and, what is worse, to place (excepting the erudite Bill Bradley, who, in *Life on the Run*, had the good sense to say that he misses "that sense of sharing that comes from people living together in one place, over time. I miss permanence." You tell 'em, Senator!)

Me, I'm here with my grill, my chops, my, asparagus, my family, and the sunshine that makes me happy when it's on my shoulders but smarts like longing itself when it's in my eyes. Ah, John Denver. One thinks of that grim NBA headline back when you came to grief: Denver Nuggets Over Golden State. Not the ending, painless, blameless, and without suffering, that we pray for. But you were good enough to ask country roads to take you home. Find me a sociologist with that much sense.

And now, Lord, take me downtown. I'm just lookin' for some toothpicks.

22

Indirect Heat: 1; Miami Heat: 0; Or, Ode to the Porcine Dead

Decoration Day was over and done with, and it was time for Game 1 of the NBA finals. The year was 2014, and I, a Pistons fan by birth, was glad enough that the Bulls were out. But that, unfortunately, was thanks to Miami and the mercenaries who just happened for the moment to be wearing Heat jerseys. These placeless opportunists were the hateful New York Yankees of the NBA, and like every other God-fearing person in my kitchen I couldn't stand the Heat. (Okay: all professional athletes are itinerant vandals, but it seemed that the Heat had really roided things up.) I hadn't watched a minute of the NBA all year and I wasn't about to start. Watching pro basketball on television is like staring up a pig's ass, as the trustworthy Jim Harrison once said of televised baseball and football.

But oh how I loved the days of the Big O, Clyde Frazier, Earl the Pearl Monroe, Jerry West, Wes Unseld, Bob Lanier, Artis Gilmore, and Dave Bing, all of them soon to yield their names to the elements. And how I abominate the game today, all tarted up and tattooed to the deltoids and hyped beyond its merits, like an Amway convention. What a cartoon of former glory days before the gladiators had outgrown the playing surface, when Kareem put his left elbow into Wilt's sternum and knocked down yet another baseline sky-hook on the man who could make it with a stadium full of women but who couldn't make a free-throw, or when Pistol Pete left off communicating with UFOs to make another pass that Magic Johnson, with slightly less paranoia, would later re-invent, and Jason Williams re-invent again.

"Dirk Nowitzky!" I remember rhapsodizing. "Our nation turns its lonely eyes to you, you big Kraut with a Polack name, you loping gym rat! Give 'em hell! Give 'em the Dave-Cowens flannel-shirted proletarian treatment! Give 'em a dose of George Ice-Man Gervin. Do what you have to do to bring down the Most Objectionable Team Money Can Buy."

Much later, when a certain LeMember of that repellent Miami team became a hometown hero by actually going home to Cleveland (which I applauded) but then later abandoned his home for Showtime (which no true localist could possibly applaud), I got to thinking about that whole 2013–14 season. And then I got curious about other headline events from that era—the death of Nelson Mandela in December, and before that the bombing at the Boston Marathon, and then such embarrassing episodes as Edward Snowden's disclosures, the Broncos' performance in the Super Bowl, and the election of Pope Francis—all of which I had to look up: vague memories, dim as the 6-volt headlights on a 1950 VW with a split rear window, or a '57 with an oval window, or a '59 with an interior wind-chill factor that kicks in at speeds of 25 mph or faster. (I had a '59 in college. Trust me. The heating system was a sleeping bag.)

But on the evening of Game 1 of the 2014 NBA finals I do distinctly remember one thing: the pork tenderloin. I distinctly remember thinking that the only good heat is the kind you rub on your tenderloin.

You can buy it any number of ways, including the right way: from your local guy at the Saturday market. It's unlikely he's seasoned it in the manner of Hormel (the name smacks of hor*mone*, or is it portmanteau for "horrible smell"?), but perhaps you'll find a reliable seller who can answer to your taste as well as to your conscience.

At any rate, heat it up with various fiery spices and lots of peppercorn. It will want you to grill it. You couldn't say for sure what round Chris Bosh was drafted in, or whether he actually is part Velociraptor, but you can tell the tenderloin wants you to grill it.

Sleepy Pie will be exhausted from coming home after midnight, four straight shifts in a row on the cardiac unit, personally enriched on poorly-fed mid-western cardiac patients but impoverished of sleep. Tell her to rest her pretty little head a while—an hour, say. Put the urchins on their bikes and send them to the public library. They'll choose volumes of classic literature. Meantime, you'll whip up the salad. All the lettuces in the garden are in now, and the spinach and the arugula, and there are even a few strawberries to slice into the toss, and you can have the balsamic vinegar / olive oil / Dijon mustard / strawberry freezer-jam vinaigrette that stops conversation if the salt and sugar are properly apportioned.

Your famous ginger / soy-sauce / chopped garlic cold bowtie antipasto left-over from yesterday will lighten the evening's tasks. Job himself would curse God and die for it, and so might you, if only you had as much as Job to lose.

Quarter some potatoes Greek-style (length-wise) and adorned them with oregano, salt, olive oil, and lemon. Imagine yourself with shoulder, neck, and back hair, but resist the urge to take a hit of ouzo.

Let your heart crack a little with love's own pang as you watch your urchins fly off to the library, helmeted according to nanny-state requirements. Soon they'll be home with *Jane Eyre*, *Old Yeller*, and *Danny and the Dinosaur*.

Mise en place undisturbed! Well, then, disturb it. But first, light the grill. Out into the liquid air that's hotter than a five-peckered billy-goat. Would that ambitious November were upon you with leaves flying and plunging. Touch the match to the fuel and retreat to the cool planks of the kitchen floor. Wash and dry a romaine heart and lots of peppery arugula.

And if your sight does not deceive you, there is a Great River Pale Ale emptying itself into a pint glass *right before your very eyes*. Chicago should be serenading you there in your kitchen!

Now that the tenderloin has been rubbed with last year's dried hot pepper and chili powder mix and sprinkled with cracked black pepper, propose a toast to the pig, the most amazing meat-producer God ever made on that literal sixth day, as recorded in the first of the two creation stories that are both literally true.

Listen to the Doobie Brothers sing about their friend Jesus. By the time they're jamming in a china grove about missus Perkins (you bet she's a game!) your charcoal grill will be ready. Let your thoughts turn to your learned children even now at the library—and to your Espoused Saint resting like God from her labors. And here you are, fully participating in the fullness of man: the incarnate condition.

Down time. Finish one more page of the nearest book review. A fine thing, the review—until like Keats you yourself are "pierced by the shaft which flies / In darkness," the arrow shot by some "noteless blot on a remembered name." Write a note to yourself: "never rush into print."

In come your urchins, flushed from peddling, and then off they go, each to his or her chair or couch and each with a classic. You take a closer look.

They're all engrossed in *Star Wars*. Ill-engaged, but quiet.

To the grill. Your little missus likes her pork tenderloin crisp on the outside; you like it slow cooked and smoked. A compromise is in order, because this is *marriage*, after all, that uneasy truce, as Michigan's Honorable Robert Traver called it. It is a supple synthesis, an holy estate, not to be entered upon lightly.

Shove all the coals to one side. Put the strip of dead pig directly over the coals. Turn it every two minutes or so until all sides are crisp. Move it off the coals. A little indirect heat for a while is what you're after. Add some apple wood and lower the lid on the grill. Sleepy Pie will get her crisp coating; you will get your slow-smoked tender dead pig—not as tender nor as smoky as it would be had you not made the concession to the crisp exterior, but good enough. Good enough especially for hymeneal peace. God is in his literal heaven, you in yours.

Down time. Brave the heat to inspect the twenty-four sunflowers started from seed in trays. The hellish afternoon heat offends you *and* them. Give them and the drooping tomato plants some water. In twenty minutes you'll both perk up. Inspect the mint, the basil, the parsley, the raspberries. Ah, salubrious seasons. Just what you banged on the literal door of heaven for.

And look you now! In the stifling air the sunflowers and tomatoes mimic your mood, thanks to the water you've watered them with and the pint of Great River you've watered yourself with. Time in this air is as motionless as a painted ship upon a painted ocean. Would that a few years back the repellent Miami Heat could have been vanquished with an ounce or two of water or a pint of ale. A gallon of contempt was needed (plus the Spurs, who by-God finished them off in five games!).

Turn the pork tenderloin. Meat thermometer says you're getting close. (Always suppose the meat thermometer is slow on the uptake, like most auditors of your jokes. Meat is always done a little sooner than you think.)

You didn't forget the secret home-made South Carolina BBQ mustard. There's a little left from that last batch. Pull it out and let it warm. Suffice it to say that this concoction of yellow mustard, balsamic vinegar, sugar, salt, butter, pepper, *and other ingredients to be named later* (see chapter 27) has the power to make Allen Tate the best pal H.L. Mencken ever had.

Tiptoe past the "readers" and up the stairs to the inner sanctum.

"Finishing the salad is up to you," you say after parting with a kiss to the cheek of the somnambulant goddess. And so Sleeping Beauty awakes, refreshed, ready to finish the salad as only she can. Look at her, blurry-eyed and still and still alluring.

Scurry down to the "reading" room. Tell the oldest to set the table. Tell her again. Tell her six more times before you get no more acknowledgment than a grunt. After several more repetitions and an ice age expect a plate to appear on the table: the day's first triumph.

Out to the grill to court a phantom tumbler of Robert Traver's Old Cordwood—a *phantom* tumbler—and to move things around on the grate. Re-imagine the back yard with a clay oven for pizza and bread and also with a smoking facility—two, rather: one for meats and one for cigars.

Like in the old hymn, come rejoicing, bringing in the pork. Sleepy Pie has found the half-glass of chilled chardonnay you left with a note: "is there anything else around here you need a man for?"

No. But it's worth a try.

And suddenly you are an unworthy man at board, your board adorned not with itinerants but with a lovely brood and a lovelier bride and food and drink aplenty. This is a day of decoration. There's a Haydn symphony on the hi-fi—an ode to the dead, blue and gray and porcine alike. You riot with your tongue and taste buds, sentinel of the table that counts us all.

23

Barbecued Ribs and "The Best That Ever Was!"

When the younger boy was about six and hadn't yet become by turns ornery and argumentative and therefore hadn't earned the many nicknames he would later go by, he saw me knocking down free-throws in the driveway one Saturday afternoon. "Dad," he said, "you're the best that ever was!"

He would see me building bird houses. "Dad, you're the best that ever was!" He would see me hanging awnings, cleaning gutters, diagnosing a noise under the hood, sweating copper, tying my tie, changing out the winter tires, telling blonde jokes on demand, reciting poetry at breakfast, making even his forearm ticklish: "Dad, you're the best that ever was!"

He was taught to say this by: The Best That Ever Was.

After making fifteen straight bank-shots from about fifteen feet I paused to see what his reaction would be. "What is it we say, buddy?"

"You're the best that ever was!"

"That's my boy!" I said. "You always *were* my favorite!"

He'd also taken an interest in cooking. He's got an ear unlike any of us—and we're all musicians of a sort—but he's got a nose and a palate unlike any of us too. Suddenly he wanted to know what was for supper.

"You're in luck," I said.

"In *luck*?" he asked. "What the heck does that mean?"

I winced and looked around. Whew! No mother in sight. "Heck" would not have gone down well with the distaff side, though I thought it was pretty damned funny at the time.

"You're gonna like it," I said. Because he was. The boy has always loved dead pig. He discovered bacon the way teenaged boys discover girls: in a mad frenzy of inexpressible confusion. Nor do the other cuts displease him (cuts of pig, not girls). And that night he was getting tenderloin ribs—brined, smoked, and chrismated in barbecue sauce.

Flashback to the day before, Friday. A school of fish filets swam on a sea of olive oil and lemon juice, each white flaky side absorbing a cayenne rub with various spices and a little black pepper showered on for good measure.

But The Best That Ever Was wasn't thinking only about Friday night. He was thinking about the next day, Saturday, mint juleps and sunshine and a Goddess, shimmering yet smoldering and apparelled in celestial light, moving in and out of his wonder and astonishment. (*I'm* with *her*, he would think to himself, utterly baffled, a classic case of a hot babe and a hurtin' dude, as Mike of blessed memory used to say.) And, of course there was the longing. Is that not right, Tom More? Always the longing.

Which probably meant taking a hit of Knob Creek or Woodford Reserve or maybe even Old Grand-Dad. They're local enough. They come from a neighboring state.

Flannery O'Connor was right. It's an arm of fire that reaches down the throat and into the gut. And Walker Percy was also right. The gears catch. Comes again the longing!

So although we were having fish that Friday night, on another platter I had put out nine bone-in pork ribs. Nearby stood a pot, and in it the water had cooled. "What water?" you may ask. That, of course, was the brine. Into six cups of boiling water The Best That Ever Was had dissolved a half-cup of salt and a half-cup of brown sugar, and, now that the water had cooled, he'd added peppercorns and thyme.

Into a zip-lock bag went the ribs, and then the flood waters of the brine engulfed them. He pressed out the air, sealed the bag, and placed the bag in a containment vessel—just in case. And then into the fridge it all went.

Refrigeration! he remembered thinking. It might kill us in the end, but it sure is convenient. Give that devil his due. Better yet, drink to it! He raised the tumbler, swirled it, tipped it to behold its color in the afternoon light (came again the longing!), and then sent another arm of fire not up but down its rightful chimney. Golden molecules went swimming in the gray matter, mingled, dissolved, became one with it. He thought: what man has joined together, let no god put asunder!

Cut back to Saturday and the basketball court. "What am I going to like?" the boy asked. "Is it carbonara?" Carbonara he fairly lusted after, even then. It's bacon and eggs, after all (and cream and parsley and pepper and parmesan and pasta). It was hard to imagine him at eighty years of age, constipated, bound and wound up like the inside of a balata golf ball, and yet preferring regular daily trepidation of the bowels to the taste and texture of carbonara.

"Not carbonara," I said. "But it *is* dead pig."

"Is it sausage? Pork chops?"

"How old are you?"

"I'm seven and a half! I'm almost eight years old!"

"You're sure you're not, say, forty-eight?"

"*No* I'm not forty-eight! *You're* forty-eight. I'm not as big as you. When I'm as big as you, I'll be forty-eight!"

"Well, buddy, you're gonna like it. Now stand here and see if you can make twenty shots. Right hand behind the ball, guide hand here on the side, just like I showed you."

"Can I start the grill?"

"You may. I'll call you. Now practice, or you'll never be the next best that ever was."

To the fridge. Ah, dead pig! With it to the countertop. Out of the brine and onto a platter. I dabbed them dry and sprinkled them with a little pork rub, this too full of heat. What was porcine now was orange, sort of like a Narcissist-in-Chief few could have bet would come along.

Zikes! The smoking chips, like my throat, were as dry as dust! (These chips came from my apple tree yonder. A branch here or there each fall, a little work with the hatchet, and there you have it: apple wood chips for smoking dead pig.)

Into a bucket of water went three hands-full of chips. I called my little Retained Flatterer, and together we went out to the grill to get the coals going. He seemed more interested in playing with fire than with a basketball.

The fire performed its ministry; so, too, the water. Back to the kitchen. But where was the lady of this manor? I went up the stairs to check the napping room. Ah, yes. There she was in the arms of my chief rival, Sleep. Friday was a late night for her, and no doubt "the staffing was terrible." I'd hear about a man my age who had a massive M.I. Not good news for how I wanted to do the asparagus.

Asparagus! I'd forgot!

To the kitchen again. I separated the tips from the thicker stalks. The really thick ends, purplish and tough, went into the compost. We'd have asparagus with our ribs.

The coals were ready. I pushed them to one side, strained the chips, put them on the coals, listened to their sibilant hiss, and then placed the ribs as far from direct heat as possible. I closed the lid, watched the smoke billow out the vents, and waited for the thermometer to stop rising. Anything above 250 would be too hot. The gauge rose to . . . wait for it . . . 250! The boy was right about me!

I had about an hour and a half, plenty of time to decide on the other dishes. Baked beans? Potatoes? It would make no difference. These ribs would steal the show. Bread smeared with butter and sprinkled with chopped garlic, crisped under the broiler, had never failed me before.

In the downtime I interrogated myself with such questions as, "How about a mint julep?" Yes, how about one. Uncle Will's recipe, of course: crushed ice, dried and stuffed into the tumbler, sugar, mint leaves, and the long golden ribbon of Kentucky bourbon. I half-expected to hear "My Old Kentucky Home." May God bless that home. And may it continue to share its finest export with the rest of the nation.

After thirty minutes I brushed the ribs with my homemade South Carolina mustard- and vinegar-based BBQ sauce (see chapter 27) and added a few more pieces of fuel to the coals. After thirty more minutes I turned the ribs and brushed their other sides. In another thirty it would be rib time.

Butter slid on its own melting in a large pan, into which went the fatter stalks of asparagus. The heat was low. A couple minutes later in went the tender tips. Time then for salt and freshly-ground pepper. No maple syrup this time. This is best done over the coals, but I had to keep a lid on the ribs, so I compromised.

Sleepy-Pie arose from what the bard called death's second self. She sipped the mint julep I made her. There was about a thimble-full of bourbon in hers, else she'd fall over. How differently we are made! The table was set. The children, filthy from play but their hands clean, were assembled. The Flatterer wanted to pray, and he was not to be denied. Add to his ear, nose, and palate a will as strong as Hercules.

"Mmm! What's that?" he asked, looking up from his deliberate cross, also a distinguishing characteristic of this peculiar boy.

"Barbecued ribs is what that is. Smoked."

"Smoked? What the heck is smoked?"

Did I dare look up? I looked up. I was in trouble. The enthymemic reasoning behind those sparkling eyes has always been decisive and swift: any forbidden word on a child's lips originated on mine.

I tried to divert attention to my boy, who was digging into his barbecued rib. "This is great! I love barbecued ribs! You're the best that ever was, Dad!"

They *were* good. You want tender and juicy pork, chicken, or turkey off the smoker? Don't forget the brine.

I looked at the Goddess Overly Censorious. So did the boy. She looked at him. "You're good too, Mom," he said. "But Dad's the best that ever was."

"Don't worry, Mom," said my daughter, the oldest, then a thirteen-year-old girl already possessed of a somewhat annoying adult judiciousness. "Dad taught him to say that."

"It's true," said the older boy in his usual delicate manner: mouth stuffed full of food, face smeared, lips smacking, napkin already on the floor, where it was likely to get more use anyway.

Expecting that wonted rolling of the eyes, I looked up, grinning stupidly.

The eyes rolled! But, lucky for me, the ribs didn't lie. Like Eve of old she appreciated the one she'd been given. But, unlike Eve, her proffered fruit is not forbidden. I remember thinking: nowhere on this unendingly intriguing earth, this goodly frame, this vast blue planet, is there a woman I'd rather be censored by.

Like the time I got The Look. Our daughter, then about four, came into the kitchen holding a screw-driver.

"Daddy," she said, triumphantly. "I found your dammit!"

That would have been a good time for me to have brined some ribs and served them with buttery asparagus, Uncle Will's best libation accompanying.

V
Vegetarian, Hell!

A lothario I know claims that vegetarian girls smell and taste better. This is the sort of claim that cries out for government- or foundation-funded research, but I am passing the project on to younger writers who, swamped in the ironies of obtaining their MFAs, are crying out to return to earth, to sink themselves in reality pudding.

—Jim Harrison, *The Raw and the Cooked*

24

Tuesdays with Jesus

Roaring noon. Shaded tables. Umbrellas that flutter lightly in the breeze. Harley riders clomping in, girls in summer dresses and flip-flops, flip-flops that slap the bottoms of their lovely bronze feet. Hard men in orange vests, construction workers, heavy in their chairs. Garroted white-collar men with neatly clipped hair, Rastafarians, derelicts, drunks, and—behold!—folks from both Chemistry and Physics. I had no idea they were human!

We're not crossing Brooklyn Ferry, it is true, but we've left all the numerous goings on of life for the Tuesday Burger Basket (and $3 pints) at Bent River brewery in Moline. My twenty-five-year-old Schwinn, its milk crate band-clamped to the back rack, leans against the brick wall of the restaurant next door. We're practically *wearing* the warm liquid sunshine out back here. The afternoon stretches out. No lectures to give. No committee meetings to feign interest in or skip. No freshman themes to mark.

Is life no more than this? asked Hamlet. Let's hope so.

O Walt Whitman, you lonely old grubber, you! Where are you now, old greybeard? What would you give for a table here, a chance to hear the summer laughter and the afternoon gossip, to partake of a little low-level early-day inebriety and maybe some first-class Midwestern American loafing by the Mighty Mississippi later on with that scrupulously coiffed fellow over in the corner naughtily leafing through *GQ*?

You'd give lilacs in the dooryard. I know you would.

Tuesdays, O Tuesdays! Where are you, Binx? Tom More, where are you? What I wouldn't give for a month of Tuesdays! Burgers and fries and sun dresses and pale ale and summer reading on the brain and the buzz of human life, men and women and weirdoes too and train whistles and pelicans aloft and Old Man River just over yonder!

Tuesday, whom I love! Tuesday, who has agreed to come round again. O Tuesday, my Tuesday!

What's that? Yes, my dear! You *may* bring me an ale and a burger basket, and the same for both of my buddies here too. We will eat and drink to life! Without provocation, without so much as imagining a canopy or a yarmulke, I almost stand and shout "L'Chaim!" We'll loaf and invite our souls. And you, my dear, you do whatever you can to increase your tips. That's *tips*, as I believe Dustin Hoffman once clarified. I tell you, the house approves of your get-up.

And I ask *you*: who would not, as I have this very day, peddle here on a mockable wicked-witch-of-the-west Schwinn for such an hour or so as awaits us? We'll talk in that way our wives, being intelligent, don't quite get: guy talk, ritual smack, taking bites out of each other's asses and yet, ere our meeting is adjourned, leaving time to be serious.

"Did you read the latest *New Yorker* yet, or are you watching season six of . . . ?"

"What was it our former governor, whom *you* voted for, said yesterday?"

"I see the River Bandits are tearing it up—*unlike your White Sox.*"

"Good God! Why are you reading *that*? You do know, don't you, that the author is a very great fool."

"No, I didn't see it. I don't go to movies except at gunpoint."

Ah! Look here. Brilliant simplicity: pickles and onions on a modest slab of ground beef draped in pepper jack cheese, all insulated between two pieces of bread, a side of mayo and fries accompanying. Who could doubt but this is part of some Divine Plan the *telos* of which is my taste buds, salivary glands, and gullet?

"I'll bet you that guy there is a Republican."

"Be careful. His bowtie is really a camera."

"We're enjoying fine weather, don't you think? I, personally, would describe it as *jiggly*."

"Did I ever tell you guys the one about the guy who wanted to start a Center for the Study of Feminist Humor?"

"Wear *that* in a place like *this*, and you could be pregnant by rush-hour."

"Do you suppose there are burgers and pale ale in heaven, or is it just bread and wine, on and on forever?"

"You're getting *what* published? *Where*? I thought that was *peer* reviewed."

"Seems there was a priest and a rabbi."

"The problem with a sabbatical is that it's over before it starts."

"That's what *she* said."

"Hey, I forget. Did Dingbat get tenure?"

"Can you narrow that down?"

"Can't remake the Middle East? Why of course you can!"

"That building right there? Lofts. Get more people back down here. Get this downtown throbbing again."

"*That's* what she said."

"LeBron? LeBoring."

"How then would going as a companion to Europe, to entertain some young gentleman with your conversation?" (For some reason we're now quoting favorite lines from "Bartleby, The Scrivener.")

And, as always, from *The Moviegoer*: "Were you intimate with Kate?" "Not very."

"I'm not exactly having a religious experience here." Apparently someone has moved on to *Tin Men*.

World Cup. The American League Central. The Tea Partiers and other cretinous Yahoos, such as Democrats. Colleagues we'd like to bludgeon with a shovel, provided it's dirty enough—and dull enough to ensure a slow painful death.

We dip our fries into the jalapeño ketchup, eat, cry, and douse the fire with golden ribbons of water and grain turned to good account. Down go the burgers (sometimes I'll bring my own tomatoes and a pocket knife to cut them with, like the divine Jim Harrison traveling with his own ubiquitous bottle of Tabasco sauce), aloft go our spirits—on the wings of the lofting spirits—and out comes the waitress once again with—could it be?—another round. How did she know? God bless the girl!

(Let not your hearts be troubled, ye wives that might still be reading: we'll observe the rule of Not Too Much. But two are not too much, and one won't fill the time God has given us. Plus there's no such thing as "one beer," as I believe the Good Book says.)

Who says this is all an accident? What but an immortal being could so adore a Tuesday in the sun amid the sweet droning buzz of local life, a little music in the air, the smell of hops, a baseball game later on across the river, the crack of the bat, the kids in the stands with their gloves and their hopes and expectations, fireworks over the Great River, and your own Sweet Precious in her own summer dress, a thin sandal dangling lightly from an elegant ankle that swings in the softening light.

Accident indeed! Accident my ass!

It winds down a little. The patrons come and go, shuffle in and out. They all have stories. We eye each other. Always the eyeing, the wondering. "What do you suppose that guy does to get to five o'clock each day?" "How'd you like to come home to *that*?" "There's a face made for radio." "Those three bores always talk about books when they're here."

It's not malice. It's a summer mood we're in. A burger and fries and a beer in the sun at noon. And to think there are people who don't do this! They're "working out" or "texting" or clutching a bag of soggy McNuggets in a parked Ford while listening to The Empire's Jaw on AM radio.

But, ah, to know *where* you are! To prefer *where* you are to where you *might* be! Those who would rather be anywhere than where they are—leave them to their ambition and their misery and there terminal peripatesis. Let them suck down Manhattans in Manhattan, tequila sunrises at the Sunset Grill. We're in little Moline. It's God's favorite day of the week, and this is Our Lord's favorite place for his three favorite guys, and I, the Bar Jester, am one of them. From out of the blue, the clear blue serene, we can almost hear Him say: "these are my bedeviled dunderheads, in whom I am nevertheless well-enough pleased. So leave them alone."

A pelican descends.

We part ways, for we do have wives to answer to—and what smart girls they are! But I peddle to Baker Street tobacconist, where I'm sure a cigar awaits me. And lo! I do indeed find a cigar there. Off to the river's edge!

What's this? A book of matches in my pocket? And look! In my milk crate is a volume of immortal poems! According to the cover, Oscar Williams has selected them just for me, for my name is written on the inside cover of the book. Jesus *does* love me. I always suspected him of this.

O, my soul! Look at that river, the Mighty Majestic Storied Huck-and-Jim Mississippi going by, the sun pouring down like honey, the cyclists and the joggers and the noontime walkers traversing its companion path. And look, you sun and river, look at me, here, on a Tuesday, not getting into any trouble at all. I half-expect Old Walt to come here and watch twenty-eight men bathe.

Not me, the upright Cheap Bastard Dumb Ass Bar Jester. I've come to read "Ode to the Confederate Dead"—for across these rolling waters there's a Confederate cemetery, where lie buried the dead of our own Andersonville, our uncelebrated Andersonville of the North.

Jesus! Let not your hearts be *un*troubled.

25

Careful Exegesis and the *Au Bleu* Ribeye

I have it on good authority—my own plus that of a few others who know more about these things than I do, including one fellow who "attended the best culinary school in the country" (a claim I take on good faith, not knowing the name of a single culinary school, good or bad)—not to mention that stern preceptor called "Experience" ("experience is the best teacher, but a fool will learn from no other," as Franklin said) . . . is this sentence going somewhere? I have it on good authority, as I say, that there is scarcely a credible reason to order a steak when you dine out.

The reason is that hardly anyone can prepare a steak as well as you can at home, and I'm not talking about doing anything particularly fancy like aging the beef or rubbing it with some mythical magical rub or any of that cowflubdubbery. I'm talking about nothing more than beef to advantage dressed, if I may steal a phrase from that diminutive splenetic, Alexander Pope.

So, as Kipling said, hear and listen and attend, O best beloved.

Choose a ribeye and bear in mind the infallible words of Jim Harrison: "Beef is a pleasure food, and we deserve pleasure because we live nasty, brutish lives." Do not be impressed by the name "New York strip" or "sirloin tip" or anything else that rhymes with "hip." The only thing hip about this meal is that that's where you're sending your calories. Get yourself a one-inch thick ribeye carved out of a locally grass-fed and locally lockered beast. If the cut is frozen, defrost it. If not, proceed to give it a dry brine. You do this by sprinkling lots of coarse sea salt on both sides and letting it sit in the fridge for at least an hour but preferably overnight. (If you have the perverse need to feel like bigshot on TV, your sea salt will be in a bowl, and you'll sprinkle the salt delicately with your fingers.)

Wait! I almost forgot! Shake a Bombay sapphire martini with a denial of vermouth. Pour it into the martini glass you've been chilling in the freezer since last week, when you began thinking about this steak dinner. Skewer a bleu-cheese-stuffed olive, rinse it, and send it to the bottom of the clear cold pool. Sip delicately. Sip again. Ah!

And some folks say there is no God! They've never seen the back pockets of a fine pair of blue jeans ding-donging back and forth down the walk on a cool fall day or beheld a shaken Bombay Sapphire martini aside the *mise en place*, where, mute and expectant, lay a one-inch-thick ribeye steak, the ivory-tickling and prestidigitation of Bruce Hornsby blaring from the hi-fi.

Dry-brined, the slab of dead cow now needs something of the green herb that fed it while it lived. Sprinkle dried oregano on both sides, then drizzle a little olive oil, again on both sides. You can crush in some garlic if you want to, and sometimes I want to, so have your garlic press poised and ready, and ignore the snide swipes taken at this noble utensil by a certain deceased celebrity chef who, though fond of parting with the confidentiality of the professional kitchen, ignored what the Almighty hath fixed his canon 'gainst.

Rub it all in or don't. There will be little influence on the flavor. You do this or don't do this depending on how tactile you want the cooking to be. Let the spirit move you. Then, says Bruce, let the spirit linger.

Cover the meat and remove it to a cool place if you're several Hornsby CDs from settling down to your dinner, which you should be. There's no hurry. This isn't fast food.

Did I mention you're eating alone tonight? You are. The family is off visiting other family, and you've been left home alone to power wash and restain the deck and build a new brick walkway along the south side of the house, which you'll do, but not this evening. This evening is given to the fullness of man: the incarnate condition.

Look out the window toward the western skyline. Observe the various mother birds at work feeding their young in the many birdhouses you've built for them: the sparrows, the wrens, the nuthatches, the titmice, maybe even a Prothonotary warbler that has lit out for the territories. Indulge the analogical imagination. How our Mother feeds us, does she not?

Sip. Sip. You're no lost soul coming down the road, somewhere between two worlds. That's worth giving thanks for. Sing it, Bruce!

The salad will have four kinds of lettuce plus arugula. . . . No! Tonight you can have straight arugula. No one's here to complain about too much arugula! You cut it from the garden not an hour ago, washed, dried, and set it by. Throw it into a big bowl, not some little bowl meant for Cap'n Crunch.

And feta! How for the least division of an hour could I have been so beguiled as to have forgotten thee?

See, here's how whole process can surprise you. You hadn't planned on this. But you crumbled up some feta—the properly soft and salty kind that only certain Greek acquaintances initiated into secret swarthy rites know how to find, and you've sprinkled it onto the salad. Ah, green and white. What colors! But now that you've got the feta out you're reminded of another noble purpose to which feta can be put. So you cut another little square off, place it on a small plate, a blue one if you've got it, and sprinkle it with oregano. You crack some fresh black pepper over it and shower it with some really fine olive oil (also procured by your serendipitous acquaintance with the Greek underworld). Go to work with a spoon on the little hunk of feta. It's your appetizer. Just don't let it blunt your appetite. Mmm-*mmm*, as the Sheriff said of Ritz crackers.

Light the charcoal grill.

But isn't it about time to shake another . . . no. Benjamin Franklin said: eat not to dullness; drink not to elevation.

To hell with that portly opportunistic fat-assed hypocrite!

Compromise. Crack open a bottle of deep inky shiraz. How it complements the colors of the appetizer and flatters the very bloodstream. You might legitimately switch over to the Ozark Mountain Daredevils and "Thank you, Lord! You made it right."

Potatoes would be good, wouldn't they? But you're on your own. Translation: no cardiac nurse is here to remind you of your soaring cholesterol levels. The words "lipid profile" will not be uttered tonight. Into the saucepan goes a half-pint of cream and about a quarter—no, better make it an eighth—stick of butter. Sprinkle in plenty of nutmeg and red pepper flakes. Stir over low heat. Let it thicken.

Boil the oiled and salted water for the bowtie pasta.

Chop up some garlic–lots of it, because there's no soft personnel to kiss tonight. Soften it in butter in another pan. Not too long. Five minutes tops. Keep the heat low. Sing to the music and ignore the ringing telephone.

Ignore the knock on the door. Whoever's there can plainly hear that no one's home but you, and you're in no mood to see your sacred rites interrupted. Probably the Jehovah's Nitwits, anyway.

In go the bowties. This is all a bowtie is good for. Beware of men who wear bowties (with the exception of your pal Kevin, who pulls it off without pretense). Step outside to spread the coals.

When the pasta is done, strain it and add the cream sauce and garlic. Cover. It'll be just fine (after you've sprinkled on the crumbled gorgonzola).

Out to the grill at last! On goes that fat slab of cow. Hear the olive oil sizzle. You give it about sixty seconds; then you turn it. You give it sixty more. Truth is, it's ready, but this isn't a night for steak tartare. You give both sides another sixty seconds and bring the thing inside *au bleu*, as the Frogs say: the only way to eat beef if you're going to bother to cook it. People who cook the flavor out of beef should just eat old shoes.

Let the ribeye sit for a few minutes. It needs to calm down a little.

Now for the place setting:

Just kidding! You're all alone! It's just you and the steak, arugula salad, bowtie pasta in thick nutmeggish cream sauce heated with red pepper flakes into which crumpled gorgonzola has fallen, and a deep inky shiraz. Read during supper if you want to. Peruse an Orvis catalogue. Vow to buy a creel even though you're a catch-and-release guy.

To the hi-fi. This calls for something of gravity: Beethoven's seventh will do. Now don't be ungrateful. Eating without gratitude leads to all kinds of mischief. And, besides, such a night calls for gratitude. There's something bigger than you out there. Make a nod in its direction.

Cut a piece of dead cow. Turn it sideways. Salt it a little (and each individual piece to follow). Stab it with your steely fork and put it in the mouth God gave you. Bite down twice, pick up the glass, swirl it, smell it, put it back down, and finish the first morsel. And, as the shampoo bottle says, rinse and repeat.

Now there's going to be a puritan out there telling you you shouldn't drink alone. But you're not alone. Didn't Jesus say, "Lo! I am with you alway, even unto the end of the world"? You, my friend, are in good company. And you're nobody's fool. You know the uses of careful exegesis. (If you're not the Jesusy type of at least Doobie Brothers proportions, there's always the providentially named George Thorogood to appeal to.)

And if irony got the best of you and prevented you from pronouncing a blessing, raise your glass to your companion. That might suffice tonight. He knoweth whereof we are made; he remembereth that we are but dust.

And congratulate yourself for resisting the urge to make a compound butter with herbs to melt over your *au bleu* ribeye. That was mighty disciplined of you. But it doesn't mean you should never prepare a compound butter with herbs to melt over your ribeye.

26

The Thoughtful Carnivore Eats Raw Beef

But man is a carnivorous production,
And must have meals, at least one meal a day;
He cannot live, like woodcocks, upon suction,
But, like the shark and tiger, must have prey:
Although his anatomical construction
Bears vegetables, in a grumbling way,
Your laboring people think beyond all question
Beef, veal, and mutton, better for digestion.

—Byron, *Don Juan*

The thoughtful carnivore lives between two opposing impulses, one to limit and one to liberate his appetites. Or, to put it another way, he has great admiration for Thoreau of Walden—"it is a part of the destiny of the human race . . . to leave off eating animals"—and at the same time significant sympathy for Rumpole of the Bailey—"never trust a vegetarian."

Between these opposing impulses there are variations of which the Mark Bittman approach is a good enough example: no animal products until the evening meal. I know people who do this and feel good about it. They also actually *feel* good.

And then there's the Michael Pollan thesis, also sensible: eat food, mostly plants, not too much.

Even the Church is helpful in recommending periods of meatlessness. These are solemn stretches of time, and not a bit fun, but they are necessary and useful and healthy in the largest possible meaning of that word, a meaning you can't expect nutritionists in lab coats or personal trainers in spandex to understand.

But during these times you can sometimes feel your incisors trying to answer some ancestral call. They want to tear into something, and, brother, it ain't tofu. They want flesh. They want smoked pork tenderloin and porterhouse and calamari. At such times you can almost believe we did come down out of the trees—that, if we are men, well then, by God, we are also animals. Thoreau himself tells us he was tempted once to eat a woodchuck raw.

But he's also the one who said that, when the body sits down to dine, the imagination must sit down with it and that both must be fed essentially.

It is unlikely, I think, that either can be fed essentially if we are not mindful of limits. I don't mean quantitative limits only, though I mean those too. I mean, mainly, qualitative limits. I mean rhythms of abstaining and partaking. At some point we must all leave off eating Death by Chocolate for dessert if we ever hope to enjoy chocolate again someday. We were not made for satiety. We were made for variety. And change is the one condition pleasure requires. Without change there is no pleasure.

If that variety includes seasons of somber meatlessness, it includes, at least for me, seasons of meatiness as well. And by meatiness I don't mean burgers on the grill, though I'm all for them. I mean raw meat. I mean mooing beef, as in "the cattle are lowing." I mean red bloody uncooked dead cow.

Listen. If you're going to pity vegetarians for missing out on steak diane but not pity meat eaters for missing out on steak tartare, you're not serious about carnivoraciousness. Your Thoreau-Rumpole ratio is seriously out of whack.

I have read around enough in the literature of *tartare d'boeuf* to know that there are disagreements about just how to prepare and eat this most elemental of heaven's gifts. Some chefs want only this particular cut of meat, others only that one. Some don't want an egg yolk added, some do. Some use olive oil, some don't. Some use onions, others shallots.

I propose to settle the matter once and for all: here I offer not only the best steak tartare recipe but also the best way to prepare, eat, and reflect upon it.

And, like Henry VIII, I will have no opposition!

- Step 1: Choose some music and put it on. *N.B.* The music you choose will depend in part upon which concoction you plan to fortify your digestive system with. The *Carmina Burana* will do if you're going to quaff something Dionysian, like, say, a quart of homemade sangria. Your manhood will suffer a little from this choice—or your womanhood (you'll be under the table ere you eat)—but there are times when the Orff-sangria option is a good one. A Bombay Sapphire martini with a lemon twist or an onion garnish will complement nicely anything baroque. (Olives are permissible during a Bach oboe concerto if they are stuffed with blue cheese and rinsed of their juice but not otherwise.) I myself like just a tiny little bit of bourbon to go along with Brahms' third symphony or The Ozark Mountain Daredevils. An Islay single malt may be taken with just about anything, including Rachmaninoff's Vespers, Gorecki's *Totus Tuus*, and "Sweet Home Alabama." An Imperial IPA is certainly okay, but you might want a more deadly concoction for the obvious reason that you're going to be eating raw beef.
- Step 2: Crank it up louder, especially if yours goes to eleven.
- Step 3: Chop up some fresh parsley. You'll want at least a quarter cup.
- Step 4: Chop up a whole shallot—a good-sized one. Under no circumstances should the shallot be sautéed. Like everything else in this dish, it should be raw. (Some want the shallot added at the finish. More on this option presently.)
- Step 5: Carefully trim the fat off a local grass-fed ribeye. A top sirloin will do in a pinch. Cut the meat into long thin strips, then cut the strips again crosswise so you have small cubes. Scrape them into a bowl—a white one.
- Step 6: Take a sip–or quaff a desired quantity–of the fortification. Repeat. Repeat again and hum or sing along to the music. Think uncharitable thoughts about vegetarians and the sissy carnivores who won't go the distance with you.

Step 7: Add anywhere from two to six tablespoons of capers to the bowl. (Some want the capers added at the finish. More on this option presently.)

Step 8: Repeat step 6.

Step 9: Scrape all the chopped ingredients into the bowl.

Step 10: Add two tablespoons of Dijon mustard; add sea salt and ground black pepper to taste.

Step 11: Add one egg yolk. (Some want the egg yolk, along with the capers and shallots, added at the finish. This is an acceptable method but should probably be used only if you're entertaining certified postmodern or gay friends who like to use the word "presentation." Otherwise, I recommend the full-mix method for reasons I'll get to presently.)

Step 12: Drizzle in some olive oil and add about three tablespoons of Worcestershire sauce.

Step 13: Stir lovingly.

Step 14: Repeat step 6 and let the ingredients mingle promiscuously while you listen to the music and behold the slow disappearance of the gastric fortification. This full-mix method does alter the "presentation," it is true, but the promiscuous mingling is, in my opinion, essential to the flavor of your steak tartare. (I sometimes let the promiscuous mingling go on overnight in the fridge.) Plus it gives you an excuse to mix another concoction and listen to Brahms' first symphony or Tchaikovsky's sixth.

Step 15: NOT TO BE PERFORMED UNTIL YOU ARE READY TO EAT. Squeeze half or perhaps a whole lemon, pour the juice into the bowl, and stir lovingly. The reason you don't put the lemon juice in until the very end is that it actually cooks the beef a little, and you want this as raw as you can get it while still availing yourself of the astringency of the lemon.

If you have finished your concoction(s) and have opened a very deep inky assertive red wine—a salice would not be inappropriate—you are ready to eat.

So—step 16—give thanks, reverently making the sign of the cross while thinking uncharitable thoughts about vegetarians and the sissy carnivores who won't go the distance with you.

Now some culinarians will suggest that you spoon the tartare onto thinly sliced pieces of French or pumpernickel bread or toasted garlic wafers. This is a fine way to enjoy tartare if you're sharing it with others—for example, your certified postmodern or gay friends—and using it as an appetizer. Nothing should dissuade you from using bread or garlic toast as your carrier. But I like to eat this right off the spoon or fork, in small delectable portions, pausing after every second or third bite to swirl, smell, and then sip the wine, all the while thinking uncharitable thoughts about vegetarians and sissy carnivores.

But here's a word of warning: people who can't believe that you would eat raw beef should probably not be allowed anywhere near you when you do it. Trust me: most of them will spoil everything—the music selection, the concoction, the climactic savoring—everything. Eat steak tartare alone or with likeminded friends but never with a dissenter, nonbeliever, apostate, or reprobate. This is as important as delaying the lemon juice until the end.

Nor would I have readers think that eating this divine dish is its only reward. Many other benefits accrue to you and your palate fine.

Among them I number the following:

3. You develop a deep gratitude for all bovines, who are very deserving of our gratitude.

2. You distinguish yourself not only from all vegetarians but also from most carnivores and therefore secure for yourself the intoxicating feeling of superiority.

1. You experience what Jonathan Edwards called the Divine and Supernatural Light. It is said that there are no atheists in foxholes. It has also been said that there are no atheists in pot bunkers (*Mulligan's Laws*, ed. Henry Beard). But I'm here to tell you there are no atheists among steak tartare eaters—or, if there are, they are profoundly disingenuous and ought to be scolded coldly by a roomful of severe and unmerciful wives. I recommend the wives of golf addicts who have never changed a diaper. Anyone who gets up from a plate of my steak tartar and still claims to be an atheist is a goddamned liar; such impertinence will elicit from me a fist upon the table as I thunder the immortal words of STC, the Sage of Highgate: "Not one man in ten thousand has goodness of heart or strength of mind to be an atheist"—especially after having been fortified by Laphroaig, serenaded by Brahms, fed by lowing cattle, and graced by a swirlable amarone in a crystal balloon glass.

Now some will wonder about the safety of eating steak tartare. My friend the parasitologist tells me that freezing meat in a normal freezer for a week will take care of flukes, tapeworms, and roundworms. He says that there are some strains of worms that have evolved in the arctic and that these can survive freezing—trichinosis worms, for example—but we can solve that problem easily enough by not eating cows pastured in the arctic.

(There are, apparently "other dangers," but they issue either from the academic left—that is, from atheists, Darwinists, and pinkos who have never been transfigured—or from the home-school right—that is, from SuperMoms and Creation Museum ticket-takers who have never been properly laid. Ignore both devoutly. Remember that you inhabit the isthmus of a middle state.)

Others will say that eating meat, cooked or raw, is simply wrong. I doubt if these people are right, though I confess that I have some interest in what their arguments look like. I would not, after all, be a mindless and unthoughtful carnivore. But I must say that vegetarianism is, I think, a luxury of the age of cheap energy and cheap transportation, especially here in the north.

Vegetarianism also has the disadvantage of excluding *tartare d'boeuf*, one of the best proofs—right up there with a really fine pair of kneecaps—that God exists.

One final word—just to come full circle: you should not eat steak tartare every day. Honor the rhythms of abstaining and partaking. Choose Thoreau over Rumpole and clear your palate over a long stretch of time with a vegetable diet and water. Work hard at being the thoughtful carnivore acutely aware of opposing impulses, one to limit and one to liberate your appetites. Then, after a suitable interval, choose Rumpole over Thoreau, clear the domicile of naysayers, and proceed again with step one. I recommend *Neck and Neck*, by Chet Atkins and Mark Knopfler, and a mint julep.

27

Cutting the Mustard

It is well-established in the authorities of antiquity that God favors those who prefer mustard to ketchup. All the trustworthy modern authorities confirm this, even Dirty Harry, who said that nobody puts ketchup on a hotdog. And to their unified voices the Bar Jester slash Culinary Plagiarist hereby adds his own correct opinion.

But having called to remembrance this incontrovertible fact, I wouldn't be mistaken for a snob. I make no special claims for "gourmet" mustard or the pretensions of Grey Poupon. I hasten to advert, rather, that there is nothing lowly or unsophisticated about ordinary yellow mustard. Behold how radiantly it adorns the hotdog when applied generously! Consider with what concord its fine tang complements the bosky bite of bourbon whiskey!

And note by contrast with what repellent gore-like attributes its hated viscous rival, ketchup, besmears and disgraces the noble bratwurst! It was a "fateful development," says John Shelton Reed, "when the Centennial Exposition of 1876 in Philadelphia introduced America to bottled tomato ketchup." (That same exposition, he reminds us, "brought us kudzu from Japan.")

And yet I would not encourage sins against propriety. There are proper and improper uses of mustard. This chaste delicacy is not an ecumenical condiment. For example, it does not belong on a burger. Anyone acquainted with the sacred canons of summer cuisine knows that there are only a few acceptable ways to prepare a burger, none of which involves mustard. In order of ascending rank these ways are:

5. With bacon, sliced jalapeños, mayo, and pepper jack cheese on a Kaiser roll (though some trustworthy men, not without reason, have substituted peanut butter for the mayo, about which more later)

4. Impregnated with blackened seasoning and blanketed with blue cheese on a kaiser roll

3. With grilled, caramelized, or raw onions, lettuce, and tomato on a kaiser roll

2. With melted cheddar, mayonnaise, lettuce, and tomato on a kaiser roll

1. With olive sauce—made of chopped Spanish olives and mayonnaise—on a kaiser roll

(This is the burger in its Highest Form. It generally goes by the modest name "Olive Burger." Seek it out in the hallowed Peanut Barrel in East Lansing, Michigan, or at the Bar Jester's Unlicensed Homebrewery & Grill in Ingham County, Michigan.)

Now those five above are the no-nonsense burgers. I intend them mainly as armature against the barrage of fussy burgers proliferating like inalienable rights at Oberlin and Swarthmore and Evergreen State. Because let's face it: sometimes when you read a burger menu at a restaurant you get the feeling that if you ever actually do get to the end of it, if you can finally close the multi-volume tome on the last tiresome busy entry—"The Hydrogen Bomb Fall-Out Shelter Everything Burger!" ("topped with a free-range duck egg fried in pigeon fat and finished with a drizzle of our own cilantro-and-bourbon infused aioli sauce aged in cedar barrels and Euell Gibbons' pine straw")—if you can ever get to that moment, it'll be time for coffee and the morning evacuation.

But I would be remiss if I did not include a brief digression concerning #5 above, which will be my one concession to fussy burgers. This might cause you, once you've read about it, to conclude that I've gone bat-shit crazy and *ausgespielt*, both at the same time. To assure you that I haven't I will even break the governing rule of this book and nod in the direction of its origin. You can get this burger in a bar in South Bend, Indiana, a place one buddy of mine calls "The *Smokey* Bar!"—emphasis and exclamation point in the original—because he can *smoke in it!* That's pretty damn rare these days in your Nannied States of America, where the ultra-censorious in sensible shoes, rehearsing their nursery-room pieties, have us all wearing undersized faux-morality strait jackets.

And while I'm at it, can I ask just one question? Where is the prophet, in the spirit of the real ass-kickers of the Old Testament, who will ride in on a whirlwind and shout to the four corners "your righteousnesses are as filthy rags!"—shout it every time a Birckenstocked sociologist, aglow with moral pride, affixes a "Safe Zone" sticker to the back window of her green Subaru—right next to "Coexist"—or every time a cop, unfamiliar with the distinction between a rule and a law, and not content merely to serve and protect, summons all the indignities he suffered as a pasty-faced junior-high fatso and settles old scores by telling you with twice the combined moral authority of a hall monitor and a Vice President of Diversity, Inclusion, and Equity to pay the Nanny State $150 for not wearing your seatbelt like a good little boy? I'm telling you, it's as if Cotton Mather knocked up Mary Wollstonecraft, and out came a humorless and sexually ambiguous Mary Poppins, snapping her ruler and scoffing at Burt's jolly holidays. Mandatory seatbelt-use is goddamned un-American, and I have no intention of coexisting with those who think it is!

Where was I? Right. Here goes: you grill a slab of ground beef—a good half-pound of it—to medium rare. (It is permissible to work fresh chopped rosemary into the ground beef, but the rosemary must be fresh from your garden.) Having fried up some thick-cut bacon, you place no fewer than four strips atop the dead cow. You drop both halves of your Kaiser bun into the bacon grease you've retained and then toast the half-buns on the grill—or, if you prefer, you toast them first and then drop them into the bacon grease. There are slices of jalapeño pepper on a cutting board, because to scare everyone else off, especially the Counter of Cocktails, you have cut a jalapeño into discs of tolerable thickness—or into wedges if high heat is your thing. You then take a shot of courage, singing along, and place no fewer than five slices (or wedges) atop the dead pig. And then—stay with me now—you spread *peanut butter* on the inside of the top half of the bun. That's right: peanut butter. I'm not going to get enthusiastic like some off-Broadway choreographer expostulating on sexual preferences—"don't knock it till you've tried it!"—but don't knock it till you've tried it. The *Smokey* Bar! calls it the PBJ for reasons that have nothing to do with jelly. I'm pretty sure jelly would ruin this marvel. So would a nanny-state bar with "no smoking" signs everywhere. I say that, by the way, as a non-smoker—a non-smoker who thinks you ought to be allowed to smell tobacco smoke in all the places it belongs in, like baseball stadiums and Departments of English, Philosophy, and Theology—that's *Theology*, by God! Not "Religious Studies," which was the misbegotten issue of Birkenstocked sociologists on whose account green Subaru would one day be manufactured. If it ends in "Studies" it's not an academic discipline. It's an ideology, and like business, accounting, and VPs of Diversity, Inclusion, and Equity, it has no place in a college or university—except, maybe, at the Jacobin rights-manufacturing plants mentioned above.

Okay. End of digression.

I'll allow that in each of the five burgers above the Bar Jester's homemade buns may be used as a substitute for the kaiser roll, but note that under no circumstances is mustard—to say nothing of its vile tomato-based rival—to touch a burger. Note also that light mayo and especially Miracle Whip are strictly anathema. I implore you not to get caught eating a burger desecrated with either of these condimental abortions.

It goes without saying, though I'll say it anyway, that the burger should be cut and ground from a grass-fed beast, locally raised and slaughtered and lockered, and that when the patty comes off the wood or charcoal grill most of it should still be as red as the ketchup so obviously ill-suited to it. Cooking the flavor out of red meat is unchristian—indeed, cooking red meat *at all* is almost unchristian. I read somewhere that in Constantine's time it was punishable by hanging and/or a form of torture known as listening to Byzantine chant intoned by someone who's a walking nasal passage with shoulder hair.

Why these prohibitions against ketchup? "His eye is on the tomato; neither will he suffer the dissembling thereof." Which is to say that ketchup should be had in a less processed form—namely, *in the form of a whole tomato*. And that tomato should be in season. Anyone who puts a rock-hard store-bought February tomato on a burger will be hanged or subjected to nasal Byzantine chant, as under Constantinian law.

And why these restrictions on mustard? Because we are creatures made in the image and likeness of God, who does not put mustard on His Burgers. Moreover, Our Lord said nothing about moving mountains with faith the size of a tomato seed.

A general rule to follow—and all the ancients corroborate this—is that if the bun you're using is round, you may apply mustard, but only if the meat is "white"; if the bun is long and tubular, you may apply mustard and mustard only—and maybe some chopped onion, but never relish, which is of pagan origin.

In the post-Baccalaureate party aforementioned in chapter 7 I recounted how I invite a few colleagues over to join me in fortifying myself against the Commencement ceremony. Everyone brings a dish, an intoxicant, and a thumbtack (for Pin the Tail on the Administrator—if Strip Poker first, and Naked Twister subsequently, don't end indecently). I fry a turkey according to specifications I lifted from an issue of Martha Stewart's *Prison Living*. I also smoke some beef short ribs cut from a grass-fed ruminant, at which ribs we pick whilst the bird fries.

Now short ribs are not generally very meaty, at least not the ones hanging on the three-eighths of a cow that I buy each year. Indeed, you won't see nearly as much fat in the federal budget as you will see on these ribs—and only slightly more at the opera. But to mitigate the disappointment of my guests, who, having spent an entire academic year demanding their pounds of flesh, count on rather a lot of it at my annual gathering, I make a South Carolina mustard sauce that is . . . I had almost said "that is to die for" and "out of this world," except that (1) it is to live for and (2) it is most decidedly *in* this world, where *we* are, fully enjoying the incarnate condition.

Like loose clothing, this mustard covers a multitude of fat.

And it's so easy even Republicans and Democrats can make it. Out of the native goodness of my large and generous heart, I hereby proffer it to the gentle and ungentle reader alike:

In a medium saucepan, combine the following:

¾ cup yellow mustard

¾ cup red wine vinegar

1 ½ tablespoons butter (margarine users will be hanged or subjected to nasal Byzantine chant)

2 teaspoons salt

1 ¼ teaspoons black pepper

½ teaspoon Tabasco sauce

½ teaspoon Worcestershire sauce

¼ cup brown sugar (granulated will do in a pinch)

Simmer 10–15 minutes on low-to-medium heat, stirring occasionally. Let stand at room temperature for about an hour and mix another drink. WARNING: Do not add Liquid Smoke. You will be smeared with jam and rolled on an ant hill. When the sauce is cool, lavish it on a dead animal and serve.

I make no special claims for other body parts, but ribs of all sorts make excellent smearing grounds for this mustard, which is also good on brats, hotdogs, pulled pork, butterfly chops, fried turkey, and on the tip of your dipping finger when your Sweet Precious isn't looking. I've even stirred it into bloody marys, wherein it does not disappoint, provided there are supplemental concoctional fires and adequate quantities of cut-rate potato-based clear fermentables to complement it.

But bear in mind that mustard is the gift that keeps on giving, and this last application of it may result in a delayed but audible and fragrant cutting of same. So air your demons the next morning with a healthy walk in the out-of-doors, downwind of her (or him) you love.

BONUS FEATURE: The mustard described above is so good that it can alter history and change the course of a life. It has even been known to make west-coast Straussians sufferable. I regret, however, that it has not yet been known to make sociologists who don't bear the name "John Shelton Reed" or "Robert Nisbet" interesting.

VI
Interlude: A Miscellany

Tolerance [is] a species of pretentiousness. . . . But notwithstanding this deep conviction of our general fallibility, and the most vivid recollection of my own, I dare avow with the German philosopher, that as far as opinions, and not motives; principals and not men, are concerned; I am neither tolerant nor wish to be regarded as such. According to my judgment, it is a mere ostentation, or a poor trick that hypocrisy plays with the cards of nonsense, when a man makes protestation of being perfectly tolerant in respect of all principals, opinions and persuasions, those alone excepted which render the holders intolerant.

—Coleridge, *The Friend*

28

The After-Dinner Cigar

Biblical scholars hotly contest a question to which there is no obvious or certain answer: on which day did God create cigars? Why this problem should be the object of such heated debate, especially given the paucity of textual evidence, is anyone's guess. It is clear that, absent anything definitive in the *textus receptus*, Right Reason alone (reason informed by *caritas*) must be our guide.

Now I'm not going to say anything more about the originary problem—for that is not my concern here—other than that I would place the creation of cigars somewhere near The Beginning for the simple reason that it's hard to imagine the *fiat lux* echoing more than a couple of times before a sentient being capable of intellection concluded that it would be a really good idea to touch the *lux* to some really fine, cured, and carefully rolled tobacco. It would have required no Miltonic Lucifer scaling the walls or crouching toad-like in the garden to convince *me* to do it.

So: light, then vegetation, then men. Cigars almost certainly followed fast upon these three.

The problem is, so did women, which is why in the fullness of time Chesterton was obliged to say, "most of us have heard the voice in which the hostess tells her husband not to sit too long over the cigars. It is the dreadful voice of Love seeking to destroy Comradeship."

Notwithstanding the small number of women who willingly suffer their men to linger over the cigars (my sainted mother, for example), and indeed the even smaller number of women who actually smoke them (I'm not sure where I stand on this—for obvious visual reasons), it is generally the case, near as I can tell, that, among the many reasons women were created, one stands out: to keep men from enjoying themselves too much over the cigars. Remember the old joke about why women close their eyes during sex? It's because they can't stand to see a man have a good time.

This cigar business is another one of those problems that only Reason informed by charity is equipped to deal with, and once Reason has sufficiently turned the problem over it will certainly pronounce in a man's favor. "Ladies," it will say, "mind your own business." (Right Reason doesn't know what it's up against, but that's another matter altogether.) Whereupon the men will adjourn. They won't fully enjoy themselves, of course, because they know that what they're about to do will set them back a bit, but they'll adjourn nonetheless. Consequences are something they've learned to suffer willingly.

Now if you're going to risk the consequences, there are three things you must keep in mind as you buy your three or four nights in the doghouse: the third is the *kind* of cigar itself; the second is what to put in the *snifter*; the first is *where to go*.

As for the third: if you're rich, buy good cigars—really really good ones. But if you are not rich, find a middling cigar that won't scorch your tongue or send you reeling. On these two commands hang all the law and the prophets. And, truth be told, you don't actually need the kind of cigar you see between the hairy knuckles and gaudy rings of some fat-cat golf hack. A Churchill reject will do the job just fine. Occasionally you'll get one that won't draw, so you might want to buy two just in case, but don't break the bank just because someone in some magazine has said disparaging things about all us cheap bastards. We cheap bastards are doing just fine.

But of course you don't want an over-the-counter cigar that comes in a little three-quarter box with cellophane over it. That's beneath human dignity. It's for bait fishermen who have never wielded a fly rod. You want something that has spent some time in a walk-in humidor. (And whatever you bring home should go straight into your own humidor, which you must be vigilant to keep humid.)

As for the second: if you're rich, buy good cognac—really really good cognac. But if you are not rich, find a brandy that won't go down like flammable sandpaper or gag you because it's nine-tenths vanilla. I won't put any labels out there, because I'm a cheap bastard afraid of being called out on my tastes, but I know what does and doesn't set the gullet aflame. And I can say this: I recently scored some Armenian cognac, the label of which is inscrutable, but it's fine stuff. I heard a rumor that it's one of the spirits Stalin served to Churchill in 1942, though I should also mention what undersecretary Sir Alexander Cadogan reported, apparently from under the table: "what Stalin made me drink seemed pretty savage." (Churchill, for his part, was fighting off a headache at one o'clock in the morning, facing at least two more hours of Joe's hospitality, and "wisely" confining himself "to a comparatively innocuous effervescent Caucasian red wine"). Anyway, look for the Cyrillic alphabet and take a shot in the dark.

Or spring for some B&B. For the price it's difficult to beat. And at any rate you don't want Bo's Brandy or Karl's Konyack. You want something that will please the eyes, the nose, and especially the tongue. And don't overfill the snifter. Swirling the nectar is as important as holding the cigar at arm's length and admiring that gorgeous inch of ash that hangs from the end of it.

Finally, as for the first: if you have a barn, by all means go there.

I take that back. Don't go by all means. Go by foot.

If you don't have a barn but do have a garage, go there. A front porch is nice in a pinch, but you're pretty close to the Voice of Love. That's dangerous. So get farther away if you can.

But don't be stupid about this. Barns can go up in smoke. Avail yourself of a poured cement or dirt floor. If at all possible, have something to look out at: a field, a river, a rusting Oliver tractor in the weeds. This is called a focal point. It's like a fire only different.

And once you're there let the talk flow: the travails of home projects, especially plumbing and brush removal; the triumphs of automobile repair, especially if you are the devoted owner of an '83 Dodge Ram pickup with a slant-six engine; jokes, which don't have to be clean or given the imprimatur by sociologists and other self-appointed marmish monitors of acceptable speech; limericks, especially the dirty ones about Anglican divines; books on all topics; sports, but not the NBA unless you're in full-blown splenetic mode; wives (but remember *caritas*); campus gossip, especially if it involves the salacious behavior of colleagues, the egregious idiocy of provosts, or the golly-gee sloganeering of presidents.

But don't despise silence either. Sometimes taciturn is what's called for. Take a deep breath and exhale slowly. Say "yep" now and then, even if no one else has said anything.

And when Love gets that really serious tone in Her Voice, call it a night and head in. Unlike Right Reason, you should be smart enough to know what you're up against. The doghouse is a fine place—especially if you built it—but it's no place for a man who knows what a cigar is a symbol of.

Coda: My father was a fairly taciturn man of no little wisdom—a man, indeed, who lingered over the cigars. It was he who taught me that 7 a.m. also qualifies as "after dinner." I learned this one morning when he and I were walking down Breckenridge Mill Road in Fincastle, Virginia. We'd stopped on the one-lane bridge and were watching the water pass under it, enjoying an early morning post-coffee cigar. I was surprised to learn what a great pleasure a cigar is at that hour. But, not wishing in his presence to sin against taciturnity, I kept my surprise to myself.

"Yep," he said.

29

Men, Women, and the Dishwasher

A Non-Sexist Dissertation on Female Guile and Incompetence

"Where I come from," an ironic sort of fellow once said to me, "'load the dishwasher' means 'get your wife drunk.'" And I could believe him: his town had that "drink a beer; slap your wife" look about it. It had an ethos that any ordinarily sensible person might object to, even without the benefit of a bachelor's degree in sociology and six hours of sensitivity and diversity training.

But where I come from is different. Where I come from, "load the dishwasher" means "kick your wife out of the kitchen," for it is this Cheap Bastard's experience that the dishwasher is the one thing on earth that women, who are otherwise infinitely discerning, completely fail to understand. I mean "women in general," because of course there are exceptions: my mother, for example, daughter of a hardware man, who inherited her father's knack for knowing how things work.

But you can't base rules on the exceptions that prove them, and I for one believe we could advance civilization by leaps and bounds were we to pass legislation—local, not federal—that bans women from the kitchen after dinner and sets them free to watch reruns of *Dr. Quinn, Medicine Woman* in some other room of the house.

Consider: It was not so long ago in this country that we had distinguished and august Men-Only Clubs. That by now they have all been infiltrated by women is a fact well-known, though insufficiently lamented, for this infiltration is plainly a sign that the evil days are upon us. It is an indication that the campaign for total emasculation is succeeding, a campaign that, like an invasion of the infidel horde, would merely be gaining ground were it not, like a squirrel of querulous intent, also collecting nuts—mine, yours, every man's. But I am convinced that we could forestall the intemperance of this blatant wrongheadedness *and* have cleaner dinner plates to boot if only we would boot the booty out of the kitchen—if we would but make the post-dinner kitchen a Men-Only Club, providing, of course, for those exceptions on the distaff side who have a knack for how things work. On these venerable women we will confer the title "Honorary Guy."

Here's how it goes. My Espouséd Saint, who is equal to so many of life's challenges except understanding machinery, is putting silverware into the dishwasher, all of it covered with crud and every single piece handle-side up. Speechless, I watch. Speechlessness, of course, is exactly what's called for, because a single word from my lips could be a match to a powder keg. The top rack is completely full, and yet more bowls and glasses are being piled, unrinsed, on top of the ones already there. This woman, who apparently understands that overloading a washing machine with clothing will compromise the machine's ability to get the clothing clean, cannot transfer this intuition to the dishwasher. The thinking goes like this: if it's in the dishwasher, it will get clean. If it's *in the same zip code* as the dishwasher, it will get clean.

Part of the problem is that, like a lot of people, she hates *unloading* the dishwasher. So distasteful to her is this task that she hurries through it without noticing how unchanged things are from when she closed the door and pushed "start." I don't mean to imply she's a poor steward of the kitchen. Stewardess, rather. In fact she's indefatigable in some things, like keeping the countertops clean. But as for the dishes: the crud is still there. I've picked it off myself.

So as she drops silverware into the silverware baskets, I strain with all that is within me—and most of what's without as well—to suppress the urge to blurt out, "do you *know* how this machine *works?*" Instead I simply take the pieces out, rinse them, and put them back in the other way, the way anyone who understands how this machine works would put them in.

"What are you doing?" she asks, because only one of us has thought a few steps ahead and decided that speechlessness is what this situation calls for.

"I'm putting these knives, spoons, and forks in in such a way as to give them a fighting chance of coming out clean."

"They'll get clean."

"They won't."

"What do you mean 'they won't'"?

"I mean 'they won't.'"

"You're O.C.D. You're obsessing. Just leave them there. They'll be fine."

"I'm not obsessing. It's just that tomorrow morning, *while you're still sleeping*"—and here I make my first mistake; this, clearly, is one phrase too many, a bridge too far—"it's just that tomorrow morning, *while you're still sleeping*, I don't want to have to wash everything by hand when I'm done unloading the dishwasher."

"Why would you have to do that?"

"Because this, clearly"—and here I take out a bowl with baked shit on it, the baked shit completely shielded by a plate, also covered in baked shit—"this, clearly, has *no* chance of coming clean. How is this going to get clean? Tell me."

"It'll come clean."

"It won't come clean."

"You're obsessing."

"I'm not obsessing. I have to use these dishes tomorrow and tomorrow and tomorrow—to the last syllable of recorded time."

"Hand me that measuring cup with the dried pancake mix in it. And chill out."

Chill out? *Chill out?*

I am, believe it or not, a disciplined man, the evidence in this book to the contrary notwithstanding. But just now, standing in my own kitchen, no one to prove anything to, no one to perform for, I have been broken—nay, I have been undone and unmanned—by a mere two syllables: *chill* and *out*.

And so out it comes at last: "Do you *know* how this machine *works?*" I ask.

"Here," she says, handing me a spatula crusted with dried egg yolk. "Find a place for this."

"*Where?* For the love of God and Christ Jesus our Lord, *where?*"

"Anywhere."

Here I draw a slow deep breath. I turn to her and, with a placid but steely resolve, I take her splendid shoulders in my hands. (How I have loved these shoulders!) "This machine," I begin, to the immediate rolling of eyes I would fain spend eternity peering into, "is governed by a couple of basic principles, the first of which is that dishes come clean if and only if little tiny jets of water can actually *get* to them." I point to a spoon that is crowded mouth-end-down in the silverware basket. "Look. Do you see this spoon, spooning with other spoons, all covered with dried-on oatmeal? It's not coming clean. And do you know why? Because of all the many tiny little jets of water this machine is capable of spraying, not a single one is going to hit it."

"You're obsessing. Things move around while this is running." To illustrate this conjured and wholly imagined magical operation she moves both hands in a circular motion, finger tips down, like a double-padded floor-buffer.

"Move where? There isn't room in here for a sociologist's frontal lobe. And this bowl here," I say, lifting out the bowl in question, though I could grab any bowl from a rack that invites comparisons to the work houses in a nineteenth-century British novel. "This will be full of soapy water and food chunks in the morning. And do you know why? Because another principle governing this machine is *gravity*. Bowls must be placed in such a way as to give them a chance, once cleaned by the tiny little jets of water aforementioned, to *drain*."

"Stop obsessing."

Obsessing? That's three "obsessings" now, and as far as I'm concerned the third time's a harm. But, having broken the silence I tried so hard not to break, I cling to my back-up resolve, which is to remain calm. Not easy when you're speaking truth to power.

"Here's another principle. This machine has a discharge hose. It is not nearly as big as the *inch-and-a-half* drain pipe leading out of the sink. Why not rinse the dishes and let the nice big drain pipe bear the food scraps to the septic system, where they will be of some use, instead of relying on a *tiny little half-inch drain hose* to do that? If that drain line clogs, will you be the one to pull this machine out and fix it? Will you be the one to fix the next ten things that break? Or the next five? Or the next one?" I sound as ridiculous as Abraham negotiating with God over the number of righteous souls in Sodom and Gomorrah.

I have a brief moment of panic when it occurs to me that she might know about the screen that is supposed to prevent clogging of the discharge line, but then I see her going in a different direction and I think that maybe I detect a slight grin. It can't be said she's not a fair player.

Where this is going: I was instructed once to rip the wet bar out of the basement, which I protested doing but did anyway. She slipped out to "run some errands" and returned three hours later, by which time I had the bar ripped out. Standing in the basement, inspecting the forlorn and vacant space where a noble household institution once stood—an ugly one, granted, but one I proposed rebuilding—she said, "That wasn't so hard, was it?"

!

"Said the one who didn't do the work," I pointed out impertinently, a variation on a long-standing domestic theme played the world over: *I don't need a heated workshop because the person who doesn't have to repair things in cold weather regards a heated workshop as a luxury.* "That wasn't so bad, was it?" said the person who didn't clean the gutters, change out the coils in the engine, power-wash the sky-lights on the roof of the pole barn, move fifty wheel-barrow loads of wood chips, or cut down four briar patches each the size of Houston and more treacherous by far than Faye Dunaway's late-night drive through Chinatown.

That is to say, where this conversation at the dishwasher is going is this: "Said the one who won't have to fix the dishwasher," and she's grinning because she knows it. Plus she's a woman: she has all the power, the contrary findings of social scientists notwithstanding.

"Tell you what," I say, as calmly and reasonably as Bartleby's employer at last inviting the poor motionless boy into his own home. "From now on, I'll do the dishes. I'll do the cooking *and* I'll clean up. *You* go chill out. Do something else, something that doesn't require an understanding of how machinery works."

Oops. OopsOopsOops.

"Care to try that again?" she explains.

"What I want is for you to chill out so I can do this right, and I want to do this right so that I don't have to do it again. Leave. Go commune with Jane Seymour and that long haired proto-feminist in moccasins she's making time with—you know, that ball-less sensitive he-man with the 'Marriage Encounter' and 'I ♥ My Wife' bumper stickers on the back of his covered wagon."

It appears the suggestion agrees with her, and as I watch her walk away I am filled with admiration. Like Binx I am filled with gratitude that in this wide world, brimming everywhere with the prodigal variety that flummoxed Charles Kingsley, there should be such a thing as a woman's backside and that I, even I, here in my kitchen, on the periphery of cosmic history, should be allowed to look at one.

And at 3:24 a.m. I will awake and realize that I've been outsmarted once again.

It should be added to this faithful non-sexist account that the dishwasher is, quite plainly, an abomination, not to mention a waste of space. Marriage counseling might be obviated entirely if men and women stood together at the sink, bumping fannies and casting lascivious glances and washing and drying their dishes by hand after each meal. The only real benefit of a dishwasher is that it hides the dirty dishes of those too lazy to clean things as they go along.

But that's a whole other matter. I'm the kind of cook who cleans things as he goes along; my Goddess Excellently Messy is the kind of cook who lets dirty stuff pile up until the clean-up seems insurmountable. But of course she *would* be that kind of cook: she's also the kind of cleaner-upper who just piles everything into the dishwasher—because things move around in there while it's running, and because the tiny jets of water aren't really that important, and because the law of gravity is suspended the moment a shimmering creature presses "start."

30

Agricultural Potential, Real Wealth, and the *Gold* Gold Standard

---

There can be no successful human economy apart from Nature or in defiance of Nature.

—Wendell Berry, "The Futility of Global Thinking"

I doubt Emerson knew what he was saying when he said "a man is fed, not that he may be fed, but that he may work." Frankly, I doubt Emerson knew anything fully. He was a Unitarian, after all. (What do you get when you cross a Unitarian and a Jehovah's Witness? Someone who knocks on your front door for no apparent reason.). Emerson also had three women seeing to his domestic needs so (as he said to Carlyle) he could "sit and read and write with very little system, and, as far as regards composition, with the most fragmentary result." What could such a man possibly know about work? But I am going to attempt to relieve some pressure from that statement of his—"a man is fed, not that he may be fed, but that he may work"—by considering it in relation to real wealth.

By "real wealth" I mean nature's stock, which backs whatever paper we Moderns are habituated to mistake as actual wealth.

Nature's stock isn't gold or any other symbol. Nature's stock is available goods beginning and ending in what feeds us. There are other goods, certainly, but none as important as food (after which I would name, without ranking them, clothing, shelter, and fuel). If you aren't being fed, you're not going to be distracted into an intellectual stupor by an electronic device, much less become a coal baron or a railroad tycoon and then, if luxury affords it, a philanthropist who gives back a quarter-tithe of what he got by larceny in the first place. You're going to be a corpse with only the worms and grass and trees to thank you for your generosity. The fellowship of dust cares nothing about "texting" or donor intent.

And if we were really interested in wealth in the older and deeper sense of *weal* (whence *common weal* and *commonwealth*), we would do the intelligent thing and make health and wholeness and true agricultural potential the gold standard. There would be no such tyrant as a bottom line, because we would be engaged in a less reductive and less simplifying and less despotic enterprise than the one we're currently engaged in. We would be engaged not in selective but in comprehensive bookkeeping. A depleted aquifer would go on the books as a cost offsetting the harvest it nourished. Divorce, though it increases the unimpeachable GDP (which Ed Abbey called the "grossest domestic product"), would go on the books as a cost offsetting the purchase of extra dishwashers and toasters. These and other costs—poor health, obesity, smog, the emotional damage children inevitably bear when parents fail to love each other sufficiently—would go on the books and be subtracted from whatever gains we think we're making. And whatever *net* gain we'd come up with after doing all the math carefully and honestly might turn out to be no gain at all but, instead, the kind of loss that some people could conceivably regard as a compelling reason to adjust their behavior.

What feeds us, obviously, is food. But food isn't contingent upon piles of money, as most of us are habituated to think. It is contingent upon healthy topsoil, adequate water (preferably rainwater), sunlight, salubrious seasons, and the human intelligence and labor that encourage the issuance of food from the earth. All flesh may indeed be grass, as the prophet said, and this may suggest that our lives are ephemeral, but that's just the metaphorical sense of the phrase. There's a literal sense to it as well. All flesh is grass because we are constantly converting what the earth produces, by the grace of sunlight and water and soil, into human flesh—into *us, ourselves*.

If sunlight falls and grass grows and a steer eats the grass, and if a man comes along and eats a steak cut from the flank of the grass-eating steer, what the man is doing is precisely the same thing that the steer did: converting grass into flesh. The steer is the man's intermediary, but the man's flesh, like the steer's, is still grass. It is also sunlight, water, and soil. The body that I understand as "me" or part of what constitutes "me" is grass (or bananas or potatoes or whatever). It is as true to say that as to say that a healthy pasture, or hay in a barn loft, is stored energy. A horse that grazes and then pulls a cart has converted grass into energy. In this case all *energy* is grass, and in this case the energy happens to be solar—energy run on contemporary rather than ancient sunlight. The biggest difference between a horse and a tractor isn't horse power. It's energy. A horse uses sunlight that is falling right now or that fell yesterday or during the most recent growing season; a tractor running on oil uses sunlight that fell a long time ago—about which, more presently.

We must get used to the fact that the grass is soil plus sunlight plus water. We must get used to the fact that the steer is soil plus sunlight plus water plus grass. And as a carnivore I must get used to the fact that I am soil plus sunlight plus water plus grass plus steer. That is what I am in material terms. *Der Mensch ist was er ißt.*

But that is not all that I am. I used the phrase "part of what constitutes me" just now because I was speaking not of the whole but of a mere part; and I used the phrase because there is, unmistakably, an immaterial part of me as well. Everyone capable of saying "I am" must admit of an immaterial part of himself that is as real as a thumbnail or a kneecap; he must admit of an interior life that is as real as a life of framing houses or barbering heads. Not the spleen, not the liver, but consciousness says "I am." No one's colon ever said "thanks" or "I love you." For such an utterance you need a source actually capable of gratitude or love, and the name in English for that source is "mind." "There is an important distinction," said Michael Oakeshott,

> between a chemical process and a biochemist understanding and explaining (well or ill) what is going on in a chemical process. For mind is not itself a chemical process, nor is it a mysterious *x* left over, unexplained, after the biochemist has reached the end of his chemical explanation; it is what does the explaining. . . . Mind, here, is the intelligent activity in which a man may understand and explain processes which cannot understand and explain themselves.

But distinctions between the material and the immaterial notwithstanding, the paradigm nevertheless obtains. Call the human person what you will. I am describing a fact as much natural as theological and liturgical:

you are what you eat. I agree that man does not live by bread alone; I am only pointing out that he doesn't live without it either.

And so for the moment my emphasis is on the bread. I'm describing a stage, though not necessarily the *telos*, of a process called "eating." A man is fed not that he may be fed but that he may work: that is, that he may be.

By now, however, almost everyone who eats is as abstracted from soil and water and sunlight as from sound theology. The average lunch-goer in any diner anywhere knows pretty much nothing about the quality of the soil that nourished the wheat that the bread on his plate came from. And I'd wager that the lunch-goer knows far less about the dangerously depleted aquifer that watered the wheat.

(For the record, soil is eroding and aquifers are being depleted at alarming rates. Eating, the *unum necessarium*, is in jeopardy way beyond knowledge or apparent concern.)

And the eater's fund of knowledge about the sunlight that feeds him is no doubt equally unimpressive, but it bears saying, and saying emphatically, that by now a fair amount of that sunlight is not, as I said a moment ago, contemporary but ancient. The eater is being fed in large measure by ancient sunlight that fell and brought to life plants that lived and died and then, as decaying matter, turned into the black gold that we refine and use for pretty much everything—and which, because of our profligate use, is now in rapid irreversible decline. We eat today thanks to the massive infusions of ancient sunlight that power the machines and artificial fertility of modern agriculture. That those infusions are costly, whereas the daily infusions of contemporary sunlight are not (they're free and can be used cleanly), goes some distance in suggesting how poorly we keep our books.

And I've not yet said anything about the human intelligence, formerly known as "husbandry," that, far from being a kind of magical incantation conjuring food from the earth, is instead a place-specific kind of knowledge that encourages the earth's productive capacity, a knowledge kept in both the mind and the body, in memory as we commonly think of it but also in muscle memory as well. Ask someone who knows how to milk a cow how to milk a cow. The answer you get will be a lesson in how sometimes knowledge is more in the hand than in the head.

A consequence of this ignorance—I mean ignorance of the sources that allow us to walk around as ignoramuses—is that almost everyone who eats knows nothing not only about soil and water but also about the human intelligence that brings forth food. Eaters participate in the food economy as eaters only. It is true that they shop for food, so they're also "consumers," but a consumer in this sense is just an eater who is extra lazy and equally unresourceful. By now we're all baby birds competitively squirming in a nest, our beaks open, waiting for the pre-masticated food to drop into our mouths.

Of course there's nothing wrong with being a baby bird if you're a baby bird. But there is if you're a mamma bird.

A baby bird may think at first that food comes from his mother's beak, but he's wrong and in due time will learn otherwise, mainly because the worst thing that happens to us won't ever happen to him: he won't be duped into thinking it's okay to remain a child forever—that is, he'll grow up and learn to do something more than simply consume. He'll learn to search for food rather than merely wait for it to appear. He'll learn that a bird is fed not that he may be fed but that he may work.

We would do well to note from this scenario a natural fact: that, generally speaking, a man is less intelligent than a bird, for a bird will grow up and learn to do something more useful than go grocery shopping. Reconciled to his condition, which is to work, he'll learn to get food by the sweat of his brow, as it were. (It is always advisable to reconcile yourself to your condition.) In the bird's food economy the bird will be more than a mere eater—more indeed than a consumer who, after over-eating, needs to "work out"—and his noble fate will be to die as a bird.

The consumer's baser fate, by contrast, will be to die as a consumptive at the gym, trying to get out of life alive.

Unlike the baby bird, we who were putatively "given dominion" over the birds of the air have learned to think from infancy to dotage and deliquescence that, so long as there is money, food can be bought, for to anyone abstracted from the true source, it is money that brings forth food. Money is the new soil plus water plus sunlight plus animals. It is, as Marx taught (for he did get *some* things right), the object *par excellence*.

And it has allowed us to live the lives of the petro-chemical applicators, either actually or by proxy. Eating that we may be fed, we forget about the sources and the human intelligence that feed us. Just as the petro-chemical producer thinks that the concoction in the sprayer brings forth food, so the eater thinks that the artificial wealth in his wallet (or hiding inside his credit card) brings it forth. Both are mistaken. And what both have in common is abstraction from the *gold* gold standard: health, wholeness, and agricultural potential. Both are duped, one perhaps by artificial fertility and the other perhaps by artificial wealth, but both certainly by what is not real.

Both eat that they may be fed rather than that eating may continue. Both prepare for a future in which they will be fat, not for one in which they will be fattening worms. But fattening worms is the only real future in store for either of them. Let them reconcile themselves to *that* condition before the evil days come—if those days haven't come already.

31

Haber-Bosch and the Problem of Whom to Tickle

The civilised [sic] nations—Greece, Rome, England—have been sustained by the primitive forests which anciently rotted where they stand. They survive as long as the soil is not exhausted. Alas for human culture! little is to be expected of a nation, when the vegetable mould is exhausted, and it is compelled to make manure of the bones of its fathers. There the poet sustains himself merely by his own superfluous fat, and the philosopher comes down on his marrowbones.

—Thoreau, "Walking"

To anyone abstracted from health, wholeness, and true agricultural potential, money is the magic that conjures food.

But by now almost all of us are abstracted from the sources that feed us. We are drawn or pulled away from them, as the etymology of "abstract" suggests, and those sources have, in turn, become mere abstractions *to us*.* We buy and eat without growing or harvesting. Very few people see anything wrong with this arrangement.

My generation is abstracted—it lives at a distance—from the land because our parents, a great many of them, left the farm and then brought us up to do anything except return to it. Our own children are even more abstracted from the land, and some of them, the least fortunate, are the unsuspecting victims of educational experts who, noticing that a nine-month school year no longer makes any sense in a republic where children aren't needed as farm hands, want to send these poor inmates to prison year-round. It would never occur to an educational expert to send the children back to the farm so that they can be disabused of the superstition that money produces food (or, God forbid, so that they can learn to work). The experts are as abstracted and therefore as ignorant as everyone else; like everyone else, they get their calories from food they expend no calories to get.

I am not trying to be unnecessarily severe, and I am no more saying everyone should be a farmer than I'm saying all ignorance can be mitigated or remediated. I myself am plenty ignorant of many things. But I'm willing to go on record saying that to be an eater of food and yet remain uninterested in it—whether out of ignorance or laziness or both—is a wide-ranging pestilential scourge with consequences more serious than most eaters have bothered to consider. It is a problem because the health, wholeness, and true agricultural potential that I wrote of in the previous chapter are in jeopardy, and they are in jeopardy because people who eat—that's all of us who aren't dead—are interested not in health, wholeness, and true agricultural potential but in whether the grocery stores have Cheese Doodles and frozen chicken alfredo dinners. If they do, and if we eaters have money, then apparently there is no problem and no cause for alarm.

But this is a species of consumer ignorance caused by abstraction—abstraction from the *source* that food comes from. And the source the food comes from, which is not money but nutrient-rich and biologically diverse soil capable of retaining water through salubrious and inhospitable seasons alike—*that* source is in serious jeopardy. It is being laid to waste, and the

---

* It is a curiosity of the word "abstract," at least as we use it, that it means something immaterial or highly abstruse. "Abstract" ideas are "over our heads," but in a metaphorical sense. And yet the word implies not an immaterial but a concrete physical distance—a distance *from*, "over our heads" in a literal sense. Descriptivist grammarians and lexicographers may say what they will about the word's current use; its history insists on *spatial* relation, and that history is instructive. Its root is the same one that gives us "tractor," a thing you can actually sit on but that puts real distance between the person sitting on it and the land he drives across.

eaters don't have a clue that this is happening. People who depend on soil and water have no idea that soil and water are vanishing, that topsoil is heading toward the Gulf of Mexico and that aquifers are running dry. Meanwhile, we who remain on what's left of this once-rich land must reconcile ourselves to such absurdities as Iowa: a beautiful state, mostly farmland, that does not feed itself.

For a farm state that imports close to ninety-percent of its food *is* an absurdity. There are farmers in such states, obviously, but by now a "farmer," more often than not, is someone who, beholden to policies and forces outside his control, must overproduce annual crops—corn and soy beans mostly—on land that no one actually lives *from* and that cannot bear the pressures of overproduction, at least not for long. In other words, the farmer, in order to make whatever meager and precarious living remains to him, is coerced into feeding a cornography addiction that, by now, is about as toxic as an addiction can get: our habits demand that there be ethanol for our gas tanks and high-fructose corn syrup for our sodas so that more of us can get fat and more of our children can become diabetics, with the correlative consequence that food must be shipped in to farmland that is being shipped out to the rivers, thence to the Gulf.*

People who raise food, by contrast, are "growers" whom policy and outside forces do not favor, and the foods that they raise are called "specialty crops." Many of these "growers" live in California, which has a nice long coastline but hardly enough water—

> Water, water everywhere,
> Nor any drop to drink,

as the stammering Sage of Highgate said.

It bears repeating: "specialty crops" were once called "food" (even as "health food" was once called "food"), and once upon a time these

---

* We must guard against oversimplification, but it is instructive to note that an ever-dwindling supply of oil is the energy source that makes this bizarre import-export business possible. For again: we import food into farm states that export their topsoil. And they export their topsoil (and also deplete their aquifers) because instead of producing their own food they raise annual monocultures that are ruinous to health, wholeness, and agricultural potential. It is also necessary to point out that since the industrialization of farming after World War II (which is in some measure the topic of this chapter) farmers have had little choice but to submit to whatever price has been set by large powerful buyers and then, as the cost of goods coming *to* the farm cancels out the price of goods *leaving* the farm—that is, as metastasizing expenses have squeezed out stagnating or shrinking profits—these same farmers have had to watch somewhat helplessly as the agricultural potential of their land vanishes.

"specialty crops" were raised everywhere on diversified farms. The emblem of these multicultural farms was the old barn. As Wes Jackson has pointed out, the hay loft of the old barn was a "'fuel tank' sponsoring meat, milk, and traction energy for draft animals." The lower story had "straw or hay for bedding, which captured manure and urine (nitrogen) to be returned to the fields [as fertility] via a manure spreader." That these beautiful old barns are falling down everywhere is a sobering reminder that diversified farming has been replaced by something far more simple and simplifying. The ammonia tank—that is, the sprayer filled with nitrogen-based fertilizer whose feed stock is natural gas—has replaced the free fertility absorbed by the straw and hay or freely dropped on pastures, and the diesel tank has replaced the barn loft.

But that description of the simple and simplifying replacement is itself too simple, though it is not for this reason untrue. It is a way of saying quickly that cheap energy, cheap money, and expensive machinery replaced people, that these three "inputs" caused a farm-to-city migration not only coeval with but in a real sense made possible by World War II. The Haber-Bosch process, a method of nitrogen fixation that made the production of ammonia fertilizer possible on a large industrial scale, was originally used by the Germans for explosives. Since then this war-faring technique has been used to wage war on the farm land over which there are too few eyes to keep watch. And there are too few eyes to keep watch *because* of this very process. It evicted the eyes because it displaced and evicted the people using them. Vigilance may be the eternal price of freedom, but it is also the eternal price of other things as well, including healthy soils. And, for want of vigilance, we no longer have healthy soils. What we will do for fertility once the natural gas runs out is simply another one of those problems apparently scheduled for solution by people too clever to be wise. Progress is their religion, and they are the happy-slappy fundamentalists who practice it. Even the Jumpin' Jesus people at *Shout!* Ministries have a more sophisticated religion than this.

Thoreau said "simplify simplify!" He wasn't wrong to do so. He meant something like "reduce the distractions in your life." But the thing about life is that it is complex, not simple, and to be equal to it we must complexify our thinking. Our thinking may never be as complex as topsoil, but we shouldn't for this reason accept falsification as an acceptable trade-off for Jack-and-Jill thinking.

The wager we have placed is this: fossil fuels and the artificial fertility we have concocted from them will be available forever, even though they exist in limited supplies on a finite planet. That is, we have bet the farm not on a long shot but on an absurdity.

And it's not only that we've put all our money on this, though we have. It's that we've staked the lives of our children on the proposition that, so long as there's money, and so long as money has the magical power to conjure food, there is no need for the old knowledge that ran the diversified farm or for the intelligence that designed the barn where dwelt a genuine diversity and multiculturalism, without which the ideological kinds that our "intellectuals" are so obsessed with don't have a chance.

I pause for emphasis. Take away the real and necessary diversity and multiculturalism—the biological kind that actual life depends upon—and the ideological kinds that university careers and book contracts and course proposals depend upon will become even less relevant than they are now—which hardly seems possible, but there you have it. Only people abstracted from true agricultural potential could think themselves outside its sovereign reach and free to invent alternative versions of it. Is it any wonder that screen-addled narcissists who have never dug potatoes or bred sheep need to go on university-sponsored retreats to "find" themselves? Is it any wonder that their professors have to keep inventing new categories of identity, or that colleges and universities have to set aside safe places for young people to tickle each another in as they perform the ritual stunts of self-discovery, orphaned and untutored, cut off from all considerations of fecundity, consequence, and natural law? A migration back to the farm and its honest manual labor might obviate the need for some of this expensive therapy. And if I leave aside the fact that it might also teach the obtuse econ major something about nature's law of return, which, being nature's law rather than man's, provides no loopholes or exemptions and casts considerable doubt on the wisdom of "externalizing" costs—if I leave all that aside, it is only to say that a migration back to the farm might reduce the number of psychoses that enrich therapists, counselors, pharmaceutical companies, and Swiss surgeons, to say nothing of professors in gender studies. It might mean that we haven't altogether abandoned our children, who are otherwise being ushered into a world that would merely be meaningless were it not also false. For it's not a very productive farm where the bull doesn't know his business around the cows. He can tickle another bull, I suppose, if there's another bull that will let him, but don't expect to see a surfeit of burgers and milkshakes. Don't expect a new Gilbert White to come along and marvel at the intricate design and fecundity of *that* natural economy.

I will be accused of bigotry, of course, mostly by sophisticates who, free from bigotry themselves, have risen above the need to dig potatoes and breed sheep (though I notice they still need to eat and be clothed). But I intend no judgment of persons, who by dint of personhood merit love, respect, and forbearance. I'm simply pointing out that Nature works in a particular way and doesn't give a damn what we think. She doesn't adjust her ways to accommodate our preferences. She gets a seat at every negotiating table. The sooner we get our minds around that, the better.

But I *am* suggesting that the Haber-Bosch process has caused more mischief than has been accounted for. And this is a commentary not only on the mind-forged manacles of our academic disciplines, and not only on the illusions of progress and technology that those disciplines perpetuate, but also on the grim logic of war, whether against "enemies" or Nature herself, who, to judge by our treatment of her, is apparently the greatest enemy of all.

VII
Fasting (Sort of)

Sharpen thy sickle, which thou hast blunted through gluttony—sharpen it by fasting. Lay hold of the pathway which leads toward heaven; rugged and narrow as it is, lay hold of it, and journey on.

—St. John Chrysostom

32

Against Breakfast

Like Bruce Jenner, breakfast ain't what it used to be. (Whoops! Did I write that? I only meant to Jimmy Carter it.) I've been told it is the most important meal of the day more times than I've eaten it, and for about thirty years I have been showing my respect for the established orthodoxy by skipping breakfast. On many days two cups of strong French roast coffee do a nice job of carrying me to the evening meal, and anyone who tells you I'm killing myself works for Kellog's or some other corporation whose strength lies in exploiting human weakness.

Charity requires that we allow for diabetics, of course, and people with goofy thyroids. But if you're not a diabetic and you believe all this blather about "eating modest amounts at proper intervals throughout the day," you're a sucker. You're crediting people who are schooled not in food, which is interesting, but in nutrition, which isn't. These are the same scolds who don't drink water; they "hydrate." They also act as if thirst has nothing to do with drinking water. They'll tell you to pound water all day long until your eyeballs float away and assure you that this is normal behavior for creatures endowed with the capacity to walk upright and contemplate the heavens. They've forgotten their Thoreau: "Instead of three meals a day, if it be necessary eat but one." (It's true he also said "instead of a hundred dishes, five," but that was probably owing to too much Emersonianism in his bloodstream.) As the Good Book says, these nutrition ninnies have a form of godliness but deny the power thereof. From such turn away.

My children eat breakfast dutifully, as directed, just as I did when I was young. But when I became a man I put away childish things, such as the Breakfast of Champions. I can't point to any moment in time to mark the change any more than you can look at the human digestive system and identify the precise spot where food ends and shit begins. All I know is that for me breakfast began to lose its appeal fairly early on. It happened somewhere in that long stretch of years between the time a certain decathlete made the front of the Wheaties box and the moment he decided to set his sights on the cover of Fruit Loops.

I acknowledge that my dissent from Official Nutritional Expertise doesn't play well at your average B&B, where a smothering matron can feed you enough before 8:00 a.m. to last you the twelve days of Christmas. But I stand firm. For all across this blubbery nation of ours you can find people, all of them steatopygous, who will warn you against "skipping breakfast," as if doing so were a breach of conduct equal to knocking up a cheerleader.

Such people are deeply confused. Invite them to climb a mountain with you if you doubt this. They won't make it to base camp. I've hiked all over the Lake District on nothing more than bad English coffee in the morning and small Cumbrian beer the night before, all the while listening to undergraduates not half my age puling about where the next meal was going to come from.

The truth is, we adults need less food than we think we need. Nor is breakfast the most important meal of the day. For starters, it would be in bad taste to mix an Old Fashioned while you're stirring pancake batter, and no meal that precludes the *cocktail préparatoire* even begins to meet the minimum requirements for Most Important Meal of the Day. I'll lay good money on the proposition that people who disagree with me "struggle with their weight," which means they're also in danger of becoming dupes to the exercise gurus and are probably no more than one or two intellectual errors away from taking up the "desperate procedure of jogging," as Jim Harrison has well said. I say this as a former distance runner.

So let's be clear about breakfast fact #1: the earlier you eat, the earlier you will get hungry again. And the earlier you get hungry again, the earlier you'll eat again. And the earlier you eat again, the more you'll "struggle with your weight." And the more you do that the more likely you are to be robbed by someone selling motorized treadmills and stairclimbers, as if these abominations were adequate substitutes for the out-of-doors and the work by which we inhabit the out-of-doors meaningfully. (Harrison again:

"An adjunct wonder to an obsession with the natural world is that you don't have to become involved with exercise as a parody of work.")

For this is strict theology: whereas pressing through the first desire makes pressing through the second much easier, giving in to the first makes giving in to the second a piece of cake. Consider Hamlet, you who doubt me, and

> Assume a virtue if you have it not.
> That monster, custom, who all sense doth eat,
> Of habits devil, is angel yet in this:
> That to the use of actions fair and good
> He likewise gives a frock or livery
> That aptly is put on. Refrain tonight,
> And that shall lend a kind of easiness
> To the next abstinence, the next more easy.

Of course you don't *start* with the loins. You start with the belly and work your way up. Actually, that would be working your way down, but you get the point: crawl first; walk later. Whoso governs the belly can hope to govern the other appetites. This is not a new teaching. It is basic asceticism.

Am I joking? The Bar Jester never jokes. Not only can we live on far less. We *ought* to live on far less. Certainly we must make allowances for those of differing metabolisms and blood-sugar tolerances, but that doesn't mean that everything is therefore on the table. Take this, for example: breakfast is not the breaking of a fast. You are not fasting if you're asleep. You're *sleeping*. If you want to fast, fast while you're awake, and break the fast once you've achieved a true degree of deprivation, which can be achieved only when you are awake and conscious of how miserable you are.

I say all this fully willing to credit the dissenting view of Jim Harrison, because I take it as a matter of moral principle that you should smile upon those who disagree with you so long as their manner of expression merits your admiration. Why else read G.B. Shaw or Christopher Hitchens? Besides, they both know the truth now. Harrison scourges the French for supposing that "a croissant or baguette with coffee is enough for breakfast." This is "idiotic and certainly accounts for all the flaring tempers in France in the hour before lunch, by which time people are dazed by low blood sugar and howling with hunger pangs." With obvious relish Harrison relays the anecdote about being at his cabin and taking a two-hour walk at dawn before fishing for about twenty minutes, after which he has "the classic breakfast of beans, bacon, and trout." But he's not talking about the baguette and coffee that "must presume absolute nonmovement" or a morning of mere paper-shuffling. Eating the "classic breakfast of beans, bacon, and trout" assumes inhabiting the earth, not the cubicle. "I've been advised so often in France to save myself for lunch," he says (and here he might have added "like some blushing maiden 'saving herself for marriage'"), "but what good is that if you have to sink your teeth into your arm for a pick-me-up?"

I'll admit to doing the same myself—making a hearty breakfast after an early-morning hike or after doing vigorous early-morning work—but I've also set out working early in the morning, and I mean working, not teaching or writing or balancing a checkbook, and never stopped once until suppertime. My father-in-law, even as I write, is in his eighties, hearty as a line-backer, and he sometimes does the same thing. (And then sometimes he'll put a can of chunky Campbell's soup on the manifold of his John Deere; it makes a nice lunch once it's been heated up, provided there's a spoon and a can-opener in the cab of the tractor.) But the point is that being hungry doesn't mean you need to eat. No biological urge requires immediate satisfaction. Hamlet again:

> What is a man,
> If his chief good and market of his time
> Be but to sleep and feed? a beast, no more.

Those who answer every biological urge as if it were a pernicious "mobile device" vibrating to life and clamoring for immediate attention are nymphos, the sexual equivalents of diabetics doubly afflicted with turbocharged thyroids. We can feel sorry for them, and do, but we're not going to base our laws on their behavior. Nature, not the deviation from Nature, is the standard.

Now, having said all this, I would nevertheless say a word or two in favor of breakfast, which, as a gastronomic category, is a fine thing if you know what you're doing (it affords us an opportunity to eat bacon, after all), even though it's far less important than people say.

Perhaps you think I will speak in favor of a light fare, or a "continental" breakfast, whatever the hell that is, or a sophisticated early morning repast involving such foreign words as "muesli" or "yogurt." (Rumpole, looking in horror at muesli: "What's that? Sawdust and bird droppings?") I assure you I'll endorse no such thing. I'd sooner sing the praises of soccer, next to which even NASCAR is interesting.

Be ye an amused friend or an annoyed enemy, look for evidence of a posterial tibial pulse. Seeing one, think freely of eggs—of *eggs*—and stay tuned, for I vow to make your arse on the matins satins stir with religious fervor. You may even find yourself back in the sack for a morning frolic, all thanks to the Bar Jester, his statins, and his culinary charity.

33

For Breakfast

In my preceding treatise, O Theophilus, I spoke ill of breakfast, which many people—not a few of them nutritional "experts"—wrongly regard as the most important meal of the day. I also made plain my own correct opinion on the matter at hand, *viz.*, that two cups of dark-roast coffee are all a man needs each day to get him to the evening meal.

Coffee! As the sweet singer of Israel said, *Ecce quam bonum!* Behold, how good and joyful a thing it is, for brethren to dwell together in caffeine!

Allowances were made (and the demands of charity thereby answered) for persons of peculiar constitutions—your average diabetic and thyroid spastic—but the thrust of the piece was that breakfast, even the breakfast of champions, is for Olympic decathletes and other sissies. And trust me, you righteous ones, you white-washed sepulchers, you censorious scolds with your licked fingers held up to the winds of public opinion, you who have girded your loins and mustered up the remarkable courage to think what everyone else thinks—trust me, I say: there's nothing distinctive about being the first woman to appear on a Wheaties box.

However, I did add that breakfast "is a fine thing if you know what you're doing," and I promised that I would make your "arse on the matins satins stir with religious fervor"—all "thanks to the Bar Jester, his statins, and his culinary charity." And here we are already.

So get your eggs ready, ladies!

Ah, the egg. The chicken egg. Perfectly designed for moving smoothly through a narrow corridor and onto a man's plate. Is there anything like it in structure, function, flavor, color, or texture? There isn't (not counting the hop). As future chicken, as *pollo prolepsis*, it is excellent; as food *now* it is perfect.

Mind you, the egg doesn't stand alone any more than the cheese. It flourishes best with butter and salt and . . . well, let's get on with it.

You want farm fresh eggs. You want eggs that come from chickens that are (as I heard a guy in a bar say once, though I paraphrase) "free to run and peck and screw other chickens." If you have never done a side-by-side taste test with, on the one hand, those nasty mass-produced yellow-yolked flavorless store-bought eggs and, on the other hand, the noble orange-yolked farm-fresh eggs from farmer Jim up yonder or from your own laying hens, conduct such a test. Do one tomorrow. From the cracking of the shell to the look of the egg to the taste thereof you will notice marked differences like those that differentiate day from night, truth from error, and Lonnie from Sparky Anderson. Farmer Jim's egg, which has a brown or a green shell, will be to your tongue what the *AV* is to your ears. The white-shelled egg from the Try 'n Save will offend you like the *NIV* and the '79 Prayer Book.

Now there are many ways to prepare eggs: you can scramble them; you can whip them into an omelet; you can baste them; you can prepare them "over easy." An unscrambled egg with a yolk broken or cooked hard is an abomination, like a shapely girl in a loose sweater and baggy pants. A hard-boiled egg is another matter altogether, and although it's a beautiful thing *per se* and not to be disparaged entirely, it is not normally recommended for breakfast for the simple reason that it hasn't observed the rule of "not too much," where "not too much" means: not too much time on the heat. Or, to speak plainly, a hard-boiled egg has been over-cooked. (Nothing should ever be over-cooked, and everything except chicken and turkey should be undercooked, even pork a little.)

Another thing: whereas evening cooking requires music, morning cooking requires silence. Don't disturb your thoughts with radio or television or music or anything—except on Saturdays when "Car Talk" is on. We are talking about morning, my friend. *Morning.* Preserve and respect the morning silence that so perfectly complements the morning darkness. (Thoreau: "Morning is when I am awake and there is a dawn in me." "I have a great deal of company in the house, especially in the morning when nobody calls.") Tonight you can crank up Hornsby when you're making your carbonara and sipping your Woodford Reserve, but for now let the kitchen be still. Let the day unfold in your imagination like a cracked farm-fresh egg.

Okay. As for scrambled eggs: some people will tell you to add a little milk to them. *Big* mistake—like asking Bruce Springsteen where he was born, or asking Sting what he's sending out (or agreeing to call anyone "Sting"). You want eggs? Eat eggs, not eggs-plus-milk.

Whip the eggs in whatever's at hand—a recently-used but rinsed-out coffee mug will do just fine—with nothing more than a fork. Butter your favorite breakfast pan over medium heat, add the eggs, scramble them, and take them out while they're still good and runny. This is important. Fluffy scrambled eggs are ruined scrambled eggs. Dark and runny and orange is what you're after. Salt to taste and eat them with gratitude and buttered toast. Sausage patties are also a nice touch—and a pound of bacon a nicer one.

If you would increase your gratitude, mix the scrambled eggs with a serving of well-buttered and well-salted grits. Properly undercooked scrambled eggs mixed with grits prove the existence of God almost as much as mini-skirts and tank-tops do. You can even crumble a little bacon into the mix. Into the mix of grits and eggs, I mean. It won't go particularly well with mini-skirts and tank-tops—at least not in the long run.

(And who, I ask, in the beaten way of friendship, who could eat grits without thinking of the great Roy Blount, Jr.?

> True grits,
> more grits,
> Fish, grits and collards.
> Life is good where grits are swallered.)

And at what time of the morning in particular is this concoction best consumed? All I can say is it makes a great supper on Sunday nights, especially in the winter when the kids have been out sledding and you have been reading fireside all afternoon.

As for the over-easy egg: again, butter the pan on medium heat. Crack your eggs and leave them be. Don't flip them until you can see the whites around their eyes. But when you can, carefully flip the eggs and immediately remove the pan from the heat. Give the eggs about one *Pater Noster*, maybe less, stopping at the kingdom and the power and the glory, and remove them from the pan. Let them sit atop a pile of heavily buttered hash browns or American fries or maybe squarely on a piece of buttered toast or a buttered English muffin. Rupture the yolk and let the orange loveliness spill all over the place. Eat with gratitude &c.

You will notice that nowhere is margarine or spray or some other devilish unbuttery substitute permitted in the cooking. The reason: we were made to eat food, not chemical imitations of it.

And as for the omelet: there are many ways to ruin this great thing, chief among them adding milk and cramming in too many ingredients. The trick is to minimize the flavors. You don't want your omelet tasting like a taco or like salsa and chips. To satisfy your craving for tacos or salsa and chips there are other options, such as tacos or salsa and chips. A good omelet will have no more than four or five flavors in addition to the eggs and the butter they're cooked in plus salt, and even four or five is pushing it.

So: lay by your preferred ingredients and whip some eggs, as per the instructions above. Into a buttered pan between six and nine inches in base diameter add (for the perfect omelet) cubed ham. Toss it a bit and then add the eggs. Then add some shredded cheddar cheese. And then into the pan carefully place about a dozen capers. Place them artfully. And be sure they're spaced such that you'll get a couple in each bite.

And I guess we'd better allow for some chopped onion or shallot.

Once the egg has cooked (you might have to swirl it about a bit), flip half the omelet over onto the other half so that you've got a half circle. Grab the pan by the handle. Move the pan away from and toward you until the whole creation moves as one living being in the pan. And then flip it. Flip it by . . . well, teach yourself the motion that makes this possible. A little imagination and you'll have it.

The caper! Who would have thought it belonged in an omelet? But, O Theophilus, it does.

Add salt and pepper and eat with gratitude, &c.

For the nonce I leave aside such glorious egg-great wonders as Eggs Benedict: an English muffin in a thick garment of Canadian bacon, a poached egg lovingly placed thereon and drizzled o'er with hollandaise sauce—that yolky buttery marvel with its tangy bite of lemon and white wine vinegar subtly qualified by an implication of Worcestershire sauce—and at the end a tiny little shower of chopped chive. A man could have an accident just thinking about it! It's enough to make me change my mind about those two cups of French roast that get you to the evening meal. But I might have to postpone considering this grand work of kitchen art until after my Saw Bones has increased my statin dosage from six to ten truckloads per day.

I have departed somewhat from the usual Culinary Plagiarist slash Bar Jester formula. There is nothing in the way of aural stimulation, and there are few promissory gestures along the lines of country matters, as the Lord Hamlet called them. That is because we have been treating of breakfast, which is a lesser thing in the culinary scheme and which, as my former treatise demonstrated, is not by any means the breaking of a fast.

And that, really, is the point, I'm afraid. A really good feast is always made better by a penitential season of fasting. Sleep is no such season.

Ah, sleep—

> Sleep that knits up the ravell'd sleeve of care,
> The death of each day's life, sore labour's bath,
> Balm of hurt minds, great nature's second course,
> Chief nourisher in life's feast—

sleep, O Theophilus, is matter for another chapter. The one thing we do know about it is that there will be sleep enough in the grave, as I believe Ben Franklin once said.

34

And Now For a Little Abstinence; or, Approach to Clean Monday #1

Many good folks receive the imposition of ashes on Ash Wednesday. Across the Bosporus others will have been suffering for a couple of days already—I mean on those rare occasions when the calendars of the Christian East and West coincide.

And may I pause here for a moment to say how nice it would be if the Christian world would get its damned act together on this matter? How difficult, really, would that be? How difficult would it be to get Easter and Pascha to coincide each year? Put the Pope and the Ecumenical Patriarch together in my kitchen on, say, the Feast of the Annunciation, and after a fine repast of Michigan rainbow trout stuffed with garlic, onions, and Hungarian peppers (pre-softened in a butter-and-white-wine reduction on the stovetop—with salt and a little lemon juice added to stave off ancient heresy), then skewered back together and grilled over coals or hardwood—do all that with the biggest of the Holy Big Shots in my kitchen, and I'll fix the ecclesiastical fiasco in no fewer than two ouzos, which are permitted on the Annunciation. There will be no more regarding the high-priestly prayer as grim Johannine irony. I'll have us in full communion, by God!

Anyway, nothing like Clean Monday, clean *foodless* Monday, to remind you of the misery you're in for. Hearty souls—nay, hearty souls and bodies, *especially* bodies—may make Tuesday fully clean as well, and maybe Wednesday and Thursday right on down to the Sunday of Orthodoxy, that triumphal day appointed to celebrate the restoration of the holy icons and to vindicate the flesh, which God Himself assumed and then died in.

That first Monday in Lent can be unpleasant, especially if, like me, you usually use non-Lenten Mondays to whip up something elaborate and adorn it with an airy liquid obbligato not untouched by the juniper berry.

But, oddly enough, by Tuesday the body already somehow enjoys its abstinence and even suffers it more easily. The mind, as usual, sharpens; the intention of the inner man asserts itself more forcefully. The mind's camera is once again trained on something clearly in focus. You undergo a deliverance of sorts. You understand what the poet meant by "world's and flesh's rage," for their rage has abated noticeably. You understand what that Jewish rabble-rouser was getting at with all his righteous pique about not living by bread alone. "Clean" is the right word so far as the body is concerned. Of course cleanliness must extend to the inner man as well, but for the moment I am concerned only with the body, for the body is the first to feel the bracing Lenten slap.

And that's the proper order and direction of things—outside in; through the flesh, through the material world, to what's inside it: the athletic penetration of the finite. Even Dr. Johnson, who, according to Boswell, relished his food as no other, said that if you give no thought to the belly you won't be able to give much thought to anything else. (I'll lay odds that Dr. Johnson never skipped a meal and that he was a slovenly eater, but that doesn't make him wrong.)

How quickly, then, does the sting of that initial blow fade, and how comfortably does the joy of the season of bright sorrow settle in. According to the canticles appointed for today, this is a "light-giving season of abstinence"; "the fast shines upon all of us more brightly than the sun."

There will be days when we don't think so, for although it is true that we live not by bread alone, we live by it plenty nonetheless. Bread and cantaloupe and T-bones and IPA.

IPA! Why hast thou forsaken me?

Because, O my soul, and thou my throbbing flesh, it is too easy to forsake all others for IPA. Look you then! A grim glass of water (behold it there!) at the Barless Jester's elbow. But how elegant it looks in the dim light, how pure, how like that very thing the Great Fast proposes to us and puts so abundantly on offer.

This desert in the calendar, this frozen landscape in time, always makes me think of a buddy of mine who, nearing the end of his first Lent among the Greeks—he was a convert from Canterbury not entirely prepared for how miserably the Greeks do music—turned to me and said, "Gosh! 'Dox Lent is sodding long!" And so it is. It is longer than the one celebrated by our brothers and sisters who had to go and fiddle with the creed way back. But, long or short, Lent's genius is that it *goes* somewhere. It is a journey that, like any journey, starts somewhere and ends somewhere else. And, as always—as we learn from the Pentateuch and St. Augustine and Chaucer and Graham Greene—the purpose of the journey is transformation; the purpose is to be made worthy of the feast that awaits us.

And I know, mostly from failure, that that doesn't happen without intention. It doesn't happen without our availing ourselves of the best-kept weight-loss secret in the world. (You want to stay trim? Keep liturgical time vigilantly.)

Am I thinking right now about steak tartare and a glass brimming with an inky purple Amarone? Damn straight I am! But that's a longing proper to a man, so long as he can convert it into a true longing with a proper object. Like everything we touch and taste and see and hear and smell, meat and drink are but penultimate things, for there's always something *on the other side of them*. Or you could say they are an *outside* with an *inside*. The trick is to pass from the one to the other. The trick is the athletic penetration of the finite. I've used that phrase twice now. Since we're in a penitential season I should mention that I stole it from Fr. William Lynch. It's in a fine essay titled "Theology and the Imagination," which appeared in *Thought* back in 1954.

But first we must know, we must get it into our heads, *that the world is made thus*, made not of objects or idols (for they have no insides) but of images, images that by definition bear the stamp of something else. And we must treat these images—we must treat the world—not with contempt but with reverence. We must embrace things. It is even fitting that we should kiss them.

I knock back the last of the water, loving it for what it is and for what it is not but especially for what *else* it is and what it might become. And what do we hear in one of the canticles appointed for tonight? "O my soul, pass through the flowing waters of time like the Ark of old, and take possession of the land of promise."

But hurry the hell up, will you?

35

Lenten Humility, Bar Jester Style; or, Approach to Clean Monday #2

Or, rather, Barless Jester Style. There aren't any bars in my immediate future, because we're into it now, and I don't mean March Madness (though that's coming—and may the teams that God and I despise lose early and often). I don't mean spring either, because the cruelest month is not yet upon us, and there's always the strong possibility that it will strike like an avenging demon.

I mean the period of bright sorrow. I mean Lent: that season that seems to go on and on and on interminably. This is a journey that can make folks meatless in Seattle. It can cause men at sea to lose their beerings. In Green Bay it has been known to turn lactose-tolerant Cheeseheads into NonDairyCheeseSubstituteHeads. Were it possible, the bright sorrow would rename "Bourbon Street" "Street" and promote lentil soup from inedible to staple—all this even as the denizens of local bars go silent on the topic of my mysterious disappearance, less saddened than embarrassed, maybe, by my apparent and sudden death. Thank God there's a joke to mitigate the discomfort.

What? You don't know the one about the Irishman?

Seems there was this Irishman who went into a pub one day and ordered three pints of Guinness and then proceeded to drink them: a sip from one, a sip from the second, then a sip from the third, and then back through the sequence until all three pints were empty. He did this every time he went into this pub until one day the bartender said, "Okay, Mick. I'll bite. Why do you always order three pints of Guinness and then drink them like that?"

The Irishman said, "Well, me two brothers and me are all scattered across the country now and can no longer go to the poobs t'gether, so we all agreed that each time we did go to a poob we would arder up three pints and at least pretend we were drinking t'gether, like in the ald days."

The bartender and all the regulars agreed that this was a very sensible way to deal with the lamentable scourge of hypermobility that had separated the O'Malley brothers, who obviously loved one another very much. And so each time the Irishman came into the pub, the bar tender, being a good bar tender, drew three pints of Guinness and set them down in front of the Irishman.

But one day, before he could set the pints down on the bar, the Irishman asked for only two pints. There was some embarrassment at this, naturally, for everyone assumed that one of the O'Malley lads had died. After about two or three visits to the pub during which the Irishman ordered only two pints, the bar tender at last said, "Jesus, Mary, and Joseph, Mick. I'm really sorry about your brother."

"What about me brother?"

"Well, you've been drinking only two pints now for a while. We all figured one of your brothers had, you know, passed."

"Me brothers are fine," the Irishman said. "It's just that I've given up drinking fer Lent."

It's no fun, Lent. And, although there are many reasons this is so, one reason stands out above all the others: Lent isn't meant to be fun—in the same way that church isn't meant to be entertaining. (What, for the love of Zeus, does *leitourgia* translate into, "movie night"?) But be of good cheer. There are ways to make the bright sorrow worse, and there are people who can help you do it.

You Westerners especially need help, what with that wimpy forty-day deal you do. The smudge that makes everyone so self-conscious has barely been absorbed into the forehead, and poof! You're half-way to chocolate bunnies. What you need is something equal to what in the East, as I mentioned in the previous chapter, is called "Clean Monday"—plus the resolve to do what, frankly, few of your Dox bruthren and sistern do, which is observe the day by using your mouth for breathing and speaking only (and maybe a little water).

Now that's not much fun if you enjoy preparing food and eating it, which, I confess, I do. But it can seem like a decent idea if, like me, you opened an eye on the couch at 11:45 Sunday night, a book resting on your chest, became aware of your situation, sprang to your feet, and raced to the kitchen to make an emergency plate of nachos. After *that* midnight snack Clean Monday can seem like a really good idea, for it is very easy at the stroke of twelve, as you lie there on the couch, bloated and lethargic like a boa that has just swallowed a sheep, to say to yourself as you lick fingers eight, nine and ten, "Clean Monday"—smack, smack, smack—"here I come."

But Monday has ideas of its own, and it isn't long before you're pining for the fleshpots of Sunday (or Fat Tuesday, take your pick).

So the thing to do is *increase* your misery. When it's time for the Monday evening meal, when it becomes clear that the kids must be fed even though you've determined—and so far succeeded—to use your own mouth for breathing and speaking only (and maybe a little water), do this to yourself: chop some onion and toss a little butter in a pan over low heat. You can drizzle some olive oil over the butter if you want to. This is for aesthetic purposes mostly.

Now the kids must be taught to fast, but they must be taught piecemeal and with intelligence. You're not going to hold them to your standards and you're certainly not going to make them even more miserable than you are as the hour of homework, that Great Intruder, approaches.

So you treat them to something you'd really like to sink your carnivorous incisors into: dead pig. Mind: you must speak to them as you all sit down to eat (or not eat) about their own *askesis*, but you can't starve the children. There are State and Federal agencies that frown on this, and they're watching you. Plus you're increasing your own misery, so that's good.

Into the buttered pan go the onions and then, after about five minutes, a pound of sweet Italian pork sausage. Break it up and toss it until it's no longer pink. Sprinkle in . . . no! Wait! There's another way to make yourself more miserable.

Pour a glass of *water!* Ah, see how it doesn't catch the slant of evening light? Behold how, when you swirl it, no tempting aroma rises to your nostrils! Take three long pulls off the thick tumbler. Wait. Feel that? Feel the collision of Nothing and gray matter? That's your brain not reacting to ETOH. That's the water not elevating you a hair's breadth above the earth. It's a wretched way to spend a Monday. Suddenly you feel much better about feeling much worse.

Now back to the skillet. Sprinkle in some chopped garlic and maybe some sliced mushrooms. Stir briefly—long enough to release the scent of the garlic and multiply your dolor. Be good to yourself and take another hit of water, neat.

Into the skillet go about two cups of chicken stock and a cup of cream. For the sake of your own miserable soul you are letting the kids break the whole damn fast on the first day. Someone must think of the children. Bring this to a boil for a few minutes and then reduce the heat to simmering.

Italian seasoning? You're not having any, so why not?

And now about 12–16 ounces of rigatoni pasta: in they go. Cover. Set the timer for five minutes. After five minutes, uncover and stir. Cover again and set the timer for five more minutes. This is going to be awesome, and, best of all, you're not going to get to eat a single bite of it.

You think about pouring yourself another warm transparent water but remember that moderation is the desideratum here, so, difficult as it is, you resist the urge. You are in control of your desires and appetites.

The timer goes off. The children assemble. They notice that the table is one place-setting short.

"Daddy, who's not eating?"

"I'm not."

"How come?"

"Because I *want* to."

You let them puzzle this one out and offer up their gratitude, which they do. Then you spoon onto their plates this dish that looks and smells for all the world as if it might have been the main course in *Babette's Feast*.

"Daddy, isn't it Lent now?" asks the older boy.

"It is."

"Then how come we're having pork?"

"Isn't it obvious?"

"No."

"Because of the state of my miserable soul."

This is where the oldest one can be a pain in the arse. But pain, remember, is the point.

"So let me get this straight," she says. "You're giving us a cream-based pasta dish with pork—pass the parmesan, please—on the first day of Lent for the sake of your own, what do you call it, 'spiritual well-being'?"

And here is where your own barely-superior intelligence and slightly-greater powers of dialectic come in handy.

"No. I'm doing this for *your* 'spiritual well-being.' I want you to have someone to imitate. I want you to see what a great guy I am, all high and mighty and holier than thou. My belly's gurgling like a busted sump system with a conflicted float switch and a clogged check-valve, and still I make you this nice delicious aromatic meal only to watch you eat it. Behold my restraint, my discipline. You should grow up to be like your old man."

And here is where your oldest child's moral superiority proves inconvenient, to say the least.

"So you're using Clean Monday in an entirely self-serving manner to thwart any chances you might have at humility?"

"Who taught you to use the word "thwart"?

"You did."

"Not on *me*, I didn't."

"You didn't specify."

"*Specify?*"

"Daddy, you're losing. Admit it."

You think for a second. You're hungry. A forkful of that plus an inky wine would go down splendidly right now. It's time to turn misery to good account.

"Okay. You're right. Tomorrow you can have vegetable stir fry."

"And what about you?"

You think it over and decide one more day of Nothing might give you a fighting chance.

"The same," you say, thinking the word won't hang ambiguously in the air. But she's too smart for you, and a much better person.

"I think you'd better have *something*."

"Why?"

"We can't take much more of your humility."

"Nice supper," says the youngest one, who's been ignoring all this. "Thanks, Dad."

"What do we say?"

"You're the best that ever was!"

No. Actually, after dinner, we say the prayer of St. Ephraim:

> O Lord and Master of my life, take from me the spirit of sloth, despair, lust of power, and idle talk.

> But give rather the spirit of chastity, humility, patience, and love to Thy servant.

Yea, O Lord and King, grant me to see my own transgressions, and not to judge my brother, for blessed art Thou, unto ages of ages. Amen.

VIII
High Summer II

Oh, the luxury of lying in the fern night and the grass night and the night of susurrant, slumberous voices weaving the dark together.

—Ray Bradbury, *Dandelion Wine*

36

Cool as a Cucumber—In *This* Heat

The birds that land on our bird bath have their beaks open all the time. There's a look on their otherwise inscrutable visages that says, "what the *hell* is going on?"

And the squirrels, who only two days ago were going bat shit crazy in what appeared to be an orgiastic mating ritual, now sprawl motionless on whatever oak limbs they can colonize. And their repose isn't some opaque version of post-coital rodent exhaustion. I don't see any squirrels smoking cigarettes. These poor creatures are miserable. I can assure you as one who speaks Squirrel that they are all saying the same thing: "Jesus, take me now!"

At four this morning, when the devil decided I shouldn't sleep any more, the air temperature was eighty and the humidity at least eighty per cent. By nine-thirty, when I couldn't produce another word on whatever it is I'm trying to write, the air temperature was more than ten degrees warmer. We're promised at least a full week of temperatures above ninety-four. Explain this heat, you people so convinced by one ambiguous phrase in the prophecy of Jeremiah that God has a plan for *your* life in *particular*, because it can't be done—unless the plan is malevolent and sadistic, a design of darkness to appall, as the poet said.

There is a reason I left Tennessee in 1983 and Virginia in 1996, and, brother, *this* is it. And I'll tell you another thing: Here's one man who is already ready for God's season: winter.

Are you people who like this weather serious? Are you not in fact deranged? Snow—as in "though your sins be as scarlet they shall be white as snow"—is what the soul desires most of all, and not one second after the dog days arrive, which, let me tell you, they have.

I was in Riverside, California, once waiting to cross a street. The temperature was 113 degrees Fahrenheit. There was a local fellow standing next to me, also waiting, and I turned to him and said, "Is it always this hot here?" Astonished, he looked at me and said, "this isn't hot." Then what in the name of the mother of God *is* hot? Living in Riverside is not God's plan for my life. If it is, Mr. Big had better prepare for a battle of the wills.

Jordan Baker cried dismally, "Imagine marrying *anybody* in this heat." I'll one-up that bad driver: imagine *being* anybody in this heat.

Not to mention all my romas are getting a blight, which they are. I've tossed at least twenty young green—and partially black—tomatoes into the ravine, which I'm sure the sodding groundhog is greedily fattening himself on. (Little does he know that I've *tried* groundhog, and I know for a fact that it isn't much different from pot roast. That fat bastard had better watch his back.)

Well, under these conditions, there's nothing to do but reach for the cucumber.

That's right: cuke and tomato plus some feta cheese and crushed raw garlic. (Eat it the night before an early morning dentist appointment or a meeting with an administrator. See what kind of response you get.)

The garlic, too, is fresh from the garden. In fact, we're nearing the end of the harvest. Once again last fall we planted too little of it. Ah, garlic! How much easier it peels when it's right out of the ground. How moist! How full of "buzz off"! Is there anything better?

Now listen and hear and attend, O Best Beloved: Here is one of the best ways to enjoy the fruits of summer while pining for the stark beauty of God's season, which seems as if it will never get here. (I admit that it helps if the two older urchins have been pawned off on the grandparents, which they have, and if the little missus is at work keeping you in poker money, which she is. But these instructions are foolproof.) Tonight it's just you and the youngest, who's picky in his way but easy to please if you know what you're doing. And you do.

Observe, for example, with what alacrity and good taste you choose the music: The King's Singers Christmas album. Winter in July. If you were Richard Nixon you'd crank up the AC so you could have a fire in the White House fireplace. But the sweat rings under your arms don't quite reach Nixonian proportions, and this isn't the White House (you pay the bills, for example), so those counter tenors and a fireside tumbler will have to suffice.

You notice there are a couple of pieces of link sausage in the freezer. Jackpot. The boy will relish them. You'll chop and toss them into bowtie pasta and make a variation on bacon carbonara. He'll think you're father of the year, which you are.

Out back to cut a couple of sprigs of parsley. Quick! The Wicked Witch of the East or West or Wherever melted faster in air half this hot. (They weren't in Kansas anymore, but Kansas can't be this hot. *Can't* be.) Who—*who*—can countenance such heat? If Eden had been this hot, Adam and Eve would have disobeyed much sooner in exchange for exile somewhere north of the 45th parallel. And Aristotle? Aristotle would have said "*damn* human flourishing, Nicomachus. Nothing's flourishing in this goddamned sonofabitching heat."

If you can't stand the heat, get back in the kitchen. *Locum refrigerii!* Make a drink—one of my summer favorites: an inch of grapefruit juice over which I pour a can of Coke. Grapefruit allegedly interferes with my statins, but so does my diet. So does life, so who cares. If you haven't tried grapefruit juice and Coke, do it.

Into the pan over low heat go the sausages; into another, also over low heat, go water, olive oil, and salt. Why low heat? No hurry! People who hurry when they don't have to should be sent elsewhere, like hell, which, as their luck would have it, isn't this hot.

Okay. Sing along with "Veni, Veni." What an arrangement! And what pitch!

Chop the parsley and set it by. That's what, sixty seconds? You've got sixty seconds to give to your third-born and the King's Singers. Crack an egg, discard the whites, and drop the yolky mess into something cylindrical. Whip with a fork.

Wash the tomato. What a beautiful thing! And how it fits the lascivious hand! Cut it up into several small spoonable pieces in the way you like best. Into a blue bowl they go. Do you smell that? It's a tomato, and if it smells like a tomato you may eat it. If you cut into it and don't smell anything, it isn't a tomato. It's a red thing you bought in February or a blushing rock shipped in from far away. Feed it to the groundhog, who (you never know; times are tough) might later feed you.

And now for the cuke. Feel those spikes? This isn't like those store-bought cukes, smooth and suggestive. This is a real cucumber. Skin it in your preferred way—knife, potato peeler, makes no difference to me. Just be sure that all scraps go into the compost bucket and that none goes into the garbage or down the disposal. We must pay our debt to the soil. We must *build* soil. From the compost bucket into the compost, thence to the ground, thence into next year's growth, thence into your belly. This is how life works. Death into life, life into death, death and resurrection, on and on and on. There are people who don't think so—they are called "economists"—but they're wrong. (Don't worry, though. What harm, after all, can powerful people who don't admit nature into their system do?)

Slice the cuke lengthwise down the middle, then halve the halves. Chop up the quarters into spoonable sizes and add them to the tomatoes. Then crumble in some feta and reach for the fresh moist garlic. Peel and press. Tomorrow all kinds of people will ignore you. And this, you think, is a perfect plan. Who needs other people? *L'enfer, c'est les autres.*

Into the mix go the pressed garlic plus fresh-ground black pepper plus salt, plus—confound it! Almost forgot the fresh oregano. Back outside to cut a few sprigs of fresh oregano. Jeebus, it's hot. Into the bowl goes the fresh oregano. And into all of that goes the most local olive oil you can find. Italy might have to do. This is the Dumb-Ass's version of the Greek salad. Add or don't add Kalamata olives and red onion. I'm good with the salad as I've made it.

But shee-it! I forgot about the boy!

Whew! His sausage isn't burned, nor are his noodles over-boiled. Remove the sausage and slice it. Strain the pasta. Count forty and add the egg. Stir. Add a couple of spoonfuls of cream; add the sausage chunks and chopped parsley, and stir again. Supply him with a few pieces of salted cuke and some feta. The tomato, you know, he won't touch. The boy's good to go. He'll read to *himself* tonight. Call him to dinner.

Oh, the heart aches at the sight of him as he rounds the corner. What a boy! What a creature! He washes, settles into his chair, and, at the site of his plate, produces a smile a mile wide.

Despair is everywhere these days but not at your table tonight. You offer gratitude where gratitude is due and partake of earth's goodness. May the Earth cool soon.

Which it will, whereupon you'll ask winter to delay itself just a bit—at least until all the tomatoes ripen and the whole family is at last restored to the table it belongs to. Soon you'll all be cool as cucumbers—and soon enough as cold as the grave.

37

The Pick-Up and the Pasta

The pasta concoction invented on the fly begins in the engine compartment of an '83 Dodge Ram pickup truck, a.k.a The Babe Magnet, although to say when exactly anything begins is always tricky business.

Maybe it begins that day in January long ago when I change out the coil in air that at its zenith hits a mere nine degrees above zero—after which the truck still won't start. Or maybe it all begins a bit later, when I decide that swapping out the entire distributor in such weather ought properly to be done by someone *else*—someone who actually knows what he's doing *and* has a heated space to do it in. (After that particular decision, and what a wise one it was, I looked out the window through the snow at the motionless truck—helpless, vulnerable, forsaken—and, as if to ratify the deal, sat down by the fire to read. It was a great day in the bleak mid-winter.) Or maybe it begins when I buy the truck in the early '90s, or when my father meets my mother, or when my grandparents elope.

Hell! Maybe it begins when Eve says to Adam, "eat the apple, Bucko, or sleep in your own banana tree from now on."

At any rate, it begins. Cause leads to effect that, in turn, becomes the cause of other effects, and also defects, and somewhere down the causal chain I am putzing around in my garage, high summer at full throttle, occasionally casting malevolent glances through the rain at a truck that will start only on dry days of low humidity.

But then, as if by divine intention, "Afternoon Delight" comes on the garage radio, and *that*, let me tell you, gets me thinking down the usual tracks: there must be something wrong with that brand new distributor cap—and, to boot, we're going to need a good starchy side dish to take to dinner.

For—cards on the table—being ass-up in the engine cavity of an old truck and looking at a convoluted spaghetti-like tantalus of plug wires conduces perfectly to inventing new summer pasta dishes. How the grease reminds you of olive oil! How the grime puts you to thinking of fresh-ground black pepper!

Or, to be as plain as I can be, cause leads to effect that, in turn, becomes the cause of other effects, and also defects, and somewhere down the causal chain there I am, called upon to please two women in a single afternoon: one, my wife, who very much wants me to return the truck to its wonted reliability—so that I will quit pestering her about buying a slightly newer one; the other, my buddy's wife, who very much wants us to bring a pasta dish to accompany the pork shish kabobs her husband will be grilling and she'll be serving when we arrive at their house around six o'clock.

But oh the sins of a Sunday afternoon! How soon after partaking of the sacred mysteries can a man utter imprecations at a piece of innocent machinery when he ought instead to be throbbing with life and inventing a new (or tupping a familiar) summer dish!

Very soon, apparently. I have already come off a heavy penance imposed by a severe confessor ("my son, for your meanness you must read, cover to cover, *Atlas Shrugged*"), and yet there I am, so lately seraphic, so lately shriven and freshly fed from our Lord's bounteous table, but already accusing Chrysler workers from over a quarter-century ago of having been begotten upon female dogs that had somehow secretly scaled familial walls. There I am, asking an inarticulate coil wire (which on several occasions I have called a piece of fecal matter) why it won't seat properly. Behold me, demanding of a dumb extension cord why in the blanking blankety-blank it won't reach from the fornicating receptacle on the side of my house to the sodding battery charger . . . when lo! the new distributor cap snaps into place, and (could it be?) all the wires accord perfectly with the firing order on my diagram! I turn the key. The old Dodge jumps to life as if it had been made yesterday. Land rocket in flight! I'm ready to . . .

But wait! Ah, *damn it!* Oops. I close my eyes and bow my head. "Sorry, Christ Almighty. I meant to say 'Dodge Rammit!'" There remains the dish—and only thirty minutes until the ETD.

Well I've satisfied one woman; by God, I'll satisfy the other—even if it *is* Sunday.

Into the house to scrub & scour my hands.

"Daddy, will you play catch with . . ."

"Silence! Grease Monkey is creating!"

I paw through the pantry. Not much to work with but enough to make a safe bet if the basic principles be adhered to: (1) keep it simple and (2) keep it fresh.

Our friends and hosts, whom I'll call "Scott" and "Alexa" (because those are their names), know food pretty well and they know dullness when they taste it. Meals at their house usually sky rocket. And their bar and wine cellar are enough to make you believe in God. I have the sure confidence of a fine bourbon or a single-malt scotch or a premium martini awaiting me, so I can't exactly show up with Kraft mac-and-sleaze or Hambooger Helper.

The little missus and I are both in the kitchen now dealing with my Afternoon Neglect. It's going to be a team effort, because I've spent half the Lord's day profaning it, and she, I think, has spent the other half resting—not that there's anything wrong with that. Whatever the offenses of the immediate past, we're now complementing each other, thinking in blissful marital synchronicity about what to throw together—even as we playfully bump each other in the kitchen. Do we have enough of one kind of pasta to feed nine? We do. So exactly what will we put in it?

I think about the health of our herbs out back and say "oregano."

She agrees and asks about the peas.

"Yes!" I say. They're snap peas. I picked them yesterday. "And garlic."

"Okay. What else?"

"Do you mean, 'what else do you need a man for around here?'" (because, verily, I've fixed the '83 Dodge, I'm working on the side dish, and, as usual, she is a moving violation from head to heels).

Imagine this! She ignores what I've said!

"Capers," I say.

"The kids won't eat the capers."

I say, "your point being?"

She reminds me that the kids have to eat too.

Peas, oregano, and garlic then.

We chop up some fresh oregano from out back. The peas are already picked and waiting. We chop them in thirds, pods and all.

Chopped garlic—God's own bounty thereof—softens in butter on the stove, butter that improveth all things.

Has anyone ever written an ode to butter? (Note to self: write an Ode to Butter.)

Do we have enough parmesan? No. Asagio? No.

No matter. We have a little of both. We'll grate it all. We'll make America grate again.

The boil is done, the pasta oiled, the children summoned. We toss everything and look at it forlornly.

"The color ain't right," I say. "Sun dried tomatoes?"

We chop them up, add them, and send the recalcitrant urchins to the car. The color is much better now. Moreover, the gummy chew of the sun-dried tomatoes will offset the crunch of the raw peas. Accounts will balance.

But here's the question: will this be served warm or cold? We'll decide when we get there, which, when we get there—and thanks to a protracted cocktail hour of the sort prescribed in the New Testament, though I forget the exact reference—turns out to be cold.

And the dish ain't bad.

How do I know? Our hosts, who have no especial reason to be polite to us (we've sponsored one another's children in baptism and, like all true friends, have disagreed plenty), both take second helpings. They even *say* it's good.

Proof whereof: the next morning Nature, who pardons no mistakes, provides rain once again. I go out to test the Dodge. My old friend cranks up as if it had been built on the Lord's day. Walking back inside I catch sight of Sleepy Pie coming down the stairs for coffee in her nocturnal whites. Why, asks Tom More in *Love in the Ruins*, why did God make woman so beautiful and man with such a loving heart?

Next time I'll add chopped local bacon. Bacon *and* capers. Pork Pasta in flight—crank up the *a cappella* ending—afternoon delight.

38

Chicken Aioli with a Seventeenth-Century Wag and the Greatest Living Guitarist

(Not Counting Phil Keaggy, Tommy Emmanuel, Neal Schon, or Chet Atkins)

After a hard day at the office—I'm assuming there were people at the office; I avoided it myself—everyone could use a little break. *I* could certainly use a break. This reading chair is beginning to be a real pain under the ass.

To the kitchen—*locum refrigerii*—whence all sickness, sorrow, and sighing have fled.

Mr. Freezer, meet Mr. Martini glass.

Check the thermometer hanging on the shed. Ouch! It's hotter than a whore in the attic under six wool blankets. Do I really want to fire up the grill? I do. But first I have to fire up the hi-fi. Wolfy's string quintets cranked up to eleven will do. Eleven's a good number. It's been at least that many weeks since I shook myself a cold botanical barely-vermouthed Bombay Sapphire martini. So tonight's the . . . wait a cotton-pickin' minute! What the . . .? Damnation! No gin in the house? It's the Chief Eye-Rolling Officer's fault! She doesn't like the smell—and she has the back pockets to pull off the grim Lenten prohibition even during a festal season.

Time for an audible, Bar Jester style. I send an imperial IPA in motion. It runs a slant route into a snifter and picks up just enough yardage for me to down a first. Ah! There is a God!

But wait! Mother of . . . ! *There's no Eye-Roller here either!* No gin *and* no Eye-Roller!

You know what *that* means: massive infusions of raw garlic into tonight's repast. That's for damn sure. There aren't many benefits to sleeping alone and breathing all over no one but yourself, but the chance to consume Buzz-Off! amounts of raw garlic is surely one of them.

So: peel a whole bulb of garlic. It'll get used for something. And, for starters, crush four cloves onto a plate. Oh, I know. Anthony Bourdain, while he still walked among us, accounted the garlic press an abomination, but had he hung around long enough to read *my* book he'd've wished the Good Lord had made him an impecunious ex-jock English teacher with powder for knees and an Eye-Rolling Sweet Precious—*not* that wealthy celebrity chef that he became ere he shuffled off the mortal coil of fame.

Over the crushed garlic goes a torrent of olive oil—only the finest local stuff—while into the oven goes a baguette. And then onto the golden pool of olive oil fall specks of crushed black pepper and shredded parmesan.

You know what? Mozart was a passing good composer, and these quintets are all fine and dandy, but you can't really sing along to them. Let's go *Sailing to Philadelphia* with Mark Knopfler and James Taylor, no less than one full world away from the coaly tyne. (You don't own this album? Oh. *Oh.* I'd keep *that* a secret. See about getting a copy, just not from amazon dot hell.)

Okay. There's no elegant stemware in sight (not to mention no summer dress or back pockets or Bronze Goddess), but a floral ale seduces the nose, and I've got wee Willie Winkie and his candle stick to describe this excellent French bread to, this bread that's soaking up oiled raw garlic hotter than the air outside. How hot? Hotter than a Georgia Peach Queen sitting bare-assed on a cast-iron wood burner. That's how hot.

And into the heat I go to set ablaze the fuel on the grill. There's no soft personnel in my future, but there are two chicken breasts about to be converted into the energy that gets me through tomorrow. Would that they were thighs, the better cut, but there are no pollo gams in my fridge. (The thigh: is it not to die for? Actually it's to live for. Don't ever be fooled by the cult of the chicken breast.)

But what to adorn these breasts with . . . what to drape over them . . . what to use to achieve that necessary ratio of exposure and coverage, of revelation and concealment, about which that incomparable seventeenth-century wag Robert Herrick knew so much.

Quick! To the fridge! Eggs? Check! Lemons? Check! Both local? Eggs yes, lemons . . . not so much. Not to worry. It's time for some aioli, without which Life would merely be life.

Remove two eggs from the fridge and the yolks from the shells and let them warm to room temperature, after which into the blender they go along with the remaining cloves of garlic. (See? I told you they'd get used.) Also some salt. And now I push the button. What an invention! I chop the garlic even as I whip the egg yolks. Into this loveliness I drizzle—very slowly—about a cup of oil, half vegetable, half olive, and I sing along to the music, modifying the lyrics slightly: Do you think that you could love *me*, Aioli?

The golden mixture thickens; at length I hit the power. I squeeze a small lemon into a bowl and scrape the yolky-oily-garlicky substance into the lemon juice, then stir.

Better test this.

Oh, lord. And to think there are atheists in this world. (If there were no God, said Chesterton, there would be no atheists.) This is going to half conceal and half reveal those chicken breasts beautifully, as if they were the breasts of Herrick's own Julia. (What a girl she must have been!) Knopfler was right: You *do* look like a fine thing.

Grab two purple potatoes, wash, and slice them. I've got a hot nut for a tomato-feta salad, but the bread has gone some distance in filling me, so there's nothing left to prepare tonight but the chicken and the potatoes. They'll stuff me more than I want to be stuffed. Into a white pan I drizzle some olive oil and a little chunk of butter. I salt and pepper the blue disks and throw them into the pan.

Look at that! Purple and gold against white. Reminds me of the Minniescrotum Vikings, hateful rival of God's favorite, the Detroitus Lions. (What a shame that the Scrambler Fran The Man Tarkenton could never win the Big One with Chuck Foreman, Ed Marinaro, Carl Eller, Alan Page, Stu Voigt, Brent McClanahan, and the great MSU Spartan Gene Washington.) I'll do these starchy reminders of the glory days on the stovetop until they're ready for the fork, at which time I'll shower them with rosemary, baby.

Pull on the IPA. Don't you love the sound of a last draught going down, Mark Knopfler? I bet not, and neither do I. So I crack another. But wait! The Eye-Roller, absent and doing the lioness's share of the child-rearing, would be counting. Not good. We'll wait until it's all done—and weep when it's all done, for being done too soon—and pour a modest glass of . . . of what?

Misery! There's an opened bottle of Riesling in the fridge left here by the Eye-Roller herself. Riesling! What am I, Mark, a gullible Geordie boy? What kind of a man drinks Riesling? And haven't I made it clear that if you can see though it, it's not a beer or a wine but an article of clothing? Oh, well. I'm a conservationist. I'm not about to open a bottle of real wine when there's an open bottle of Riesling in the fridge.

Like hell I'm not! I open a shiraz-cab blend.

I arrange the coals out in the heat (how hot is it? Hotter than . . . see me after the book tour) and step back in to flip the purple disks.

Onto the coals go the pieces of chicken while Knopfler goes down in Silvertown and I go in to escape the punishing heat of a world that a few ideologues and maniacs say isn't warming; I do so to make sure all is well.

All isn't. I'm alone, and man, made in the image of the triune God, is a social creature. As Mark sings about the Sands of Nevada, it occurs to me again that I'm not made for loneliness.

"What it is is I'm older," old Mark croons, and damned if he isn't right.

I quaff another IPA, with insincere apologies to the absent Counter, Chief, and Goddess, then I flip the chicken (which I should have brined but didn't), wait, sweat like a circus lady, and bring the chicken in. The key to chicken is this: it's done before you think it is. Same as pork. (Beef is done before you cook it.)

On a white plate I place the chicken breasts and then drape them with the aioli sauce. Beside it go the purple potatoes. Into a balloon glass cascades an inky shiraz-cab blend, and the bachelor dinner is ready.

Tomorrow, Mark, when the dawn breaks even on this empty horizon, there will be something else in store, probably something meatless, accompanied by water and therefore not worth writing about, but the remaining aioli mayo will furnish forth the next dead thing. A burger? A chicken sammitch? A filet? I've never tried it on fish, and I've got some fish in the freezer.

A man cooking for one can afford to experiment as he empties out the freezer, just as a woodworker who heats with wood can afford to make a wrong cut. But a man alone, notwithstanding the chicken breasts dressed to advantage, is still a man in his unnatural condition. What is it he tries to outrun? What is it, Mark? Dice like red rubies? Be careful, O man, lest you fail to see time running out with your roll.

39

O Summer! O Saturday!
O Barbecued Chicken!

Five o'clock on a summer Saturday morning and not a minute to lose! Soon it will be suppertime. Out of bed and down the stairs. The knees snap and crack. The left plantar loosens in muted shrieks of agony. But so what if the flesh be weak? The spirit is willing. This body—this failing creaking tomb-doomed body—will have its moment this very day in the summer sun.

The fullness of man! The groaning rag-weed-sneezing splendor of the incarnate condition! Tonight's meal will remind us that the labor of six days, and not only The Lord God Almighty's, was all *very* good.

5:02 at the coffee pot with its built-in timer, an invention to rival instant replay. First the smell and now the taste of French roast. How it greets the chief of sinners!

> Amazing love! How can it be
> That O these beans have found out me?

The synapses fire. Brain and mind alike jump to life. Nabokov, you were right. There is nothing like coffee in an empty stomach to clear and jumpstart the head.

In no less than twelve hours I'll be cooking for five. What to do first. What to do. . . . I know! Read!

VIII: High Summer II

Ah! My chair, my footstool, my end table, the birds at their matins outside my window, the rosy-fingered dawn creeping up on me. Who does not adore so great a thing of beauty as Dawn's early crack?

The pages turn to count the clock that tells the time; hideous night rises to brave day. Where has this novel *been* all my life? And what is that I hear? What but the stirrings of my first-born son. He wants me to himself. And who wouldn't? I took him and the others, one and all, for local ice cream last night. I'm Father of the Year.

No "good morning, Dad." No greeting whatsoever. It's a waste of time for the child of my right hand, and joy. He wants to know if we're going to the market.

We are.

On bikes?

Of course on bikes.

"Yes!" he says, and off he goes to dress himself. If I am not mistaken, he'll come back down in shorts, a t-shirt, a ball cap, and Converse All-Stars. He'll also have some loose change in his pocket for the musicians down at the market, who deserve his largesse.

He descends in shorts, a t-shirt, a ball cap, and Converse All-Stars, and out he goes to get the bikes—his new Schwinn, which somehow made it down the chimney last Christmas, and my old one, which is so ugly and old that not even the hobos will steal it. You may have seen it before. It's an antique machine, and a beautiful-ugly one at that, with a milk crate band-clamped to the back rack. It weighs more than anyone tall enough to ride it.

We check the tires and off we go into the morning air! Down into the river valley and up onto the bridge. O Mississippi, thou storied river! Speak! Sing to us ere you roll to that warm sunlit hypoxic catch-basin for ancient Iowa topsoil and ancient Iowa sunlight and nitrogen and other Big-Ag run-off. O muddy waters! What soil and oil await thee in the troubled, the too too sullied gulf. Soft you now! Slow be thy flowing, thou river of all my days and ways!

We whiz down the nether side and coast along the bike path. It fairly throbs with life. Ahead of us two young studs are out for a morning run. I catch in them the image of my former self. They are swift and light and unconquerable. What beautiful strides they have. My knees call out to them. Nay, to the skies they call out. Why must my days be three-score year and ten but only two-score minus five allotted to my joints? Why the treachery and treason of cartilage?

Never mind. Nor do I envy these glorious runners their youth. Let them run and eat and love. I'm peddling with my boy to the market and looking out at the river as the sun grows round this very day, my heart vibrating to the iron string of a summer mood. There will be plump tomatoes and stiff cukes, sweet corn a-plenty and garlic and onions and cilantro and chickens and buffalo meat. There will be music and smoke from the grills and girls in summer dresses, wine and honey and pastries, friends to greet, enemies to avoid, peaches to taste, bird houses to admire (and copy), and my boy tugging at my shirt and saying, "Daddy, can I have a lemonade?"

O, my handsome growing infuriating boy, you may! Here. Get two. We'll toast the numerous goings-on of life.

Aging heart of mine, if you should throw a calcium deposit now.... Don't do it, foolish foolish heart. Not now. Not yet. Beat on, old heart. I've got to cook for five tonight. Heart of gold, keep me searching. And I've got another boy, a boy full of piss and vinegar, it is true, but a boy all the same, and a graceful girl, and a bride these many years ready to say, "I know you of old, you old goat! Come here, you!"

(And, God help me, I will.)

To the chicken man I go. A whole fryer, a dozen brown eggs, and a little banter with the banty rooster man—until a more shapely patron steps up. I know when I'm beat. I'm off to get my beans, my sweet corn, my tomatoes, my white onion, my blue potatoes from the ragged boys calling themselves the Mad Farmers.

So they know, then! Well they're getting *my* money, I can tell you. Long may they thrive. May they live to write their own manifestoes and sow their timothy in the moonlight and come into the peace of wild things.

My boy! Where is he? Ah! There he is, listening to the jazz combo and scaring up the nerve to toss them a few quarters. Which he does.

"So, how much did you give them?"

"A few quarters."

"Of your own?"

"Yes."

"Good for you, buddy." (The bass player was once a student of mine.) "Now let's hit the bikes."

And we do, and my milk crate is loaded for bear. It'll be a tougher ride across the river and up our side of the river valley, but we make it at last. Into the fridge go the frigeables. I leave the fryer out to defrost. Foghorn Leghorn, I tell you verily: Old Square Britches will be our main fare tonight.

God bless the gal for what she laid and for what (and whom) she didn't and for giving herself to our board this very night. How I shall relish her!

But it's not night yet. It's not even eleven o'clock in the morning.

O to be standing in the kitchen now, pressing garlic, sautéing yellow onion in butter. To be at the grill turning the plump breasts and the dark thighs and the damn-nigh meatless back over the glowing coals.

But the day's work lies ahead: grass to cut, traps to check (and, perhaps, dead groundhogs discreetly to dispose of), oil to change, this and that to fix, and—damn me to the outer darkness—did I really promise to make Inigo Montoya swords for the boys? I did.

So then to cut the grass, to check the traps, to dispose of the groundhog (it's a 25-pounder if it weighs an ounce), to change the oil, to fix the derailers, and at last, after cranking up the garage radio to "The '70s with Steve Goddard" and pouring some lemonade, one for me and one for each boy, to design swords on a scrap of plywood. Jigsaw, clamps, and sandpaper at the ready, boys poised—nay, bated—and I (no longer Father of the Year but of the Decade) about to go to work.

And after the careful cutting (too careful: my old impatient neighbor watching me wield a jigsaw once said, "I bet you'd separate black from white in pigeon shit, wouldn't you?") and after the sanding we discover that the swords, which are made of plywood, look like plywood, whereas they're supposed to be silver.

To the hardware we go for paint and, no doubt, a jawbreaker apiece and a promotion for yours truly to Father of the Galaxy, while the beneficiaries of the jawbreakers are sworn to secrecy from You Know Who.

The painting done, the swords dry, the work pronounced "very good"—it can only mean that the fighting may now begin. And so it does (. . . you killed my father. Prepare to die!). So be it. I at last am ready to do the day's real work, which begins with cutting the chicken.

Some people buy their chickens already cut—to "save time" or "cut down on labor." I confess I don't understand this at all. I want to *increase* my time in the kitchen. I want *more* work to do. There's music to listen to, and a drinky-poo to get through, and a shimmering vibrant woman to nudge and pinch and bump up against. Shorten the time for this? Inconceivable!

Michael Bublé's birds fly high on the hi-fi. Old Grand-Dad's in the tumbler where he belongs. I begin cutting the chicken my way: first the wings, then the legs, then the thighs. Then I separate the back from the breasts, and then I separate the breasts. My spirits soar.

Now a careful chef might have done this the day before in order to brine the chicken. Great idea. But on a summer day like this it's okay to cut the bird you bought that morning and carted home on your old ugly Schwinn. So I do. And then I salt the bejeezis out of it. Shake shake shake. Shake shake shake. Shake your shaker. So sing I as I salinate the bird, and if I am not mistaken the jewel of my eye, passing through the kitchen, rolls her eyes and disappears. Her scorn and indifference can mean only one thing! What a lucky devil I am.

And then I husk the corn and lay it by. And I snip the beans and put them in the steamer and lay them by.

I light the water on the stove and then I light the grill. You grillers with gas, I extend my hand to you in friendship even though I cannot credit your way, for I'm a charcoal and/or wood man by birth, training, and moral commitment. But Old Grand-Dad has kicked in; the gears are turning nicely, and I, so long a worshipper of charcoal, greet you in brotherly affection. Let us not quarrel on this splendid summer Saturday.

Back to the kitchen. There must be salsa. So I chop the tomatoes, the white onion, the cilantro, and a wee bit of heat off a fresh cayenne pepper newly plucked from the garden. Squeeze the Key limes, pour on the salt, and we're ready for the chips.

We? Lo! I'm alone! I'm Mr. Flood. I raise the tumbler to no one: "here's to no one's showing up."

Great Scott! I almost forgot the Greek salad! Cut some fresh oregano from the crop out back. Chop more tomatoes, cukes, red onion, and feta cheese. Grind in the pepper, shake in the salt, press in the mother lode of raw garlic, and shower on the oregano. (You users of dried oregano, I extend my hand to you too.) Drizzle on the olive oil and toss the colorful mix. (Place the vinegar at hand for those who use it. You users of vinegar, join the ranks of those who grill with gas and dabble in dried oregano. For—O magnanimous me!—I befriend you this very day.)

Bread? Why not! A simple baguette will do.

Into a bowl goes a bottle of barbecue sauce—I'm ecumenical on this score: let local tastes prevail—and out to the grill I go, heavily armed with a dead chicken, sauce, a brush, grill tongs, and the residue of the Old Grand-Dad (with maybe a little more added for good luck). I ring the dinner bell. This signifies that it's time for someone to set the table, toss in the corn, and for everyone else to move tableward, a process that includes rebellion, tantrums, urination, and protracted hand-washing.

I, for my part, am going to look out upon the waning summer light, watch the finches and the hummingbirds, question the squirrels frolicking on the redbud tree, commune with Grand-Dad, reflect upon the glorious day, congratulate myself on my promotion to Father of the Galaxy, and grill my bird in solitude.

Once the pieces are nearly done, I start brushing them with sauce, turning them in order to cook the sauce in, and then I brush them some more. When at last they're done I put them on a platter and drown them in more sauce. This is called Grilling on the Premise of S.T.E.M: If a little is good, a lot is better. And then I present myself to the table—now set and laden and peopled—as Lord of the Grill and Father of the Galaxy.

No one notices. There's a fight over who gets to pronounce the blessing, a fight about which, at this point, I'm agnostic. Once arms and hands and fingers have duly crossed the torsos, chaos ensues.

But above it all I hear Mozart speaking to me across the centuries, and oh how I relish the tastes, the joys of the fullness of man, the incarnate condition.

And suddenly there is only carnage before me. The children are out in the warm and never-ending summer evening; their mother, whom I fain would toss upon the turnips, is knocking about in the kitchen. I kick her out of doors with an amorous foot applied to a splendid bottom. What a lucky foot!

The reward for my labors isn't what you're thinking, you lecherous reader. My reward is to be left alone to clean the *mise en place*, to listen to what I want to listen to, and, at long last, after baths and stories and resistance thereto, which is the way of things on long summer evenings, to end the day as I began it—in my chair with my book. Where has it *been* all my life?

IX
Adult Beverages

There's a lot of liquor in the world, even Scotch, but I took it and gave a pull, feeling too that it was something special.
—Robert Penn Warren, *All the King's Men*

40

Beer: It's What's For Dinner

The topic of drink, like drink itself, is not without its dangers. No doubt there is a time when it should be treated without smartassery. This is not that time, but I'll allow that seriousness sometimes ought to be brought to bear on almost all objects of consideration, even beer. Pete Hamill, for example, tells us that he started writing *A Drinking Life* when some of his friends, "physically ruined by decades of drinking," began to die. (He himself had been dry for several years.) Scott Russell Sanders has a fairly sobering piece that begins without any indirection whatsoever: "My father drank. He drank as a gut-punched boxer gasps for breath, as a starving dog gobbles food—compulsively, secretly, in pain and trembling." Such sentences portend a grim narrative, and what we get, though characteristically thoughtful, elegant, and affectionate, is grim enough to last us a while.

And my wife! Let us not even rehearse the nights she comes home having had to affect charity toward the drunks who end up on the cardiac rehab floor—and she's more charitable than I by a long shot. On such nights you don't dare whistle a beer jingle. To hear the tune issuing from my lips is to smell the beer on them. I know what time it is, and, brother, it ain't Miller Time. (It's never Miller time.)

But bearing in mind the Kingsley Amis doctrine set down without hesitation in his short book *On Drink*—"that conversation, hilarity and drink are connected in a profoundly human, peculiarly intimate way" and that "the collective social benefits of drinking altogether . . . outweigh the individual disasters it may precipitate"—let us not spoil the summer mood if we can help it—not today. Let us now praise famous beers—or not-so-famous-beers. For not-so-famous-beers are what concern me here. I grant that there are some very fine beers that also happen to be famous. Jolly good for them. But what makes beer interesting, here and abroad, is anything but fame. What makes it interesting is the local nature of it.

When I'm in the Lake District, as I sometimes am, hiking with students through Wordsworth and Coleridge country, we drink Cumbrian beers. When I'm away from home but here in the country, I ask for the local stuff.

More and more you can get the local stuff in the local restaurants and bars, and more and more you realize what a vibrant beer culture we've got in this country, which is otherwise spiraling into the maelstrom of confusion. Good thing we've got beer to help us withstand the mischief. It's true there's some real bat piss out there, and no one except bats should be required to be loyal to bat piss, local or not, but lots of small places are making some really fine beer, all of it better than Keystone and Bud Light and Natural Scheit.

The Quad Cities responded to my moving there in 1996 by quadrupling the number of breweries in the area. All are unaccountably thriving. All were within walking distance of my house (my kind of walking: four or five miles) and all of them brew beers good enough to vacuum my wallet occasionally.

My home state, Michigan, to which I have repatriated, has more breweries than most states in the union, all of them doing exactly what they're supposed to be doing: providing their region with really good beer. One of them I regret to say went the way of the dodo: Michigan Brewing Company. Its High Seas IPA could stop planetary motion, and one year at Christmastime the seasonal barley wine was paradisiacal. The former owner has resuscitated the project at Michigan Brewing Works, a little unmarked farmhouse that has the benefit of looking like a barely-legal place designed and maintained for the handful of people who know about it. (It's fully legal, and saints be praised I know about it.) Bobby, the man behind the bar, always has something else going on, usually a smoked meat of some sort, and he's generous with whatever he's experimenting with. He keeps a garden outside and a half-acre of hops as well.

Almost everyone knows about Bell's, not so small now, thanks to its well-named Two-Hearted Ale, a reliable beer that passes for both a pale ale and an India pale ale, depending, I gather, on which contest it's entered in. It's good, but it isn't the best that Michigan has to offer in either style, and for my money Bell's's Third Coast Old Ale is its crown jewel.

There was a place called Duster's in Lawton, which specialized in beer and smoked meats—imagine walking into a place that smells of both wort and hickory—that, as I heard the story anyway, Bell's bought in order to move some of its production to in order to maintain its micro status. I don't know if this is true, but Duster's became Top Hat, as I recall, and is now something else. North of there in the great little town of Paw Paw there's a brewery that proudly bears its town's great name. It was once a right proper little dive—just my kind of place—now expanded (without injury) and still crafting beers that can cure acedia. And then there's Arcadia, Dark Horse, New Holland, Greenbush, Short's, Shed's, Bifferhaus, Griffin Claw, Bad, EagleMonk, Grand River Brewery, Ellison, Dead Bear, Paddle Hard, Poison Frog, Lost Nation, Lansing Brewing Company (the script on the logo makes you think of classic baseball uniforms), Brewery Vivant—it pains me that I cannot name all the breweries in my native state, where once again you can get Stroh's and even Carling Black Label, both in their original recipes and both pre-dating the beer boom. My dad would avail himself of one or the other of these, usually on Monday nights, when he and I sat down to catch a least a half of football with Howard Cosell, Dandy Don Meredith, and Frank Gifford, the highlight of the evening always being Cosell's halftime highlight reel of Sunday's games.

I won't touch anything but the local stuff—here or anywhere, provided local stuff is available.

Obviously weather and mood will sometimes determine your desired beer style. Who can account himself a man, or herself a woman, and refuse a crisp pungent pilsner on a hot summer day? Show me the scoundrel who can refuse a barley wine and a cigar of a fall evening and I'll show you someone who thinks Charles Bukowski wrote poetry.

Stouts? Brown Ales? As the Scriptures say, for everything there is a season.

But for my money Housman was right: ale's the thing. More specifically, India Pale Ale. It's hard to imagine the Holy Trinity sitting down to ecumenical council with anything but IPA.

Some time ago a friend briefly allowed me the society of her good husband, and in our quickly passing exchange this fine upstanding and erudite man tipped me off to 3floyds Imperial IPA out of Munster, Indiana. Forget that business about "no atheist in a foxhole." Show me an atheist who can drink 3floyds IPA and still persist in his error, and I'll show you someone who fell out of the stupid tree and hit every branch on the way down. *This* is an IPA. O to be a Hoosier! You denizens of the Crossroads of America have more than basketball and a good movie about it to be proud of.

Think of all the little-known but tremendous beers out there! And then think of the Anheuser-Busch flunkies drinking long-necks and listening to Garth Brooks. Missionaries to Africa? We need missionaries in the honky-tonks and neighborhood bars! We need earnest people blitzing them and admonishing the locals to leave off born-on dating to drink locally.

(A worthy aside: not long after Buttweiper launched its "born-on dating" scam, Mike of blessed memory and I were in a bar on which an Andhowsyer Bush promo truck had descended. A rep wearing a Bud Light shirt and sporting hair gel—no doubt one of the millions of college grads too unimaginative to major in anything but business—came up to us and asked us if we were "familiar with born-on dating," to which one of us, probably Mike, said, "no, but I'm familiar with bullshit.")

When I was in college and on choir tour my buddy and I sneaked out of our hosts' house in New York and stumbled upon Genny Cream Ale—and that, as I write, was over three decades ago.

In Louisville I once baptized my tongue with the American Pale ale from Bluegrass Brewery—and then amazed others with my charming personality and erudition.

In Seattle I went ape snake.

Something happened at Jackson Brewing Company in Jackson, Michigan (now, alas, no more). I'm fairly certain it was preceded by a miserable round of golf at The Grand or maybe Cascades. Grand River Brewery in that same golf mecca is a step-off on the pilgrimage to heaven.

Now defunct Big Buck in Gaylord, Michigan, did not disappoint me—even though earlier that day my golf game did.

This is what I'm talking about. Dispersed, small-scale, local beers. This is what we mean by "democratic." Micro-breweries as model of government: decentralized, local, small-scale, and kick-ass, full of happy people, people who are glad enough there's a beer that made Milwaukee famous, or a walk that made Milbeerky shame us, but who happen to live in Bad Axe or Soddy Daisy or Willamette or Roanoke or . . . where do you live? What's your local potable?

My fellow localists, lend me your beers. Would you have an active and informed citizenry that knows where it is and cares about its place? Would you have young men and women devoted to something rather than to everything (which is to say *nothing*)? Would you meet on that beautiful shore—your own local brewery—in the sweet by and by?

Then see to it that good local beer gets brewed and that you buy it, that you spend your money not with your enemies but with your friends—for example, the good people who run your local hardware. Love baseball too and poetry and pottery and local music and a blues festival during the dog days of summer. But make or be a part of something worth caring about and defending. Do you live in a noplace? Get the hell out of there and settle in a someplace. Drink beer and belong.

And should your sons or daughters find themselves far from home, pray that their thoughts will turn to neighborhood baseball lots and creek beds and hamburger stands. Implore heaven that when they come of age they'll turn to local copper tuns and brassy neighborhood taps. And when they come home at last, when they finally come home where they belong, feed them local beer for dinner.

41

The Neighborhood Bar and the Chief End of Man

One of the great casualties of the poorly-built human environment is the neighborhood bar. Due to a number of sinister influences both terrestrial and sidereal—from urban planners drunk on cheap oil to unhappy planetary alignments in the post-geocentric cosmos—the mixed-use neighborhood gave way to such unsustainable, inhuman, and inhumane living arrangements as suburbia. These are arrangements that, thank God, have no future, but in the meantime, as we wait in far too many places for the energy-scarce years to rearrange things, we lack, among other blessings, meaningful destinations in walkable environs.

Such as neighborhood bars.

The well-built college or university town will sometimes accommodate the odd professor who wishes to slip out of his office, walk across an amply wide and tree-lined carriage-way, stroll half a block in a summer mood, and take the hit that will get him through a department meeting later that day (I don't happen to work in such a town), but the neighborhood he lives in will probably not be so accommodating.

It will consist of other houses, probably with no front porches, and certainly no barbershops or butchers or general stores or public houses amicable to conversation, places where jokes fly and beer flows. And this, some would say, is a travesty, except the truth is that it's a damn shame. At their best such neighborhoods are cartoons of the well-wrought human place.

The Neighborhood Bar and the Chief End of Man

Long ago, in the days before good beer existed, when I was paying my bills by fixing irrigation leaks on a golf course and studying for comprehensive examinations in areas of literature about which very few people care anymore, there was a neighborhood bar I would occasionally visit that, oddly, was home to two disparate groups of people who got on famously: blue-collar men like me and women of the sort sometimes lampooned by Foghorn Leghorn. (I gather by their attire that they played a lot of softball.) Could it be that these two groups got on famously because they shared two interests in common—cheap swill and women? Be that as it may, this was a smoky bar with pool tables, a juke box, and a regular crowd for the shuffling-in part of the narrative. And on a certain stool you could count on seeing an amiable drunk who, though he was never sloppy, was never quite sober either. He lived on the golf course and would often offer me a beer if I happened to be edging the bunker near his back deck or changing the hole location on the green nearby or mowing the fairway on the temperamental lightweight diesel fairway mower we named for the superintendent's ex-wife. (It was a piece of perpetual perplexity to this local boozer that there were men in the world who didn't drink on the job, or all day long, or every day, or at breakfast.)

But now, in the era of good beer, now that I'm armed with enough money to afford it, there are precious few signs of human flourishing—by which I mean neighborhood bars.

There was a place on my walk home from work that, in the years before the smoking ban, you could talk yourself into visiting (*because* there was no smoking ban yet), even though it wasn't always hospitable in the necessary ways: there wasn't anything but see-through swill, and sometimes the unstable woman in see-through clothing serving it—the wrinkled rode-hard woman who drank on the job—wasn't quite able to grab the tap on her first attempt. It was a place for old men mostly, and you could count on hearing good gossip or seeing a card game *in medias res*, but in it you never quite felt oriented toward your true end.

Now there's a smoking ban—not an absolute good by any stretch—and the tap is keeping up with the inevitable social improvements that accompany the rise of craft beer, but, not having been habituated to frequenting this place, I have found it difficult to school myself in the particular virtue of entering it during that dismal part of the year—the academic part—when I'm back earning my keep.

Then along came an ale house and nano-brewery a half-block away. There were zoning issues at first, and the folks in the neighborhood objected, perhaps understandably, to plans for a *Biergarten*, but this very small brewery and alehouse is, so far, flourishing in accordance with what the earnest people who patronize the Creation Museum call "God's plan for my life." There are about ten taps, and not a bummer among them. The owner / brewer lured the best bartender in town away from his long-held job at a downtown bar, and there's hardly a beer-drinker in the area who can resist the urge to stop in when he sees the bartender's Jeep parked outside. He's quick with a joke—but, under the current ban, not to light up your smoke—and if there's someplace that he'd rather be, you'd never guess it. So hospitable is this place, and so deserving of success, that during the liturgical fasts you feel as if you should go in there and pay for beer you're not drinking.

Now one of the great things about beer, aside from its unerring capacity to achieve its true end, is that many iterations of human flourishing manifest themselves around it. There are days when you can count on seeing a few colleagues in this new establishment eager to share campus gossip (gossip being the one thing that makes academic life bearable). There are days when you can count on seeing the same two retirees and long-time residents of the city reliving their hour of splendor in the grass. And I know of two women, wives of younger colleagues, whom I can count on seeing each week on one particular evening. There they sit, attractive in their way, not entirely oblivious of scrutiny, pacing themselves through a single ale each, enjoying a brief reprieve from young children and childish husbands.

I may say hello to them if I happen to stop in, which is unlikely, because I prefer the five o'clock beer to the nine o'clock beer, but I'll otherwise leave them be. It's girl-time they're after, and they deserve it. And they deserve a place like this, and now they have one.

The neighborhood also features a coffee shop usually filled with people you know, though they're staring at laptops rather than conversing with other human beings. More and more you see them at the latest stage of evolution: with wires hanging from their ears. And there's a barber shop across the street, and a couple of antique and collectibles stores—the residue of former days when thinking was an important component of the urban plan. But walk a little farther and soon you enter a newer development, and a worse one.

I wrap my scarf around my neck, don my coat, and pull up my gloves. Outside the ale house the wind congratulates me on my good behavior with its wonted friendly slap. I walk past a restaurant and a hardware store and a church, also remnants of bygone days when urban planners knew how to design neighborhoods and city administrators knew how to zone them (that is, for mixed use), and then soon I've left, on foot, the well-built environment and entered the travesty or parody or perversion of it—take your pick. Now it's all cars and businesses with objectionable names frequented by people who think their legs were made for sitting on, as Thoreau once put it. (They should be congratulated, he said, for not having committed suicide long ago.)

Ignatius J. Reilly opined that the world is in ruins for want of geometry and theology, to which I'd add walkable neighborhoods, craft beer, and good neighborhood bars. How, without them, can we achieve *eudaimonia*?

42

Bourbon

Balancing there, her oval face aglow in the dark vestibule, hair combed flat on her head and down into the collar of her suit, she looks like a college girl. She drinks, pressing fingers to her throat. "Lord, how beautiful."

—Walker Percy, *The Moviegoer*

Colonel Joe Nickell's *The Kentucky Mint Julep* sits on my shelf alongside Henry Crowgey's *Kentucky Bourbon: The Early Years of Whiskeymaking*. Near them are various companions to bourbon that pass judgment and rate this exquisite gift from above—or from down south, rather—and that tell me what I should think of this or that mash. (It's not enough that every news source has decided to tell me what to think.) In fine, my shelf features much that concerns bourbon but, alas, no bourbon. I have bad luck with it. Every bottle I've ever purchased has had a hole in the bottom of it.

Speaking of pork chops on the grill, which I wasn't: now *there's* an occasion for bourbon. Your favorite pork rub on a thick butterfly chop and a little swirl of Four Roses Single Barrel by the glowing coals—these are all you need to keep warm out back beneath the swirling December snowflakes, the late ones, *after* the Nativity, for Advent is theoretically a bourbon-free season, longer in the East than in the West, as usual. (Some ecumenical council should have appointed not a bourbon-free but a free-bourbon season, complete with several days of obligation.)

Ah, bourbon, the dear throat's golden ribbon. Does not the catechism teach that we should glorify God and enjoy bourbon forever? I think it does. And, if I recall correctly, we believe in the resurrection of the dead and the life of the barrel to come. Amen!

Who has not sung its praises? From Lawrence Block's *When the Sacred Gin Mill Closes* to the pixeled "pages" of the Front Porch Republic, bourbon, like mercy, first and last brightest shines. And as for that storied region known as "every place in between," think no further than *Love in the Ruins*, wherein Percy's hero, Tom More (no saint, he, but we'll leave that for the moment), would do aught but sit in his office, listen to *Don Giovanni*, watch the martins swirl about in the afternoon sun, and pull on the Early Times. Talk about civilized.

What does a man live for, asks the unsaintly St. Tom, but to listen to music, love a woman, read a book, and drink a drink? There are other things, such as confess and commune and struggle for that elusive firm purpose of amendment, and Tom knows it, but that is not presently the point.

It's a good question, Tom's, no less to the purpose of a short winter's evening than of an endless summer's night. No time of year, no season, spurns what unsaintly St. Tom calls the "bosky bite." And St. Walker knew whereof he wrote. *Signposts in a Strange Land* has a splendid little essay on the golden elixir. Read it.

I don't think snobbery is called for in a piece on bourbon. No need from high atop the scotch bottle to make the Charles Emerson Winchester crack at the expense of Colonel Potter's noble preference. There are harsh bourbons, to be sure, just as there are rot-gut scotches. But the American liver deserves its own whiskey (or "whisky" if you're a Maker's man or woman), and I would not have a nation divided against itself, unless the Federalists are out front.

I've sprung for Noah's Mill and Rowan's Creek and Blanton's and God knows what else (or maybe God doesn't know, or has tried to forget), and I've also been known to keep on hand a supply not only of Old Crow but also Benchmark, which must be among the cheapest and worst bourbons known to man. And in sooth I can usually tell when I am sipping one of these top, and now one of these bottom, shelf bourbons.

But, to go back to unsaintly St. Tom, it is still, as always, the bosky bite—the bosky *bosky* bite. And praise be to the God of all Grains for it. Praise to the Lord, the Allbosky.

Now I would not, like Milton's Satan, make all speeches about Me, but suffer me to say a word or two about my own prime bourbon moments. I have mentioned the grilled pork. No scotch, gin, or beer for me when pork sizzles above the red coals. There's something about a dead pig that wants a thick tumbler of bourbon—neat.

Same goes, I think, for fried turkey, all smoked meats, and grilled shrimp. I'll allow all manner of potables for burgers, steaks, and the various manifestations of grilled poultry. But some dead animals simply call for The Bosky Bite, and there you have it.

Is there a vegetarian who has read this far? Let me say to you that I honor you—if for no other reasons than that (1) Thoreau thought we would eventually leave off eating animals, and (2) you can still grill vegetables with a bourbon in hand, which I sometimes do.

Bourbon also serves a man, as might a very dry martini, on a rare night out. I can't say as I especially like nights out, because I usually pay a lot for food I can prepare better for less money at home, but, given the option, I will take a night out now and again. And, when I do, I will usually order myself a top-shelf bourbon, neat. The Goddess Excellently Displeased with me will order her "house Chardonnay" or, on an especially adventurous evening occurring once in six blue moons, something that I can't pronounce or delineate the ingredients of; but I myself, for the most part, am predictable. Give me a Good Bourbon Neat. ("Double," I mouth, if the missus is distracted by a particularly handsome young waiter in the periphery. God bless the boy and his temporary usefulness to me—and damn the bastard bantam rooster and his youthful good looks!)

And let's not forget the quiet night at home: three fingers of bourbon, a reading light, a book, and some music.

And, *pace* Tom More, there is the stolen drink in the colleague's office. Oh, I know. We're not supposed to do this. But seriously. Does anyone expect us to endure the slings and arrows of outrageous academe without the bosky bite? So, in the failing sunlight, or drowning, rather, in the bleak midwinter's darkness and fighting off the malaise of everydayness, trying to figure out how to tolerate a world in which "text" and "friend" are verbs, we sometimes sip, surreptitiously, the delicious stolen tumbler of Old Grand-Dad or Early Times or Elmer Lee or Elijah Craig. We gossip. We share stories of classroom failures and triumphs, agree on the relative demerits of certain sloe-eyed slow-wits whose names keep showing up on our class lists, talk politics ("The governor's doing a good job"; "No, he's a peckerwood sonofabitch sucking the plump tit of the farm bill"), compare hende Nicholas to Donald Trump and puzzle over how a certain kind of grab—"and prively he caughte hire by the queynte"—can be funny in the Miller's Tale but offensive on the campaign trail. We, the loose-collared journeymen, complain about the garroted managers, while garroted managers, schooled in Management Jargon, do whatever it is they do, which in English, I'm fairly certain, goes by the name "mismanage."

I have just pilfered a bit from Walker Percy's essay titled, simply, "Bourbon," which is a beautiful little flash, a perfect blend of whimsy and insight. Percy tells us he doesn't write for connoisseurs or for people worried about alcoholism, cirrhosis, or other ailments. "I, too, deplore these afflictions," he says.

> But, as between these evils and the aesthetic of Bourbon drinking, that is, the use of bourbon to warm the heart, to reduce the anomie of the late twentieth century, to cut the cold phlegm of Wednesday afternoons, I choose the aesthetic. What, after all, is the use of not having cancer, cirrhosis, and such, if a man comes home from work every day at five-thirty to the exurbs of Montclair or Memphis and there is the grass growing and the little family looking not quite at him but just past the side of his head, and there's Cronkite on the tube and the smell of pot roast in the living room, and inside the house and outside in the pretty exurb has settled the noxious particles and the sadness of the old dying Western world, and him thinking: "Jesus, is this it? Listening to Cronkite and the grass growing?"

Ever the Kierkegaardian, Percy insists that the "pleasure of knocking back Bourbon lies in the plane of the aesthetic but at an opposite pole from connoisseurship." You have to balance the "Epicurean virtues of cultivating [your] sensory end organs with greatest discrimination and the least cost to [your] health," but you do that against "the virtue of evocation of time and memory and of the recovery of self and the past from the fogged-in disoriented Western world." And he minces no words in saying what's at stake: "the use of Bourbon to such an end is a kind of aestheticized religious mode of existence, whereas connoisseurship, the discriminating but single-minded stimulation of sensory end organs, is the aesthetic of damnation."

You ignore Percy on bourbon at your own peril. One thing you'll miss out on is Uncle Will's mint julep recipe, to say nothing of Percy on the topic of college girls and nurses, where he's without rival among the writers of the century he graced and helped make bearable. *Ipsis, Domine, et Walker Percy et omnibus in Christo quiescentibus, locum refrigerii, lucis, pacis et bourbon, ut indulgeas, deprecamur. Per eumdem Christum Dominum nostrum. Amen.*

I can think of five other essential bourbon moments or circumstances. I'll rehearse them quickly.

One requires that there be a bourbon cabinet in the barn and either a couple of glasses or clear plastic cups there with it. On cold fall afternoons, or during those respites between jobs when you're trying to figure out what to do next, a quick hit of bourbon helps to clarify things. The bourbon cabinet is also hospitable. Your father or father-in-law, if either or both are puttering around, might could use a pick-me-up; both would certainly be glad to know there's a bottle of delight nearby.

A second is out by the brushfire or campfire, especially at night. There isn't anything like the way bourbon catches the glow of an outdoor fire in a deep surrounding darkness, except of course the way your tongue catches its taste.

A fly-fisherman should have a flask of bourbon with him on the stream. He could make good use of a belt if the fish aren't rising for anything. He also deserves one right after he's landed a really nice brown or wild brookie, the darling of Michigan's incomparable Robert Traver, whose books no one should die without having read.

Same goes for the morel hunter.

And, of course, there's "ding-ding." "Ding-ding" is code for an infusion of bourbon in your coffee. Not with frequency but now and then a man might rightfully say to himself of a morning: "It's my day off. I want some ding-ding in my coffee." I don't happen to like coffee with bourbon in it, but I can respect those who do.

The uses of this most versatile, this most American, of beverages are not unlimited but they are legion. You scotch and gin and (gasp!) vodka drinkers may dismiss it. But you should know that you're mistaken. As Jim Harrison has said, "in this case I'm right and anyone who disagrees is wrong."

43

James Bond, The Poet Laureate, and a Plagiarized Drink

Among the many things I have in common with James Bond, a wide range of experience with beautiful women is not one of them. Nor is vodka. My experience is limited, happily, to one beautiful woman and, not always happily, to gin. And whereas one of Bond's girls ends up taking her own life, in part because she loves him, my girl sometimes wants to take mine, also because she loves me.

But notwithstanding these differences, there are some obvious similarities that cannot be passed over lightly. I can be depended on to live and let die; that is a strategy for surviving committee meetings. And my advanced degrees are, in essence, a license to kill, for no one can kill a good poem like a scholar. ("All cough in ink," said Yeats of such tedious fools. "All think what other people think.") But, more to the point, both Bond and I have the distinction of having given a distinctive name to a drink. Bond did it in *Casino Royale*. I did it in a restaurant in Okemos, Michigan.

But the story begins in a little English place called Thirsk, James Herriot's hometown. In the early years of my marriage to the C.E.O she had no need of such coping strategies as eye-rolling, for I had not yet become tiresome and predictable. I was in graduate school at the time—getting credentialed in tiresomeness and predictability—and we had several pre-children routines that we didn't fully understand the joys of. One was availing ourselves of a Friday happy hour or dinner at a place in East Lansing called Pistachio's, which, alas, despite our patronage, did not survive. The place served an excellent chicken aioli (see chapter 38) and an even better blackened planked whitefish. This was before the era of craft beers. Heineken was the better of the two drafts on offer, and at happy hour you could get a 22-ouncer—a "horse's leg," as my grad-school pal Rob called it—for a buck-fifty. It was served by a guy named Will, whom you could call "Sammy" if your Cliff Claven imitation was good. Will had an M.A. in English from SUNY Binghamton, as I recall, and at the time he was tending bar to help put his fiancée through graduate school in one of those soporific sciences you sometimes hear about. He was soft-spoken and unassuming, and you could talk books with him if you wanted to. You can't always say that about a bartender.

One Friday my wife picked me up from campus, as she often did, and I assumed we were headed to Pistachio's to meet my brother, who was an undergraduate at the time and just getting out of orchestra rehearsal. She kept driving right on past the restaurant, much to my consternation, until it became clear on U.S. 127 north that she was kidnapping me for a weekend in Acme, which is near Traverse City.

O the things in our pasts, including the past itself, we didn't fully understand the joys of!

She was a reader of the James Herriot stories back then, and when I told her I'd been awarded a dissertation fellowship to do some research in England, she proposed that the research include something that would actually be interesting, like a day or two looking for the famous but reclusive veterinarian who'd written the stories she and so many others had come to adore. She had no trouble convincing me. Interesting is always better than Not Interesting, which, I gather, is why on the last page of *Don Juan* C.S. Lewis is said to have written "Never again!" I believe this included a double underscore for emphasis.

We would discover in the end that Thirskians were properly taciturn about their local celebrity, and therefore trustworthy denizens of their place. They hid him well. But we didn't know that when we started planning, and so Thirsk went on our itinerary—and probably would have anyway, even had we known that a bad English breakfast (but I repeat myself) with Herriot himself was not in our future. And I'm glad the itinerary included Thirsk: it was the beginning of my brief stint as Bond, James Bond.

"So where does James Herriot *live*," my wife asked our hostess at the B&B, taking even me by surprise with her wonted knack for cutting to the chase. Our hostess looked off into the distance, perhaps not without annoyance, I thought, and then probably for the thousandth time said, "Oh, hereabouts." And thus by indirection did we find no directions out. I read in those four English syllables an answer the whole town had been instructed to give. The remark was, to be blunt, the end of one half of the research trip. We did find the clinic, naturally. There isn't much room in Thirsk for a veterinary clinic to hide, and somewhere in our basement there are photos to prove that we stood before the sacred and reveréd shrine. But finding Herriot himself was going to require dumb luck, which we had none of until dinner that night.

But don't get too excited. The luck led us not Herriot but to an ersatz poet laureate instead. We were sitting down at a table to dine at a place called the Three Tuns Hotel, a pale three-storey building at 54 Market Place that dates back to the late seventeenth or early eighteenth century and that had apparently been frequented by Wordsworth, though I could detect no lingering whiff of dullness in the air. In all likelihood I was having a Yorkshire beer that evening, perhaps something from Samuel Smith, but whatever it was it became the topic of conversation between me and a man standing alone at the bar—now with his back to it—who found my conversation engaging precisely because of what talking to me allowed him to look at: my dining companion, the Goddess Excellently Direct and Subtle.

Americans don't hide any better in Thirsk than the veterinary clinics of famous veterinary writers do. The stranger at the bar drew from us that "part of America" we called home, Michigan, which he knew to be "near Chicago," the North American to-and-from point for almost every Brit I've ever met, though this man's geographical knowledge was a bit better than your average crooked-toothed Yorkshireman's. It was better for the plain reason that, as he was eager to explain, he'd spent some time in America while in the employ, he said, of Mitsubishi. I detected in him an effort to pass himself off as an intriguing driver of fast cars. He wore an ascot, after all. I asked him his name.

"Ted Hughes," he said.

"I've heard of you."

"Not *that* Ted Hughes, I'm afraid," he admitted.

"Well then," I said. "That's saves you the Sylvia trouble, doesn't it?"

I think he must have replied, "Yes. Quite."

Our food arrived, if "food" it could be called. This was back before England realized that it is located somewhat permanently near France, where food means something other than Bangers & Mash.

"That looks rather appetizing, now that I look at it," he said, and I was not entirely sure which dish he meant by that—mine, my wife's, or my wife—until he wondered whether we'd mind if he joined us.

We didn't, so he joined us and ordered boiled beef or sheep shit pie or shoe tongue sausage or some other equally awful English culinary nightmare, and we had a pleasant conversation that came back around in the end to drinks. He asked if we'd ever had a Graham's and Guinness, and I said I'd never heard of one.

"It's a Guinness stout poured over about an inch of port," he said. And to this day I remember his chiasmic description: "The Guinness cuts the sweetness of the port perfectly, and the port perfectly cuts the bitterness of the Guinness. It's really quite lovely."

He ordered some up, and when they arrived I took a sip and allowed that it was quite lovely indeed, though I don't normally go in search of ways to corrupt Guinness, and I have been a port man only in an on-and-off sort of way, mostly off, for most of my life.

We did not make much of a night of it. I think my Espouséd Saint grew tired of male talk and the fairly transparent male admiration attending it. She had not crossed an ocean to listen to Ted Hughes, whether poet or Mitsubishi laureate.

Back in the states—and here I leave off rehearsing the details of a trip to Edinburgh, where I was so damned cold I *had* to buy a wool sweater, another to Swansea, where a Welshman along the Gower coast said to me "Trout streams? No. I mostly fish the sea," a night in Reading memorable for being distinctly unmemorable, and a visit in East Grinstead with that neglected genius Owen Barfield, who had a picture in his modest room at The Walhatch of Walter de la Mare and who asked me to deliver greetings to the poet-critic R.K. Meiners, now of blessed memory—back in the states (as I was saying) we found ourselves in similar circumstances at another favorite spot, Dusty's Cellar. Remember: this was before the beer boom. The draw at Dusty's back then was Watney's Red Barrel at a mere two-fifty per pint. Plus the food was good, though being poor as synagogue mice we seldom sprang for it. My Counter of Cocktails was especially fond of their *torta rustica* and, later, a crisped skin-on chicken breast stuffed with Gournay cheese, etc., oft-replicated in the Bar Jester's kitchen (see chapters 4 and 10).

James Bond, The Poet Laureate, and a Plagiarized Drink   239

Why "similar circumstances"? The manager at the time, whom I'll call "Scott" (because that's his name), seldom missed an opportunity whenever we ate there to take a long break from work and sit down with us. He'd sit next to me the better to avail himself of the scenery across the table and he seemed to understand that he owed me something for allowing him to do this, so he would usually scratch one of the meals from the ticket—a good example, I thought, of the barter system or what would later be called Fair Trade. He'd also bring out drinks we hadn't ordered. He was especially fond of Duvell. Whenever I went there, not for the Watney's but for the food, I knew there was a good chance that a Duvell would appear in front of me, *gratis*—except of, course, when I went in with grad-school Rob. On those occasions Scott would look right past us, like a dog searching for his household favorite as the whole family traipses in. Not seeing the goddess of my youth, Scott would first become downcast, then aloof. The room would go dark. It was as if the power had gone out all across the city. In the absence of scenery, what good is sight?

Scott was swirling a sangiovese in a balloon glass and listening to stories of our trip to England. Travel was something he took an interest in. His own wife was a travel agent, and the two of them, also *sans* children, got around a little.

At length we came round to the business of the Three Tuns Hotel. Scott especially liked this story because, as I pointed out, he was in it in the person of his British counterpart, the admiring—nay, gawking—Ted Hughes. I described the Graham's and Guinness, whereupon Scott instructed his bartender to make one. He liked it well enough to decide on the spot to put it on the menu. But he said it needed a better name than "Graham's and Guinness." I suggested "The Poet Laureate," which he wasted no time rejecting. I went through all the local Thirskian features I could think of that might provide the sort of name he was after but only came up with several other losers: "The Thirsk-Quencher," "The Yorkshireman," "The Three-Tunner," "The Herriot." Scott rejected them all without apology and also, in my view, without much thought as well. I don't know what possessed him at that point to ask after my middle name, which many of my old pals still call me by, but he did.

"You're not seriously going to call this drink 'The Randall,' are you?" And, again, without much thought—indeed, as if receiving direct revelation from above—he said, "I am."

Bond's drink was "three measures of Gordon's, one of vodka, half a measure of Kina Lillet," shaken until "ice-cold" and adorned with "a large thin slice of lemon." He gave it the name "Vesper," after Vesper Lynd, the double agent who fell in love with him. It's a better name for a drink than for a girl, and better still for a poet and an evening star. "Assume thy winged throne, thou Vesper of our throng!" That's Shelley (*Adonais* XLVI; *q.v. OED*, def. 1). And, of course, it's a good substitute for evensong.

Now Ian Fleming doesn't tell us that Vesper Lynd was an artful blend of passion and treachery, but the fall menu at Dusty's described one of its autumn specials, "The Randall," as an "artful blend of Graham's Port and Guinness Stout, perfect for . . ." well I forget what it was perfect for.

But that, at any rate, is a faithful account more or less of how I plagiarized a drink from one of my wife's many unlawful admirers whose name was plagiarized from a British poet who, I gather, was far less happily wed than I.

Who will play me in the movie is, I understand, a matter of considerable debate at the moment. In his younger days Robert Redford was almost good-looking enough.

44

The Teleology of Vodka

The martini glass and the garnish, O Best Beloved, were made for nobler spirits than vodka, nor did the lime and the tonic water have need of better company once gin joined their *ménage*. And yet to this day both God-fearing and God-smearing men and women order drinks, make drinks, and drink drinks with vodka. Unbelievable.

It's time for some right belief and right worship. It's time for some orthodoxy.

I would not willingly offend the whole Alexander Nevsky choir or five-fifths of its audience, but it is incumbent upon someone to say that the true end of vodka is not a glass, because vodka is not really a drink. So used it is more like an excuse or a delivery system, much as a cigarette is a delivery system for nicotine. For although vodka may please the brain and the bloodstream, it can never fully satisfy the nose or the tongue—and will quite often offend the one and make offensive the other.

No, friends. Even once we have made allowances for the differences between rot gut and premium vodka and the two drinks that (I suppose) it *must* go in (a pomegranate "martini" and a bloody mary), still we must ask a fundamental question: to what end is vodka?

Put aside your stemware and your tumblers, for as St. Paul saith (or "Paul," as his modern commentators call him), yet shew I unto you a more excellent way.

Let the weather turn cold, the sky slate-gray, and your inner weather gloomy. Put a deep skillet on the stove and a requiem on the hi-fi. Or, if you're breaking one of the fasts, throw on some Russian choral music, for there's vodka in your future. Just don't be so impertinent as to drink it. Remember: we're considering its true end.

Over low heat melt some butter—as little as a quarter stick or as much as a half. Watch that beautiful solid fat turn slowly into liquid as the music swells. But don't watch too long, because you've got some chopping to do.

Strike that, Willy. Reverse it. You don't want the butter to separate. So be sure that before it hits the skillet you've chopped up a yellow onion: small, medium, large—doesn't matter. Quantity is up to the chef. Let old scolds worry over their tea about quantities, or deans and provosts over theirs about "outcomes." What you're doing right now is making sure the kitchen smells good. And, reader, believe me: there's nothing like an onion sautéing in butter to prepare you for discovering the teleology of vodka. You want incense, you've got it.

Oh, and garlic! Make sure you've chopped up lots of garlic. Four minutes or so after the onions have gone in, dump in the garlic. Mind that you keep the heat low. And should someone you love walk through the kitchen, imprison her soft hand and gaze deep, deep into her peerless eyes. Or give her splendid bottom a friendly little smack. Think of it as a promissory note and dismiss her to her business. You've got yours to attend to. We're doing teleology here.

But as a cross-gartered thespian might say, look you now! Mark the lack of contrast in the skillet. What you need is good eighth-of-a-cup of Italian seasoning or straight oregano if you prefer. Ah, yes! If your nose is happy, why then shouldn't your eyes also have their pleasure? Behold the pale garlic, the translucent onions, the golden butter, and now the green herb for the service of men. What but these was the eye made to look upon?

Yes, there are other things. I can think of two. But these will do for now.

And presently you'll hear, beneath the music, the low sizzle as the heat rises, and soon enough you'll taste the harvest of your labors, and of course you've been handling the ingredients all along. That's five-fifths of your senses at work here—and you're thinking of even more touch later on—the erring lace, the tempestuous petticoat . . .

The incarnate condition! The fullness of man!

But knowing that the *Dies Irae* is coming, best get yourself a little drinky-poo. Not Vodka, though! It wasn't made for drinking! A Russian stout would do the trick if you've got a good one at hand—and it would also lend a little justice to the occasion, but by now the kitchen smells so good, and you're feeling so ecumenical, you could possibly find yourself imbibing a little sherry even! I'd try to keep that a secret if I were you, but do treat yourself. You're learning something tonight.

By now you should have some salted water heating up in a separate pan, because you've got pasta to boil. As always, drizzle in some olive oil. Good local stuff.

Now the next thing you're going to need is a nice big can of plum tomatoes—fourteen, sixteen ounces, plus the juices. Slice 'em up good, throw 'em in, and turn up the heat a little.

N.B. The disadvantage to doing this when the weather turns cold and the sky slate-gray is that you can't use fresh tomatoes, for which there's no substitute. But this is a good cold-weather Rachmaninoff kind of dish, so some sacrifices must be made. Do remember, however, should a vodka mood o'ertake you in summer's prime, to use fresh tomatoes.

You are stirring with a *wooden* spoon or spatula, are you not? That's good, because stainless doesn't quite sit right with the imagination or the moral sense, and Teflon or plastic could get you drawn and quartered and served to the hyenas or the sociologists.

Chop up some shaved prosciutto and toss it in. A half a pound is plenty. You could get away with less if you're feeling especially guilty about breaking an ecclesiastical fast, more if you're not, but at any rate get some dead pig into the skillet. And then carve out some time to meditate on what a truly wonderful animal the pig is. If you're the praying kind, as I try to be, give thanks. And stir.

Though it may be you've been listening to Rachmaninoff's Vespers, or to some of Tchaik's liturgical pieces that never made it into the great Opus 41, here's where you'll note Russia's true contribution to your evening: you're going to pour about three-quarters of a cup of vodka into the skillet and watch it mingle promiscuously with all the other ingredients. This is what vodka was made for: promiscuous mingling. (I understand there's a dispute about the origin of vodka. Did the Ruskies or the Polacks give it to us? For the nonce I'm going with the Ruskies. In the next short chapter, which offers a variation on this repast, I'll credit the Polacks.)

And just when you think the picture can't get any prettier, you dump in about a cup of heavy whipping cream, because, brothers and sisters, the only thing better than a tomato-based pasta dish, or a cream-based pasta dish, is a tomato-and-cream-based pasta dish. The white against the red, the red against the white, the translucent onions, the green herbs, the pink meat, and all those beautiful little rivulets of vodka!

Quick! Another drinky-poo! (But not vodka.) Ah! A ribbon of Russian stout like the *lachrymosa Christi*. Oh, this life! The poet was right. Who, stepping toward his grave, would not cast one last longing lingering look behind?

Break into apostrophe: Thicken, thicken, toil and juices! And now into the boiling waters toss your penne or rigatoni pasta. Ten minutes and counting. You step back and think and listen. The strings rise; the music builds. Two pans on the stove, one moving slowly over low heat and the other quickly over high heat, meet in the final cadence. How it all conduces to thoughts of . . .

Cheese! You've forgotten to shred the Asagio cheese, which will be the finishing touch once you've brought everything orgiastically together. (Cheese be at my end—and in my departing!) So you shred some quickly and put it into a dark bowl. There *must* be contrast.

And now you drain the penne or rigatoni, toss it in with the vodka sauce, and, having learned vodka's true end, you now consider your own—and hers!

45

Variation on the Theme of Vodkaean Teleology

As promised, the Polack variation: put on Górecki's third symphony. Let the fat in the pan accompany the soprano in a fragrant sizzling pianissimo.

Why Górecki's Symphony of the Sorrowful Songs? Consider that in recent memory there have been serious contenders for the POTUS who answer to such names as "Mitt" and "Newt" and that at present writing the White House toilets are being scheissed in by an orange narcissistic real-estate scheisster. Consider also that congressional minorities are harboring fantasies—however disingenuous—about climate change in spite of pronouncements to the contrary from radio talk-show hosts with impeccable scientific *bona fides*. These are tough times. Many evils have been visited upon Winthrop's exceptional City. You can't even tell a good Polack joke anymore. So what you need is good Polack music and an onion sautéing in butter, because face it: if Nutt, Mutt or Donald Cluck doesn't destroy the free world, someone else will. And he'll probably be a vodka drinker.

Now don't boil any water for the penne or rigatoni. At the appropriate moment, when you dump the vodka into the sauce, add a cup or so of chicken broth and stir lasciviously. Once you've added the heavy whipping cream, add the penne right into the pan. After about eight or ten minutes the pasta will be *al dente* and ready to serve, provided you have grated the asagio cheese.

On the hi-fi Dawn Upshaw will come to her moment of crisis. Close your eyes, cock your head, and grimace like Keats's god in pain. Then take two hits of Warka, one for Dawn and one for Henryk.

46

Concerning Spite;
or, Metaphysics as a Guide to Porters

Aristotle advised studying the soul, Machiavelli war. In the *Ethics* Aristotle (lacking the benefit of a certain catechism) identified *eudaimonia* as our chief end. In *The Prince* Machiavelli (anticipating congressional behavior) pointed to power and the retention of power as a chief desideratum. Aristotle would have us trained in the virtues, Machiavelli in *not* being good—when occasion calls for it.

I have sometimes been able to persuade myself that there is a difference between these two kinds of advice, but the question is a hard one, and I'm just a poor country English teacher, which is why for this little chapter I propose asking a different question. I have many options to choose from:

Why is there something rather than nothing? That's an interesting question in its way, and it has the benefit of having flummoxed some fairly smart people who aren't quite smart enough to consult the first paragraph of St. Augustine's *Confessions*.

Another: why don't the shampoo and conditioner run out at the same time? Again, one of life's deep questions, certainly, but Occam's Razor can make short work of it: we don't disperse and use them at the same rates. And the reason for this is that the shower is a woman's demesne, and women don't need as much shampoo to wash as they need conditioner to disentangle their long hair. (If, like me, you're assigned your own shampoo and conditioner—a white bottle with black letters that read "Hare Kleenin'

Stuff"—the answer is that, like me, you're simply inattentive to quantities beyond the gin/vermouth ratio and that when you're in the shower you are probably thinking about where you can get away with building another work bench, or which dish would be a good one to prepare while looking out at the finches—Tom More style—and sipping a toddy and listening to *Don Giovanni*.)

Why does the choke on the '83 Dodge, a.k.a. The Babe Magnet, stick? An even better question, but the answer is that it's an '83. And a Dodge. And actually a Babe *Repellent*. If it ran like a gazelle it wouldn't be an '83 Dodge. It would be a gazelle, which does run like one. Or it would be a younger man than I wearing adidas Gazelles, which I wore when I was younger and could run like a gazelle.

Why do birds suddenly appear every time you are near? A question, I warrant, that has bothered mankind since the dawn of carpentry. But the fact is they don't. Things that happen in bad songs don't usually happen in the world of sticky chokes.

Will a drink appear somewhere in this chapter? It will, but then that's as predictable as an Indian in a cigar shop. Will there be spleen? Almost certainly. The Bar Jester is still an unreconstructed splenetic: He'll never be happy so long as some people are.

Why is America so great? Another good one—if begging rather than asking questions is your game.

What's better, ale or porter?

Well, now! At last, a real question, a real object of study, which in the academy would be called a "subject," because folks in the academy get everything bass ackwards.

In the normal everyday run of things I'm going to order an ale, an exceedingly hoppy and floral India Pale Ale if one's available. And, thanks to the mutually beneficial relationship between supply and demand, an IPA often is available, and it often pleases the nose and palate in terms that answer to a man's scruples. But when the second round comes around—as, not infrequently, it will, especially when attention flags and you find that you've placed an order without realizing it—such ales don't always answer to the transcendent localist criterion of "place," much less of "limits," whereupon a true localist is obliged take the tenebrae option: a local dark beer.

Now when it comes to beer, the word "local"—like *virtu* in 1513—is slippery, because being at your local brewery doesn't vanquish the brewer's problem of using local ingredients, which more often than not he isn't and can't, with the exception of water. So for the sake of conscience-vacuuming let's consider personal transport. If you can get *to* the beer, it's local enough.

And if you're in Chicago you have the beneficent option of drinking not only locally but spitefully. I am speaking, of course, of Spiteful Brewing company, which, if you're a localist Chicagoan, you should patronize. Believe me: you should patronize these guys. By means of a short chain of acquaintances leading straight to the power structure itself at Spiteful I found myself in possession of a couple of their bombers, and God put me here to tell my readers, especially you hog butchers in the city of the big shoulders, that the boys at Spiteful know what they're doing.

My introduction was to their peanut butter and jelly porter. I didn't think it possible to put a PBJ sandwich into a porter, but these guys managed to do it. I'm not saying I want my porters to taste like a PBJ sandwich, but I've had a porter that does, and the feat itself is impressive.

Next I tried (and here I must apologize to my mother, who taught me to use better words) the God Damn Chocolate Banana Pigeon Porter. I had this in the front pasture when I was clearing brush one cold December morning (another apology to my mother), and it proved to be a most delicious and satisfying breakfast.

(It was *late* morning, circa 11:59 EST, when the bottle cap inexplicably flew off the bottle of God Damn Chocolate Banana Pigeon Porter, after which I was pretty much helpless to do anything but drink it, so don't anyone plan an intervention. Churchill's morning consumption, I hear tell, exceeded the intake of a man let loose on the twelve days of Christmas.)

Wow! What a beer—and what a breakfast! Are you bothered by nothingness rather than somethingness or by the shampoo/conditioner ratio? Do you find yourself inexplicably puzzled by the sticky choke? Get over it, because you've got your paucity of God Damn Chocolate Banana Pigeon Porter to worry about. That's one lack you've got, as Miss O'Connor once put it. I'm not saying this porter will change your life. I'm saying that, if your life needs changing, you should give this porter a chance. At the very least it will put within reach the blessedness Aristotle sought, perhaps even the power so dear to Machiavelli.

Which brings us full circle, as all metaphysical inquiry should do (because the conclusion is usually lurking about in the premise): by "virtue" Aristotle meant one thing, Machiavelli another, and both were worried silly. But the semantic slippage there is an evil that God Damn Chocolate Banana Pigeon Porter can make disappear. Its explanatory power is equal almost to that of the nude. And, were it to fix the slippage, we would be left with one less theodical problem to worry about. Moreover, if truth is at the bottom of a well, I can think of one well all truth-seekers could do worse than look down. My own view is that if we could give everyone in the world a bomber of Spiteful, we would forthwith turn our bombs into plowshares and get on with the salutary business of living well.

Will it help Michigan State win its third national championship in basketball? Well, now you're in the region of a woman's fury and pigs flying and what wild horses can drag. Now you're talking Churchillian quantities, which are out of my league.

47

How to Write History and Practice Bourbon Politics

Your personal library should include a book by Gerald Carson titled *The Social History of Bourbon* (1963), reissued by the University Press of Kentucky in 2010 with a new forward by Michael Veach, author of *Kentucky Bourbon Whiskey: An American Heritage* (2013), also from UPK. You don't have to like bourbon to like Carson's *Social History*. All you have to do is like good writing. Teetotaling prudes whose hemlines have never risen above their shoelaces will like this book if they like good writing.

It opens with a splendid sentence that all historians would do well to give their full attention to, especially if they have any interest in breathing life into that futureless discipline of theirs. Here it is: "Long before recorded history, primitive man discovered that the molecular readjustment of the carbon, hydrogen and oxygen atoms in a watery solution of fruit pulp which had been allowed to stand, produced a beverage which made the world seem a wonderful place."

Of course primitive man discovered no such thing. But if you yoke him to "molecular readjustment" you execute a joke in first-rate fashion. What primitive man did discover was booze, ushered into this sentence by the magic of its absence.

Carson's gag is a good one—it too makes the world seem a wonderful place—and the jokes keep coming. Almost very paragraph sets up a happy turn-of-phrase:

> There is nothing in alcohol itself which is poisonous or injurious to man's health, despite a large propagandistic literature to the contrary. Indeed, the blood stream of the average healthy human normally contains a small amount of it. William Jennings Bryan, the advocate of unfermented grape juice, John B. Gough, the great anti-whiskey orator, when he was sober, even hatchet-wielding Carry Nation—she, too, had .003 per cent of alcohol frisking through her arteries.

"Frisking"! Give me the contemporary historian who will risk using that excellent word—*and* take a jab at the unpatriotic rabble-rouser Carrie Nation!

But let us listen again to Mr. Carson.

> The first settler to plant a peach orchard on the Broad River was Micajah McGehee, who set up a small country distillery and consumed most of his own product. But so hard was his head that it took him all day to get capsized. In a moment of religious excitement he joined the Methodists; so, of course, he was spoken to about his drinking. McGehee replied that his peach brandy was necessary to the preservation of health. But as a gesture of good faith he agreed to limit himself to a quart a day.

Now that's good comic timing. But then Carson extends the joke: "The allowance proved to be too small, for Micajah lost his battle with the angel of death at the age of eighty."

Those who consume a quart a day—think of the morning half-ration allotted to such legends as Ed McMahon and Dean Martin—should all hope for so long life. Even Pat Summerall of blasted memory made it to 82, albeit with a teenager's liver the last dozen or so years.

Carson continues with a sentence that would allow most of us to die happy had we merely drafted it: "Firm information on the applejack distilling industry of the state [of New Jersey] is fragmentary and difficult to come by, since local history was usually compiled by emeritus pastors to whom the moral stance on total abstinence was more compelling than the moral imperative to write objective history," which imperative Carson obeys with all the moral conviction of an emeritus pastor.

One Owley Lemon, reports Carson, drank a quart of applejack a day "without inconvenience." Elsewhere Carson says, "The arduous occupations of lumbering, coopering, shipbuilding, grubbing out the farms, fishing on the Grand Banks all called for strong drink to wash down the Indian corn and salt provisions. So did the rigors of the American climate. Rum, and later whiskey, offered an attractive form of central heating."

I see several historians in the hall each day, but no such Gerald Carson do I see. Not a one of them would think to compare spirits to a furnace and duct work, probably because, like sociologists, they're too busy providing the Ur-Narrative that Explains Everything.

Of the Irish in Pennsylvania of the 1790s: "When the new federal government taxed their Monongahela [whiskey], the western counties exploded with oratory and the squirrel hunters began to oil their guns."

There ought to be a comma before any coordinating conjunction that introduces a subject change, but that's a sentence to make you get down on your knees and thank God for guns and oratory.

Carson's account of the Whiskey Rebellion during those grim years of the late 18th century might make you long for the Articles of Confederation, but it will also make you glad you learned to read. The resistance was staged by a bunch of brave decentralizing proto-Front-Porchers, which is to say a sturdy band of true Federalists whom we know as Anti-Federalists. Unlike the Fed, they had no interest in asking the things they loved most to do the work they liked least—namely, discharging the debts incurred during the Revolutionary War. So Carson writes of Geo. Washington's Secretary of the Treasury, Alexander Hamilton, who

> proposed, to the astonishment of the country, that the United States should meet fully and promptly its financial obligations, including the assumption of the debts contracted by the states in the struggle for independence. The money was partly to be raised by laying an excise tax upon distilled spirits. The tax, which was universally detested in the West—'odious' was the word most commonly used to describe it—became law on March 3, 1791.

Later, in *Kentucky Bourbon Whiskey: An American Heritage*, Mike Veach would write: "About the same time that whiskey came into favor with distillers, taxes came into favor with legislators." (It's a wonder the gummint hasn't figured out a way to tax sex, which would get us back in the black by nine o'clock Monday morning. True: not everyone would pay his or her fair share, but the phrase "do it for your country" would acquire a certain felicity decidedly lacking at the moment.)

IX: Adult Beverages

Whiskey makers, responding to the whiskey tax, regarded a distant government arrogating itself to tax collection as being "no less oppressive than the one seated in London, and often drew the parallel."

David Bradford, prosecuting attorney for Washington County and avowed enemy of the so-called "Watermelon armies" assembled to suppress the whiskey rebellion, "was a rash, impetuous Marylander, ambitious for power and position. Some thought him a second-rate lawyer. Others disagreed. They said he was third-rate."

Now *that's* timing. It makes you think of the old birth-control joke originating, I think, with Woody Allen but improved upon in this variation: "She used an oral contraceptive: she said 'no.'"

After the rebellion was squashed, "the punitive army moved forward in glorious autumn weather, raiding chicken coops, consuming prodigious quantities of the commodity which lay at the heart of the controversy."

You Ph.D. candidates in history who are told by your thesis advisors not to use such words as "punitive" and "glorious," point to Gerald Carson's fine example and make creative use of your middle fingers. Then write with your ears and spleen and funny-bone—not, like most academics, with your feet.

And how's this for delicacy? "Faded diaries, old letters and orderly books preserve something of the gala atmosphere of the expedition" surrounding that punitive army. "At Trenton a Miss Forman and a Miss Milnor were most amiable."

If the rising was a failure, reports Carson, so was the liquor tax. The military adventure alone, without ordinary costs of collection, ran up a bill of $1,500,000, or about one third of all the money that was realized during the life of the revenue act," whereupon that great agrarian decentralist, Mr. Thomas Jefferson, came to the rescue:

> The excise was quietly repealed during Jefferson's administration. Yet the watermelon armies and the Whiskey Boys made a not inconsiderable contribution to our constitutional history. Through them, the year 1794 completed what 1787 had begun; for it established the reality of a federal union whose law was not a suggestion but a command.

But out on the frontier, says Carson, and amid all this, "Ministers of the gospel were paid in rye whiskey, for they were shepherds of a devout flock, Scotch Presbyterians mostly, who took their Bible straight, especially where it said: 'Give strong drink unto him that is ready to perish, and wine unto those that be of heavy hearts.'" I'll bet these Prostiterians (as I once heard the word pronounced by a sturdy Christian woman of impressive credentials) took their scripture "neat" as well. No God-fearing man would take his whiskey on the rocks—nor his gospel neither.

Along the western rivers, where there was little currency to speak of, "a gallon of good, sound rye whiskey was a stable measure of value." O for a sound and stable barter economy now or, failing that, the gold standard of the old rye whiskey measure, by means of which we might have averted such embarrassing misrepresentations of value as were assigned to pet rocks, Nikes, vinyl-clad suburban houses, and professional shortstops in pinstripes. Gerald Carson, our nation turns its lonely eyes to you.

There's not only a lesson in *The Social History of Bourbon* for those who aspire to write history; there's also a moral for political economy—if only sobriety could divine it or divinity find it out. But I have my doubts about this ever happening. It's impossible to read Carson's history without an ample pour at the elbow.

X
Back to School

Already? Damn it!
—The Author

48

Something's Fishy—But Not Very
—At Suppertime

As darkness falls upon what a friend of mine charitably calls "Jack-Ass Acres"—that is, my Michigan domicile—and as the promise of rain comes with the moving clouds at the end of one of the few really warm days we've had this summer, a man on the downward slope toward the grave might be tempted to indulge the lyrics of an Eagles' song: "another summer's promise almost gone."

Not exactly "they shall come with jollity," as the Psalmist said and as the hi-fi now proclaims. It's "Turn our Captivity," from a collection of William Byrd's motets and anthems. These divine settings will serve to lift the spirits for a while until the moving parts of "Plorans Plorabit," one of the great lamentations in all of English choral music, resolve into a touching but unconvincing picardy third. Then, with the school year looming, it's back to that grief without a pang of which the stammering unlucky English bard wrote.[*]

Or not!

---

[*] A man shouldn't always be cryptic, I reckon, and if he's going to mention Coleridge (the stammering unlucky English bard) he should probably open up a footnote (or at least a parentheses—the "drama of reason") in honor of STC. I take it that some music historians see in "Plorans Plorabit" a complaint against the English Catholic captivity akin to the lament that some Shakespeareans hear in the "bare ruin'd choirs, where late the sweet birds sang." So King James I and Queen Anne, who keep captive the flock, are being given What-For: *Dic regi et dominatrici: Humiliamini, sedete, quoniam descendit de capite vestro corona gloriae vestrae.*

It is certainly a terrible thing to send a man back to work after three months off, but think about it: a summer during which the temperature has mostly been in the seventies—and the fifties at night; the great privilege of having real work to do and therefore of falling dead tired and sore into bed at the end of each day; sporting fauns in the field; turkeys among them providing comic relief as they run in fear of the fowler—or "fly," as it were; room aplenty for foul toads to knot and gender in and then go to work, along with their colleagues the bats, eating down the mosquitoes to a sufferable number (a number we've not yet reached, but we're getting there, notwithstanding the fact that drought is the only significant predator mosquitoes have); children chasing fireflies, swimming, playing one-on-one, and shooting B-B guns; the Bar Jester cutting herbs from the garden and watching the summer vegetables ripen, especially the sweet corn; and there amid it all the Eye-Roller and Goddess Excellently Longsuffering, worrying herself over curtain rods and valences and mirrors and towel hooks, and inhabiting her worry and her fuss in those splendid back pockets of hers!

Who would have it any other way?

Well, for starters, I would have the denizens of this chaotic place more favorably disposed to a repast of real fish, but they all seem intent upon eating only the mildest and least assertive of the ichthyological creatures: the tilapia filet. Hardly local and hardly interesting, but then that's where the Bar Jester slash Chief of Dumb Asses steps in. This is a job for the Culinary Plagiarist.

It happens like this: onto a platter go the filets.

But wait a fly-floatin' minute! Where in tarnation is my iced tea? To the antique hutch I go, where awaits a goodly, not to mention Godly, selection of "iced tea." A thick rocks glass with no rocks awaits the coppery cascade of Rowan's Creek. Here at Jack & Dumb Ass Acres we might be sucking left hind tit, but we take our bourbon according to the divine pattern: neat. And we believe with all our hearts and souls and bodies in its apotropaic powers—for believing a thing makes it so.

Back to the platter. Onto the filets goes a shower of Konriko. (Conrad Rice Mill: I'm still waiting for my free case of this.)

Next a golden drizzle of olive oil on each filet. After about a half hour—but not into the second bourbon, for the Counter of Cocktails has come in from green-thumbing her flower boxes and hanging baskets—I'll flip the filets and repeat the process.

To the wi-fi. No one's around, so I can get away with blaring a little Arvo Pärt. How about some *Totus Tuus*? Yes. How about it.

Something's Fishy—But Not Very—At Suppertime

The Konriko and oil are going to give the filets two things they generally lack: character and flavor. But more can be done, and more will be done—on earth as it is in heaven. Normally I'd put these little fishies on the grill, but I've got the *mise en place* in order here in my kitchen, whence all sickness, sorrow, and sighing have fled, so I think I'll stove-top the flaky sides that once swam in either Indonesian or U.S. waters. (The label tells me they're a product of one "place" or the other but is otherwise non-committal. I just hope someone got the lead out.)

Speaking of getting the lead out. I'd better move the cream sauce along. This is "key," as the color commentators say.

Heavy whipping cream falls into a sauce pan with just enough cream reserved for swallowing the bedtime statin—because that joke never gets old. On low heat I thicken this once white, now dun, elixir. Why dun? Because this is going to be a lemon-pepper cream sauce, and you don't make a lemon-pepper cream sauce without putting into the cream several times more black pepper than you think is necessary. I fairly coat the whole top of it and then stir lovingly, always with a wooden spoon. A dollop of butter is also necessary, or else the statin later on won't be, and we want to keep both the dairymen and the pharmaceuticals in business. Toward the end of the thickening I'll add the juice of a whole lemon, because if half a lemon is good, a whole lemon is better. That's the law of quantities—unless you're the Tabulating Goddess, in which case it's the law that, like the quadratic equation, can't be made plain.

A little oil and butter into a large pan over low heat, and I'm not very far from allegedly having Indonesian (or U.S.) impurities cooked out of my tilapia. These little inoffensive shingles of fish flesh cook pretty quickly. On the grill they get maybe two minutes per side, depending on the heat, but here on the stovetop I'll give them a little more time.

But not before (as our Lord once said) I prepare a place for them, which is to say a bed of rice. The Breath-Taking Breath-Sniffer and I like our rice done in one part water, one part dry vermouth. But there are children to feed—at least I've seen some around here somewhere, though not in the vicinity of any work that's being done—so we'll back off the vermouth a little. They're not crazy about the taste. Bring the caldron to a boil and cover the rice. We're twenty minutes away.

Of course risotto with chopped mushrooms, shallots, and sun-dried tomatoes is a good variation on the rice. But be sure to use chicken or beef stock instead of water.

Down the gullet goes the last arm of golden warmth dipped from Rowan's creek. What a lovely stretch of moving firewater it is! If only bourbon really did flow like streams in the desert—or, better yet, like a trout stream across Jack-Ass Acres. And if only tilapia could be brought in on a dry fly. I might be the Chief of Jack Asses, but I'd be the luckiest of them as well.

A chopped kale salad with chopped red and yellow peppers and some shredded carrots added for color, baptized in a peanut dressing, and we're close to supper time. What a thing it is to cut kale from your own garden! It beats hell out of just about everything.

And, when the time comes, I lay out the fish, each on its couch of rice, spoon on the lemon-pepper cream sauce, and, at the last, punctuate each filet with a spoonful of capers. Don't forget the capers. You've pretty much wasted your time if you do.

From across the table, above a raised glass of chardonnay, I get not the rolling of the eyes but a wink. Mine eyes shall *not* weep sore. There's something in this for me. Another summer's promise? They shall come with jollity?

Money says I'm going to get to install more curtain rods later on.

49

On the Conversion of Grass and Sunlight; or, Round Steak in a World Gone Mad

That the world's gone mad may be deduced from the recent failures of my favorite sports teams, not to mention from undergraduate preferences for Ginsberg over Vaughan. Clearly, the overwhelming tendency of the world is toward anarchy and ruin. If we're not vigilant, soon perfectly sane men, men of impeccable tastes and reasonable sports loyalties, will begin to prefer vodka to gin, spinner to fly fishing, The Birds to Byrd, and new things to old. Their light hearts will darken. And then what will become of us? Mark me: soccer over baseball will be the *kurz und lang* of it. The *horror!* The *horror!*

But a local cattleman who actually lets his grass-eating beasts outdoors to feed on the grass they were made to feed on and who has apparently read his Thoreau—"the very cows are driven to their country pastures before the end of May; though I have heard of one unnatural farmer who kept his cow in the barn and fed her on hay all the year round. So, frequently, the Society for the Diffusion of Useful Knowledge treats its cattle"—a local cattleman, as I was saying, has recently slaughtered another of his grass-eating beasts, and now that a local locker not much bigger than a milking stall has hung, carved up, packaged, and frozen all the beast's edible guts, I'm fully reconciled to the growing madness, for I've paid my processing fee and carted my portion of the beast home. My freezers are loaded with converted grass and sunlight: ribs and rumps and rib eyes, steaks and stewing meats and the miracle of ground beef, fundamental ingredient of the olive burger, the burger above all burgers. All of it awaits my deliberate prep and careful undercooking. Thanks to highly complex processes both natural and cultural, an animal with four stomachs is on its way to an animal with one.

To eat is human; to feed me bovine.

Take the "problem" of round steak, tough as old leather and not very attractive: "gnawgahyde," I call it. But there's no need to waste it when you can *waist* it. This is real lips-to-hips cuisine, plenty good for weekdays not set aside for commemorating betrayals or crucifixions.

Season the round steak according to your tastes (blackened is good; Cajun is good) and then steel yourself for a difficult decision: either roll it in flour and sear it quickly in a pan, in which case you're going to have more burned flour than seared meat, or sear it first and then roll it in flour, in which case you're actually going to have seared meat but meat less inclined to absorb anything else, including flour. Flour is flour, so I prefer the second method, but do as your conscience dictates. Then put the round steak on the stovetop in chopped onions awash in a forty-ounce can of cheap beer or malt liquor, covered. You know you've always wanted to buy a big can of Colt 45 anyway, so do it. Buy two, in fact, and put one in a brown paper bag. Sip from it as you walk home from your local Discount Liquor & Lotto.

Make sure the heat is low. Simmer the round steak slowly for a couple of hours but be sure to add about six wheel-barrows full of chopped garlic half-way through.

Serve your round-steak-in-beer with mashed potatoes to which, in the mashing, you've added not plain milk, and not heavy whipping cream, but buttermilk. Don't forget you've got garlic chives still growing out back, even at this late date. Chop some up and sprinkle them atop each serving. Hear your youngest say disapprovingly, "hey, what's this green stuff?" before he picks it off piece by piece in that finicky and exceedingly annoying way of his. But rejoice at his moxie and exchange lascivious glances with the missus, because lasciviousness is what got you in this attitudinal mess in the first place.

What? You don't want to be seen buying a forty-ounce can of cheap beer or malt liquor? Not to worry. After someone has given you the clubbing you deserve, defrost your round steak, salt the bejesus out of it, sprinkle it with dried oregano, drizzle some olive oil over it, and let it sit covered in the fridge overnight.

Next afternoon, maybe at about five, pull it out, put a little Neil Young on the hi-fi, pour yourself an Amstel Light—or, if the clubbing taught you anything, a bourbon—and cut the fat off the piece of dead cow. Toss the fat into a pan lightly oiled on medium heat and release some of that beautiful sizzling fat.

Start some water for the angel-hair pasta.

Once you've collected a fair amount of the beaded fatty wonder, the arterial impedimentia, remove the chunks of fat, take them out back, and give them a fling. A critter will bless you later on. Let the pan cool a little while you cut the meat into strips no wider than a half-inch. Then cut the strips cross-wise a couple of times. You've got not cubes but short strips now. That's what you want. Into the pan drizzle some olive oil and then toss in a half-stick of butter, bearing in mind that you hydrate meat not with liquids but with fats. The round-steak-in-beer was good, but you were tenderizing the gnawgahyde, not making it juicier. Tonight your approach is a little different.

Tell the kids to stop fighting or else. Observe how they ignore you. Toast yourself: Head Chef and Resident Irrelevant.

Lo! The missus appears in that pair of jeans you haven't seen since last winter! She's clearly pre-occupied with something having to do with the kids' homework. (Monstrous Intrusion!) Make a pass at her and watch her roll her eyes as she walks out of the room mumbling something to herself. No harm in thinking that the way she ignores you can mean only one thing.

Obviously it's not quite time to heat your meat, but you can get the butter melting if you want to. So leave off what you were about to say to those splendid head-turning back pockets, turn the burner to low, and then pull out a sauce pan. But first: another hit of bourbon (or, if you're a slow learner, a mouthful of some rice-based abortion, like Sapporo). There *is* a God! (Or isn't.)

Into the sauce pan goes a pint of heavy whipping cream and *at least* a tablespoon of nutmeg. Hot red pepper flakes too. The other half-stick of butter wouldn't be unwelcome in the pan. Bring it slowly to a boil, turn it down a little, and let it thicken. Stir. Sip. Sing along. You're searchin' for a heart of gold—or, having already found one, a way to turn the round steak to good account.

As the sauce thickens and the water for the pasta comes to a boil, it's time to get serious about the timing. You've probably already made a salad from the late fall greens out back—something else for the green-averse youngster to object to (the little monster will probably develop an affection for such offensive combinations as maize and blue)—and so you're into the home-stretch here. Into the pan goes the meat. You move it about with a wooden spatula until it begins to brown on the outside, at which time you've got to put the angel-hair pasta in. Six minutes to Charlie, as they used to say at the four-o-double-seven.

Sample a piece of the buttery meat. If it's red in the middle, you don't want it over the heat much longer. Take it off soon, a minute ago if possible, and put it in a covered serving dish. It's still going to cook a little, and you don't want it cooking much more. God didn't put grass-eating cattle on this earth so man could kill, carve up, and cook the flavor out of the poor ugly beasts. Onto the table it goes, mooing and chewing its cud the while. It's plenty done.

Into the strainer goes the pasta, then into a bowl. Over the pasta goes the lovely nutmeggy cream sauce. Mix it all together and cover it. Grated asiago cheese stands by. Everyone's going to get a pile of pasta topped generously with small pieces of perfectly undercooked round steak sprinkled with grated cheese.

This ain't Chateaubriand with béarnaise sauce or a wine-and-shallot reduction, but you've turned the round steak to good account. All you need is a fairly assertive red wine to make you forget what more wasteful (and waistful) beefeaters are having. That and another roll of the eyes from you-know-who.

Meanwhile, out in the freezer, converted grass and sunlight rest poised and cold and ready.

And you still get to clean up! Clear the kitchen, brew yourself an after dinner coffee, and crank up a requiem. Make it Brahms, not Britten—in honor of your having avoided boiled beef.

50

Skillet Penne Sausage and The New Year's Dissolution

"There are Klingons orbiting Uranus!"

That, I decide, is what I should have said to the puppy earlier today when at last my teenagers had roused themselves from their chaotic dens of slumber and provided me with an audience unappreciative of my subtle humor and rapier wit. Another missed opportunity at the end of another year.

But it's the one-year anniversary of my breaking an ankle and some ribs and, notwithstanding the many close calls since then, there are no newsworthy casualties to report, for which a thankful man might give thanks—and for which even such ingrates as I give thanks.

A man might resolve not to do anything dumb-assed enough to imperil his life in the coming year, but the Chief of Dumb Asses doesn't see that happening. Pillows were made for sleeping, not walking, on, and there will be sleep enough in the grave, as I and Ben Franklin have both well said. Life is for the living and the wide awake.

These and other thoughts rattle around in what passes for my mind as the low December sun, oblique in the southern afternoon sky, smiles on but fails to warm me in the back pasture, where an unmerciful northern wind whips and lashes this solitary figure so stubbornly unresolved. At last, after Olympian feats of procrastination, I've begun clearing out the little copse of wild cherries that last winter's ice storm ravaged. By now someone will have taken the puppy for what the groomer calls—unhappily, in my view—a "sani-trim." I gather it is meant to reduce floaters around the dog's nether eye.

But I'm cold right through to my bones and the screws holding them together, and I'm dreaming of a white kitchen and the Goddess Excellently Smoldering who warms it. The tractor and the chains used for dragging out the larger limbs are put away; the chain saws and other tools of my erstwhile trade are in the bed of the '83 Dodge, a.k.a. The Babe Magnet. I put my trophy vehicle in the barn, close the barn doors, and head for warmer climes and better scenery.

I kindle a fire, instruct the children to keep it fed, hold out no hope of being heeded, and head to the stove, where waits the twelve-inch pan in which I'll concoct a piece of culinary genius for which I'll be summarily ignored. Would a Dumb Ass have it any other way? He wouldn't.

Into the pan of olive oil and butter warming over low heat goes a chopped onion.

The onion! What a marvel of creation is this bulbous thing! My soul magnifies it! How right you were, Robert Capon, to exalt it in rhapsodic prose!

It's the fifth day of Christmas, that short festal season between Nativity and Theophany, and it would be a damn shame, probably even a sin, at this of all times not to honor the fullness of man, the incarnate condition. Besides, fasting *ist verboten*. So where in carnation is the music? The libation?

As the Manhattan Transfer fills the festive air, a cataract of Beefeater cascades into the shaker—accompanied by two drops of vermouth, one for each of the two natures of the erstwhile babe wrapped in swaddling clothes and lying in a manger. A single lemon twist, vivid as the star above Bethlehem Ephrata, reposes in the bottom of that eternal shape—the frosted 1939 World's Fair triangle, stately and still atop the elegant slim narcissus stalk. And what to my wondering eyes should appear at the sound of my shaking?

It is she whose glittering taketh me!

I espy what she's wearing, its brave vibration each way free, as the divine Robert Herrick said of Julia's silks, and I barely forestall a fainting spell. "You do know, don't you," I say as I give it a pat, "that I already have a weak heart and occluded arteries." If I were Frost's horse I would give my

> harness bells a shake
> To ask if there is some mistake,

Skillet Penne Sausage and The New Year's Dissolution

but she, as if reading my mind, gives *herself* a playful little shake, and I nearly fall to the hardwood in a swoon.

"A very weak one of these, if you please," she says, pointing to my glass, by which she means that girly concoction involving pomegranate juice and some insufferably sweet liqueur bubbling in a stainless steel piece of stemware, the which I have at sundry times and places immortalized in amorous apostrophe.

I oblige and return to my pan, where the greatest smell on earth—an onion sautéing in butter—rises to the old factory. Ah, yes. The fool hath said in his heart there is no God, and all because the fool never sautéed an onion in butter. Over the onion goes a pile of sweet Italian sausage and, when all that is pink has turned brown, a mountain of chopped garlic and a mound of sun-dried tomatoes. I follow this with two cups of turkey broth, conveniently positioned on the stove already, a benefit accruing from the remaindered bones and scraps of the bird fried and ravaged on Christmas day, and then a cup of heavy whipping cream.

(An interesting variation is to add about a half cup of dry sherry at this point. Be sure to try it sometime.)

I can add the penne pasta to this and stir while the broth reduces or I can boil it separately. Today I have opted to boil it separately. And when at last the stock is reduced to my satisfaction, I add the penne, now strained, and about five ounces of chopped spinach. A sprinkling of shredded hard cheese would not be unwelcome.

There ought to be someone to share this with, and, as it happens, there is. Or are. The urchins gather round, each from his or her Christmas day distraction, which includes a new basketball hoop newly assembled and erected for cold-weather drills with a new ball that won't bounce in this chilly air. My own concentration has been tested by an even greater distraction: the shimmering creature next to me, who in stretchy finery that some women wrongly think is a right when in fact it's a privilege has been preparing a salad of kale, brussel sprouts, radicchio, cranberries, and parmesan cheese, all a-drizzle with olive oil and the juice from a couple of freshly squeezed lemons.

Second only to an onion softening in butter is that stirrer of eros, a whole lemon in the hand: "the lustiest to look upon," as the venerable Dutch pomologist put it so many centuries ago.

Who needs the ontological argument when there's all this proof everywhere around? And to seal the deal the puppy trots by, his little tail curled up over his waddling hind end. Binx would call him "Rosebud." To make the yuletide gay he dangles no mistleturd. I don't know if the clippers tickled his yonder socket, but the fifteen bucks for hedge-trimming and nail-clipping were, in my view, well-spent.

During the clean-up, which, generally, I enjoy as much as the preparing and partaking, my mind returns to the copse of trees, now dark, and the cold labor therein. You can't help but think about the new year, and I was thinking about it myself out there. In Chaucer's day the new year began at the Annunciation. The liturgical year in the East begins September 1. For me, as for many others, new life is sometimes no farther away than the next tee or the back nine. Golf is a game that lends itself easily to renewal, mainly because pretty much everyone plays it so badly. Golf is a resolution waiting to happen.

But golf was far from my thoughts this afternoon, out there in the cold, and I see no point now in irritating my glands by thinking about that pretty right-to-left turn that's a good four months away. (It'll most likely be a snap hook anyway, if I can even get a club head on the ball anymore.) And, in any case, the new year for me has never quite been about resolutions. Am I going to be kinder? More thankful? I hope so, and of course I'll try, though it does seem to me that each man is a creature incorrigibly himself. Emerson said that "all men plume themselves on the improvement of society, and no man improves," and there I think he had it about right.

No. For me the new year, more often than not, is a sad reminder that there hath passed away a glory from the earth, that nothing gold can stay.

> We and the trees and the way
> Back from the fields of play
> Lasted as long as we could.
> No more walks in the wood.

So the late great erudite John Hollander.

When the last days of December roll around it's hard not to think I'm in the fourth movement of Tchaikovsky's sixth symphony—late into it, the final bars. These splendid trips around the sun, these amazing pilgrimages with my Espoused Saint—fair creature of an hour!—and the urchins she bore me, are grand journeys all, thrilling white-knuckle rides full of hard turns and terrifying plunges, and yet another one is over and done with. Gone. Out, like a brief candle.

Afterword

Curiosity Killed the Keg: A Tribute

Half of earth's gorgeousness lies hidden in the glimpsed city it longs to become. For all its rooted loveliness, the world has no continuing city here; it is an outlandish place, a foreign home, a session in via to a better version of itself—and it is our glory to see it so and thirst until Jerusalem comes home at last. We were given appetites, not to consume the world and forget it, but to taste its goodness and hunger to make it great.

—Robert Capon, *Supper of the Lamb*

Hunger is more than a problem of the belly and guts.

—M.F.K Fisher, *Here Let Us Feast*

O n any given Saturday, sometimes with a propane heater hissing away in my garage and a thirty-year-old TV showing what appeared to be a football game even though it looked more like a snowstorm, my friend Mike would stand sentry over the keg of IPA chilling inside my old refrigerator. I had drilled a hole in the side of it for the CO_2 line; Mike had discovered what good company a guy with draft beer in his garage can be.

There, amid the floor jacks, bar oil, framing squares, and box-end wrenches, we'd capitulate to hops and barley and let them lead us wherever they might. There was obligatory campus gossip to get through, but we'd always get round to books, and we'd talk them through pretty thoroughly until a second pint facilitated a question to take us elsewhere. I remember asking him once: when in the march of western civilization or the evolution of western consciousness do you suppose irony became a necessary mode of consciousness—and then its default mode? It pleased me that he thought it a good question. We worried over that one for a while, as I recall, though if we came to a conclusion—or, what is more likely, a disagreement—I can't say that I remember what it was.

Now bear with some tedium for the moment and consider the keg as a vehicle in the Augustinian sense of that word. You will remember that in *The City of God* St. Augustine speaks of the vehicles we may use but not enjoy on our way to the heavenly city, which he takes to be the *telos*, the end, of the human pilgrimage we call "life." And, says St. Augustine, we are not to mistake the means of the journey for its end, nor the vehicle for the city. He says this because that is precisely what we are prone to do when our fallen eyes are set on things below.

So it is that Hazel Motes, the protagonist in Flannery O'Connor's first novel, says to a rival street preacher that no one with a good car needs to be justified, for Hazel, who claims to believe in nothing, prefers the car he owns to whatever place it might take him to. But, though he doesn't realize it, he is on a journey, and to get to his destination he must learn to differentiate between the means and the end, the vehicle and the city. He must learn to use but not enjoy his high rat-colored car. In fact the car in that novel must be destroyed if Hazel is to set his sights on the end, not the means. And eventually the car *is* destroyed; in a moment of high drama Hazel renounces it and embarks upon an internal pilgrimage to a place he has not yet imagined, much less comprehended.

I have often thought of the keg in these terms because—and here there will be some disagreement from our wives—for Mike and me the beer was the facilitator of the point but never the point. It was a vehicle the purpose of which was to get us to the problem of irony as a default mode of consciousness—and with luck direct us toward a solution. It brought us together on Friday nights or Saturday afternoons and it bore us up upon its wings toward an answer, but it was never itself the answer. And this, I take it, is strict theology. Perhaps we violated St. Augustine's injunction to use but not enjoy the vehicle, but at any rate we could justifiably say of the keg what a charitable and mysterious auto mechanic says to Hazel Motes: the mechanic is unimpressed by the car Hazel has put all his trust in, but he says "Some cars'll get some folks somewheres." Hazel has no idea where his will get him—mainly because, like all of O'Connor's dim-witted heroes, and probably like most of us, he's being undermined by a thing called "grace." He has no idea that the car he drives, lives in, preaches his creed of unbelief from, and eventually renounces will get him where he's going; he has no idea where that place is, but then in O'Connor's fiction no one ever knows what hits him. In this respect her characters are just like us.

There is a scene in one of Evelyn Waugh's novels, *Brideshead Revisited*, that illustrates well the point I'm trying to make. The elder Marchmain son, who goes by the name "Bridey," asks a guest, Charles (who is also the narrator), whether he's been adequately provisioned with wine during his stay. Charles says he has and that he is very fond of wine. Bridey then says, "I wish I were. It is such a bond with other men. At Magdalen [college] I tried to get drunk more than once, but I did not enjoy it. Beer and whiskey I find even less appetizing."

The conversation then turns to art and architecture and then at last to religion. Bridey and all the Marchmains are Catholics, and all conversations among them culminate organically in religion. Bridey asks Charles, who is an artist and an agnostic, whether the chapel at their house is good art.

"I think it is a remarkable example of its period," Charles says. "Probably in eighty years it will be greatly admired."

"But surely [says Bridey] it can't be good twenty years ago and good in eighty years, and not good now."

"Well it may be good now," Charles says. "All I mean is that I don't happen to like it much." And Bridey replies in this fashion: "But there's a difference between liking a thing and thinking it good?"

This is the kind of point Mike would have considered worth pursuing, especially in my garage, where the beer was free, at least for one of us: "But there's a difference between liking a thing and thinking it good?"

At this point in the novel the younger Marchmain son, Sebastian, impatient with strict theology and fast on his way to becoming a dipsomaniac, says, "Bridey, don't be so Jesuitical." But the artist Charles breaks in again: "Isn't that just the distinction you made about wine?" he asks Bridey. And

Bridey says, "No. I like and think good the end to which wine is sometimes the means—the promotion of sympathy between man and man. But in my own case it does not achieve that end, so I neither like it nor think it good for me."

Someone says, "Bridey, do stop," and Bridey says, "I'm sorry. I thought it rather an interesting point."

Which of course it is. It is Augustinian through and through. It is sacramental. It is a view of things in which things themselves matter, in which *matter* matters—such that wine, for example, may be a vehicle of grace. And if you think you hear in Bridey's remarks the *Spiritual Exercises* of St. Ignatius Loyola, that's because you do: "All the other beings and objects that surround us on the earth," St. Ignatius writes, "were created for the benefit of man and to be useful to him, as a means to his final end; hence his obligation to use, or to abstain from the use of, these creatures, according as they bring him nearer to that end, or tend to separate him from it."

Moments later Bridey can't help himself. He says to Charles, "Of course you are right really. You take art as a means not as an end. That is strict theology, but it's unusual to find an agnostic believing in it."

I'm not saying that I played the dull tedious believing (and also chaste and sober) Bridey to Mike's agnostic Charles (who, by the way, will eventually get one of Bridey's sisters between the sheets and, owing to her, ultimately convert to the ancient faith). I am only saying, at least for now, that there is a good end to which beer or wine or a high rat-colored car or any other thing, even a penchant for quilting, may be a means. And the tradition from St. Augustine all the way on down to Waugh and O'Connor supplies us with authoritative examples. Mike, who was a curious but unbelieving Catholic, and a big fan of O'Connor (to say nothing of Walker Percy), could have been a character in the novels of these or any other writer in the Catholic tradition.

I have drifted from curiosity and the keg into something like the theology of beer, and that is precisely my intention, for I want to say a word or two now about something Mike did when his father was sick. And what Mike did was give me a pay raise. He did this by giving up beer. He said to me very matter-of-factly one day that this was an act of solidarity with his father and that he was going to do it until his father made a turn for the better.

A mutual friend of ours once said that religion, for Mike, was a vaccine that didn't take, and I think that this is true to some degree, although I'll dispute it in a moment. I doubt that in adulthood Mike ever mumbled any words to the close and holy darkness, to use Dylan Thomas's nice little circumlocution for prayer, and I'd be surprised if he ever darkened the door of a church during that long dry stretch that rendered my keg so lonely and me so friendless and our wives so hopeful that we had started down the road to temperance and moral improvement.

But he undertook this Lenten-like discipline, this physical but also spiritual *askesis*, to *some* effect and for *some* purpose. He was unwavering and purposeful. I want to say—without presuming to name the destination—that the vow he took *took* him somewhere, and I kept wanting to quote Flannery O'Connor to him: some cars'll get some folks somewheres. For to the Catholic novelist there is no such thing as a mere action. You can renounce a car or beer or anything else, but you cannot conceive of such discipline as mere action. It is always something *plus* something else, something *other* than itself. It happens on one plane of existence but strikes on a higher plane as well.

I will not make more of this than is reasonable for an onlooker to make, except to say that Mike's failed inoculation was administered from within a tradition that has coursing through it no small measure of intellectual respectability. I am talking about the tradition that reminds us of the goodness of creation, a tradition that remembers that the world was declared very good and found worthy of a dying God, a tradition that had the good sense to condemn the Gnostics, that apparently deathless sect that is wreaking such havoc on us today under the names of technology and evangelical Christianity. I am talking about the tradition in which "The mud in man," as Thomas Lynch once put it, "the lowermost point in the subway, is nothing to be ashamed of. It can produce (St. Thomas would call it *potential oboedientialis*) the face of God. *Aperiatur terra et germinet Salvatorem*," proclaims the introit for the fourth Sunday in Advent: Let the earth open and bud forth a savior. This is the tradition that would go so far as to see salvation redound on man himself, or rather on a woman who says in perfect synergy, "be it done unto me according to thy word."

I mean that tradition descending (as unlikely as it seems) from Aristotle and passing to us through St. Thomas, the Great Dumb Ox. It is an intellectual and spiritual tradition always concerned with the place of knowledge, ethics, and politics in the locus of human thriving: the city. According to this tradition (and I quote now from my friend Philip Bess in *Till We Have Built Jerusalem*), knowledge originates in the senses conjoined to an active intellect. . . . Knowledge of the world—including the understanding known as 'science' and the know-how known as 'art'—and of any particular thing in the world, while never complete, can nevertheless be true; and a rudimentary understanding of anything includes knowledge of its efficient, material, formal, and final causes. Ethics and politics in this tradition are related to each other, and the subject matter of each is the good life for human beings—which itself is related intrinsically to life in a city (polis). The good life of any individual human being is the life of moral and intellectual excellence lived in communities,

which are groups of "persons who pursue a common end. The ultimate human community is the city, Aristotle's community of communities, the foremost purpose of which is the best life for its citizens."

I hope I will not be asked to demonstrate that this is slightly more respectable than the hollow therapeutic American religion that seems to get so much air time whenever some newsman, desperate for a strawman, has decided that it's time for another public thrashing of religion.

And, having said all that, I will now say one more thing about this tradition. It understands itself in terms not merely of devotion and feeling but of efficiency and fact, and I will illustrate this point by examining an unpopular word: "Christian."

The word "Christian" denotes not someone who feels a certain way or who has recited the right words, as the therapeutic do-it-yourself religion holds, but "someone to whom something has happened," as Martin Thornton has well said, something that is "irreversible" and that "penetrates to the very roots of his being." And that something is, quite simply, baptism, which, when understood in terms of efficiency and fact, implies an ontological shift, a change in nature that doesn't really give a damn what we think about it and probably smiles at our attempts to undo it.

I am not concerned for the moment with whether any of this is true. I am only saying something—a very *small* something—about what a particular system of belief and thought assumes to be a first principle. You don't go down into the water and come back out the same person. That's not up to you. Thornton has said it with good humor in *Christian Proficiency*, so I will hand the point over to him (the humor comes toward the end of this quotation):

> In practice, being a Christian means accepting both a job and the tools with which to do it, and a Christian can be plainly,

fully, and accurately defined as 'one who has been Baptized.' The baptized soul can 'lose his faith,' refuse the sacraments, give up prayer, and constantly commit the most scandalous sins; which would make him a very bad and inefficient Christian, but a Christian nevertheless. Baptism remains the irrevocable act of God which has 'happened to him' as surely as he has been born of particular parents in a particular place: extreme excitability, a loathing for cricket, and a passion for garlic may be a little odd in a Yorkshireman, but they do not turn him into an Italian.

(He also adds: "Then there is the man who prefers the radio service to his parish church, which may indeed be more edifying; but Our Lord seems to have omitted to tell us on which wave-length sacramental Grace is purveyed.")

Now one of Mike's favorite words was "horseshit," which for Mike was usually preceded by the word "what" and followed by an exclamation point: "What horseshit!" He had a pretty good nose for religious nonsense, and I heard him on more than one occasion turn the expression "what horseshit!" on contemporary Protestant hymnody, which, quite frankly, is horseshit. (C.S. Lewis called it fifth-rate poetry set to sixth-rate music.)

But partly because of the example of our mutual friend, and perhaps even because of my own example, Mike remained interested in religion. As I said, he was a curious unbelieving Catholic. And the reason I have drifted from curiosity and the keg to the theology of beer is that such a theology is not unworthy of the attention of a curious unbeliever—to say nothing of the fact that many of its practitioners (O'Connor and Walker Percy, for example) regarded irony as a necessary mode of consciousness at this point in the long march of western civilization.

But all that I have said here, regardless of whether any of it is true, I have said because I think it is, and for a long time has been, a powerful explanatory system for understanding that sympathy between men of which Bridey spoke, for understanding the friendship I happened to have shared with Mike, and for Mike's little act of solidarity that helped extend the life of at least one keg, if not also of one man, his father. I'll stop short of speculation here to make this modest observation: it was my privilege simply to observe the lonely isolated keg always poised to serve as the vehicle, not the destination, of an intellectual journey that may, for all I know, have been a spiritual journey as well, but an earthly journey at any rate that for Mike is over now, as it will be for me one day.

So I return now to Bridey:

"No. I like and think good the end to which wine is sometimes the means—the promotion of sympathy between man and man. But in my own case it does not achieve that end, so I neither like it nor think it good for me." "Of course you are right really. You take art as a means not as an end. That is strict theology, but it's unusual to find an agnostic believing in it."

I goaded Mike plenty about the vaccine that didn't take, and he goaded me plenty about its taking too well. I regret many things (regret is another aspect of that default mode of consciousness), but I especially regret that I can't get his reaction to this book, especially its final pages. I would have enjoyed hearing him say "what horseshit!" and then seeing him puzzling it out in that unbelieving but honest manner of his, often in my garage, where curiosity killed the keg.

www.ingramcontent.com/pod-product-compliance
Lightning Source LLC
Chambersburg PA
CBHW032100220426
43664CB00008B/1075